THE HUNT FOR MOORE'S GOLD

THE HUNT FOR MOORE'S GOLD

INVESTIGATING THE LOSS OF THE BRITISH ARMY MILITARY CHEST DURING THE RETREAT TO CORUNNA

FRONTLINE
BOOKS

THE HUNT FOR MOORE'S GOLD
Investigating the Loss of the British Army's Military Chest
During the Retreat to Corunna

First published in Great Britain in 2019 by Frontline Books,
an imprint of Pen & Sword Books Ltd, Yorkshire - Philadelphia

Typeset in India by Vman Infotech Private Limited
Printed and bound by TJ International

Pen & Sword Books Ltd incorporates the imprints of Pen & Sword Archaeology,
Air World Books, Atlas, Aviation, Battleground, Discovery, Family History, History,
Maritime, Military, Naval, Politics, Social History, Transport, True Crime, Claymore
Press, Frontline Books, Praetorian Press, Seaforth Publishing and White Owl

For a complete list of Pen & Sword titles please contact:

PEN & SWORD BOOKS LTD
47 Church Street, Barnsley, South Yorkshire, S70 2AS, UK.
E-mail: enquiries@pen-and-sword.co.uk
Website: www.pen-and-sword.co.uk

Or

PEN AND SWORD BOOKS,
1950 Lawrence Road, Havertown, PA 19083, USA
E-mail: Uspen-and-sword@casematepublishers.com
Website: www.penandswordbooks.com

Contents

Acknowledgements		vii
List of Maps		ix
Introduction: The Quest for the Chest		xi
Chapter 1	Cintra Shame	1
Chapter 2	Blind Confidence	15
Chapter 3	Portugal Adieu	31
Chapter 4	The Fate of Spain	49
Chapter 5	In Fortune's Way	73
Chapter 6	Risking too Much	91
Chapter 7	Retreat	115
Chapter 8	The Loss of the Military Chest	135
Chapter 9	At Bay: The Battle of Lugo	155
Chapter 10	A Melancholy Aspect of Affairs	173
Chapter 11	'I Hope the People of England will be Satisfied!'	191
Chapter 12	Consequences	209
Chapter 13	The Hunt	235
Notes		261
Appendix I	*Reasons for the loss of equipment during the Corunna Campaign*	279
Appendix II	*British Losses in the Corunna Campaign*	283
Source Information		293
Index		299

Acknowledgements

I am grateful for the time and effort contributed by D. Jesús Manuel Núñez Díaz, Consuelo McMurdo, Professor Javier Gomez, Alfredo Erias Martinez, the director of the Archives of Betanzos, and Laurie Dennett, whose combined knowledge of the Lugo region proved invaluable. I am especially thankful to Luis Coedonova for his warm hospitality.

The trip to the mountains of Galicia simply would not have been possible but for my son, Marcus, who somehow managed to drive along the narrowest, rockiest tracks imaginable while maintaining his perpetual optimism. Military artist David Rowlands was the man behind the lens, taking photographs of almost every point along the line of the retreat to Corunna. His knowledge of British military history is quite exceptional. Thanks to Charlotte Rowlands for her Spanish translations.

My thanks also to Robert Mitchell and the historian and Peninsular War tour leader Nick Lipscombe for their assistance, and Hannah Fadairo for all the support she gave me.

Most especially, the one person who has devoted very considerable time talking to almost everyone he could find in the Becerrea region and, as I write these acknowledgements, is still investigating, is Angel Rodil Perez.

Martin Mace deserves particular credit for telling me to stop talking about the loss of Moore's military chest and to go and look for it – and for publishing this book.

List of Maps

1. The Peninsula Campaign 1808–1814   xiii
2. The Retreat to Corunna and Vigo (Dave Cassan)   114
3. Nogales to Cereixal (Dave Cassan)   248
4. Cereixal to Baralla (Dave Cassan)   249

Introduction

The Quest for the Chest

'"Oh, beg pardon, sir", said the blue-coated officer; "I am paymaster general … The treasure of the army, sir, is close in the rear, and the bullocks being jaded are unable to proceed."' The officer that the paymaster general had addressed was General Paget in charge of the retreating army's rear-guard. Paget had no time, or men, to spare to deal with the paymaster general's problems, for he had an enemy to fight.

That enemy was creeping round the rear-guard's right flank and the military treasure chest, heavy and immobile on the carts of the exhausted cattle, was certain to be overtaken by the pursuers. Paget had no choice. The money had to abandoned.

The Light Company of the 28th Regiment was ordered to the rear in double-quick-time to hold back the French cavalry as the remainder of the regiment drew up in close order around the two the paymaster general's carts. The military chests were then opened and the treasure of the army, silver and possibly gold specie, was thrown over the snow-covered cliff into the ravine below. 'As they rolled down the precipice, their silvery notes were accompanied by a noble bass,' wrote a young officer of the 28th, Robert Blakeney 'for two guns were thundering forth their applause into Soult's dark brown column as they gallantly pressed forward.'

Anyone who has read the history of Sir John Moore's retreat to Corunna will know of the story of the army's military chest being thrown into a deep ravine rather than allowing it to fall into the hands of the enemy. But just how true is this tale and exactly how much treasure was lost? How much of it was seized by the passing troops and was any recovered by the local Spanish peasants when the snow thawed and coins were exposed? Perhaps more importantly, is there any of that treasure still sitting at the bottom of the ravine?

For years, I have pondered these questions, indeed my personal journey began when I purchased a copy of Blakeney's memoirs at a table-top sale at a gymkhana in the New Forest whilst on a farm holiday with my family. Remarkably, the book was signed and dated July 1900 (just after the book had first been published), and was given as a present to Fanny Blakeney. It cost me just 10p!

After decades of wondering what had happened to the military chest I had to accept that there was only one way to find out – by looking for myself. Thus began this quest to discover, once and for all, what happened to Moore's gold.

The approach I am taking in this book, is to retell the story of the retreat to Corunna in as great a detail as I possibly can. This, I hope, will enable me to understand the circumstances around the loss of the military chest, and its exact location. The retreat to the coast of northern Spain and the battle outside the port of Corunna to hold back the French before the battered and bloody British army was able to safely embark on the ships that would carry them to England, is also one of the most dramatic tales in British military history and well worth the retelling, drawing on the standard accounts of the retreat, as well as some that have not been presented to the public for more than 200 years, and a number that have only recently become readily available.

The second part of the book will focus on the events of that cold winter evening of 5 January 1809 and culminate in an expedition to Galicia to investigate in person the possible site where the sacks holding the military chest were discarded. As I write this introduction I do not know where this journey will take me, or where it will finish. It might be that I can positively identify the location of the lost treasure but that the slope is too steep to be climbed, I simply do not know.

My search for Moore's lost bullion may end on the top of a precipice staring down a ravine I will never enter, or in an Assay Office as the coins bearing the image of King George (or more likely Carlos IV) are weighed. Please join me on this journey, it should be quite a trip.

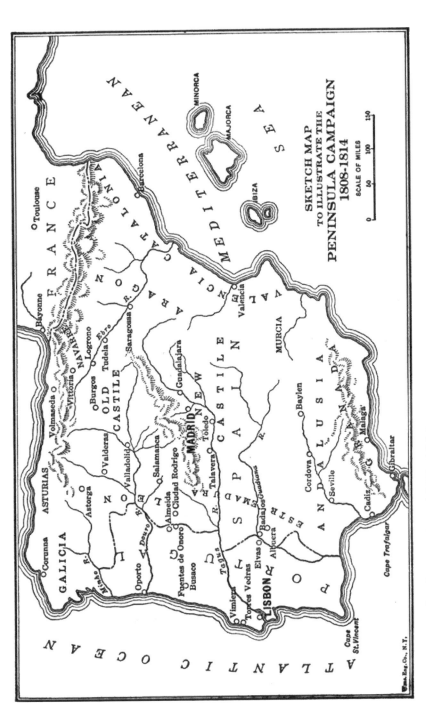

SKETCH MAP
TO ILLUSTRATE THE
PENINSULA CAMPAIGN
1808–1814

SCALE OF MILES

The Peninsula Campaing 1808–1814

Chapter 1

Cintra Shame

The raft swayed gently on the slow-running waters of the Niemen. Napoleon's boat was the first to arrive, the Marines of the Guard proving swifter oarsmen than their Russian counterparts. Upon the raft had been built a magnificent apartment, the imperial eagles of both countries proudly adorning the doors and the roof. A few moments later, Alexander I, Czar of All the Russias, stepped onto the elaborately decorated craft. Napoleon courteously opened the door flap for the young Russian autocrat and, for the first time, the two most powerful men in the world stood face to face.

They were there, anchored in the middle of a neutral river, to formulate a treaty of peace after years of antagonism. But one obstacle still stood in their way – Britain, Russia's ally and financial backer, France's implacable enemy.

Acutely conscious of Napoleon's growing strength and Britain's increasingly isolated position, the Czar made the first move: 'I hate the English as much as you do yourself,' he declared. 'If that is the case,' replied Napoleon, 'then peace is already made.'[1]

For more than an hour the two emperors bargained over the fate of Europe as a host of dignitaries and the massed ranks of the French and Russian armies lined the banks of the river. Twenty-three days earlier, on 14 June 1807, Napoleon's seemingly invincible horde had crushed the Russian Army at the Battle of Friedland and the despondent Czar had begged for an armistice. After ten months of almost continuous warfare the last two major continental powers in arms against France, Prussia and Russia, had been beaten and humiliated. Only that small nation of shopkeepers, sitting remote and secure behind the 'wooden walls' of the Royal Navy, refused to pay homage to the new Charlemagne.

Now, with almost all of Western Europe under his control, Napoleon could turn the full weight of his empire's vast resources upon those 'Perfidious Islanders'. A direct assault upon Britain, however, was beyond even Napoleon's means, for although France dominated the land, Britannia still ruled the waves, and the frigates of the Royal Navy cruised the Channel with an unrelenting vigilance. Unable, therefore, to come to grips with his enemy, Napoleon had resolved upon warfare of a different kind. On 21 November 1806, five weeks after defeating the once-mighty army of Prussia, Napoleon issued a decree from the captured Prussian capital, Berlin, in which he outlawed all trade and correspondence between Britain and the French-controlled areas of Europe.

Britain then, as now, relied upon international commerce to maintain the expansion of its manufacturing industries. The restriction upon its trade caused by Napoleon's 'Continental System' caused some discomfort throughout the United Kingdom and export figures fell. Many countries in Europe, including alleged allies of France, nevertheless, disregarded the decrees and openly, or secretly, continued to trade with the 'Workshop of the World'. Napoleon was determined to stamp out this illicit trade and close off every Continental port to English shipping. So, when the two emperors met in the middle of the River Niemen at Tilsit, Napoleon was prepared to use every possible expedient to persuade Russia to participate in his embargo of British goods. Alexander, though, did not need much persuading. Anxious to achieve an honourable settlement, he readily agreed to ban English goods from his domains. Napoleon had no wish to humiliate Russia. His real enemy was to be found in London not in St Petersburg, and he needed the support of this huge northern state to bring the few wayward countries into line. Denmark, Sweden and Portugal still trafficked in British merchandise, the first as a neutral, the latter two as allies of King George.

Publicly, the Treaty of Tilsit proclaimed the advantages of harmonious relations between the two countries, the new opportunities for enterprise that this would bring, and the now mutual affection of the two emperors. The treaty, however, contained a number of secret clauses. Europe was to be split into two spheres of influence. Russia was to add Finland to its growing list of conquests and exert pressure upon King Gustavus of Sweden to sever his links with Britain. France agreed to abandon its traditionally friendly relations with Constantinople and allow Alexander to seize parts of the European provinces of the Ottoman Empire. In return, Russia would stand aside while France took possession of the Ionian Islands, the Dalmatian coast of what is now Croatia, and 'The Bourbon dynasty in Spain and the House of Braganza in Portugal shall cease to reign; a prince of the Bonaparte family to succeed to each throne.'[2]

News of the Russian defeat at Friedland and the diplomatic manoeuvring at Tilsit reached Westminster by mid-July. Although the content of the secret clauses was unknown to the British Government, dark intrigues were immediately suspected. Considerable suspicion also surrounded the motives of 'neutral' Denmark and its ability (and determination) to withstand the mounting pressure from France to close its ports to British vessels. Fearing that the Danes might soon be overwhelmed and their valuable navy fall into the hands of Napoleon, the British cabinet decided upon an audacious scheme to capture the entire Danish battle-fleet.

With uncharacteristic speed the government assembled a force of 30,000 men and seventeen battleships, under Lord Cathcart, and despatched them to Copenhagen. This armada was preceded by an English diplomat, Mr Francis Jackson, who demanded the surrender of the Danish fleet in return for an annual payment of £100,000, with the ships to be returned to their owners upon the cessation of hostilities.

The crown prince naturally rejected Jackson's offer, and on 16 August 1807, British troops landed at Vedboek and marched upon Copenhagen. Powerful batteries were erected and, after four nights of devastating bombardment, the city was surrendered and with it forty-five warships.

However piratical this act may have appeared, it was in fact a brilliant piece of anticipation. The combined naval strength of France, and her Dutch, Spanish, and now Russian allies, stood at 129 ships-of-the-line. The Royal Navy had, at the most, 113. Despite this slight numerical advantage, the French and Spanish fleets had spent much of the war blockaded within their own harbours.

Man-for-man the inexperienced French sailor was no match for Jack Tar, as Nelson had so emphatically proved at Trafalgar two years earlier. If Napoleon still nurtured any hope of driving his old enemy from the seas he would have to considerably increase the size of his navy. It would take years to build such a fleet, but what Napoleon could not manage by construction he might yet achieve by force. Only days before Cathcart's men began their advance upon Copenhagen, Napoleon had told the Danish Emissary that his country must ally itself with France or face war, and that a large force under Marshal Bernadotte was concentrating in Holland for the invasion of Denmark.

When the French Emperor heard of the British coup his rage was uncontrollable. Yet there was once last chance. Lying idle in Lisbon harbour was the powerful Portuguese battle-fleet. At a diplomatic reception a few days later, Napoleon threatened the Portuguese Ambassador: 'If Portugal does not do what I wish, the House of Braganza will not be reining in Europe in two months! I will no longer tolerate an English Ambassador in Europe. I will declare war on any power that receives one two months from this time! I have 300,000 Russians at my disposal, and with that powerful ally I can do everything.'

On the last day of November 1807, two months after Napoleon's prophetic tirade, General Junot marched through the crowded, cobbled streets of Lisbon. Behind him trailed 1,500 ragged and exhausted men, the remnant of a magnificent force of 25,000 seasoned French troops who had crossed the Pyrenees only a few weeks before. They had encountered no organised resistance from the Portuguese but the invaders had suffered terribly from the ravages of the weather in the barren and inhospitable country-side. Many had died through exposure, others simply starved, the rest staggered on at whatever pace they could. Nevertheless, Junot had crossed the northern Iberian Peninsula at astonishing speed, covering the last 300 miles in fourteen days. His objective was to seize the Portuguese fleet before the British could once again intervene. Unfortunately for Junot, only forty-eight hours earlier a terrified and confused Prince John had submitted to the entreaties of the British Ambassador and, in the company of a Royal Navy squadron, he had sailed to set up court in the Portuguese colony of Brazil. With him went the Portuguese fleet and Napoleon's last hope of naval supremacy.[3]

Over the course of the next few days the stragglers hobbled into the Portuguese capital and soon Junot had more than 24,000 men under arms. Dispatching strong columns to occupy the principle fortresses, Junot quickly and bloodlessly subdued the population. The subjugation of Portugal was, however, only part of a far grander design. Napoleon was under no illusions as to the efficacy of the Continental System, for while large parts of the old world were denied to the British traders, the UK's unrivalled naval strength allowed those traders to open unlimited new markets in the developing countries of Asia and America. Napoleon, consequently, planned a series of massive assaults upon British-held posts throughout the globe.

The first of these attacks, aimed at India, was to consist of '50,000 men, Russians, French and perhaps Austrians,' Napoleon announced, 'marching into Asia by way of Constantinople [who] would no sooner reach the Euphrates than England would tremble and go down on her knees'. The second part of the scheme was designed to drive the Royal Navy from the Mediterranean, thus depriving the ships of their vital supply bases and compelling them to lift their blockade of the southern European ports. This would enable the combined fleets of France and Spain to execute the third phase of Napoleon's master plan, and sail against the British colonies in South Africa and the West Indies.

By far the most important of these measures was the one directed at securing control of the Mediterranean. Gibraltar, Sicily and Malta, all garrisoned with British troops, provided the Royal Navy's Mediterranean Fleet with food, shelter, and essential stores. So Napoleon's brother Joseph, King of Naples, was to be ordered to seize Sicily, while a second army marched through Spain, besieged Gibraltar, and took possession of the free ports along the North African coast.

This last task could not be safely entrusted to the Spaniards. Although nominally an ally of France, and at war with Britain, Spain had shown herself to be a fair-weather friend. In October of the previous year, when the Grande Armée was about to face the feared

Prussian Army, Godoy, the Spanish Prime Minister, believing that Napoleon had finally met his match, issued a proclamation evidently designed to raise an army against the French.

Godoy, as it transpired, had backed the wrong horse. When news of the sensational French victories at Jena and Auerstadt reached Madrid, he rushed off a letter to Napoleon in which he promised unending allegiance to 'the most perfect model of a hero that History has to show.' With such a fickle neighbour as this, Napoleon's southern flank would always be in danger. The Spanish authorities had also proven to be unable, or unwilling, to stem the regular flow of British goods into the country and the once-proud and formidable Spanish fleet lay idle and rotting in its blockaded harbours. Much, then, could be gained by the military occupation of Spain, particularly if this could be achieved without great loss or expense. Already thousands of French troops were pouring into Spain under the pretext of reinforcing Junot in Portugal. By the Treaty of Fontainbleau, signed on 27 October 1807, Spain had agreed to the passage of Junot's army across its northern provinces and to the occupation of some of the key towns along the route to secure the French line of communication. A further 40,000 men were to be held in readiness at Bayonne close to the Spanish border, to support Junot in the event of British military intervention. The Spaniards themselves were to provide a strong force to garrison many of the Portuguese towns and to assist Junot if the Portuguese offered any resistance.

Napoleon had manipulated the situation extremely skilfully and Spain lay open at his feet. But Napoleon wanted to avoid another costly war and, if possible, add an air of respectability to his actions. The political situation in Spain at the time offered him every prospect of accomplishing both those aims, as the royal family was bitterly divided. The regal disputes were brought to a head when French troops marched into Madrid.

King Carlos sought Napoleon's help to adjudicate in the family squabble, giving the Emperor the opportunity to intervene in Spanish affairs with all the appearance of legitimacy. He managed to persuade Carlos, his son and heir Ferdinand, Prince of Asturias, and most of the leading royals, to travel to Bayonne to settle the dispute. Once in France, the Spanish royal family was removed into the heart of France.

While the attention of the Spanish authorities was distracted by the regal wrangling, French armies had taken control of most of the northern provinces. The fortresses of Pamplona, San Sebastian, Barcelona and Figueros were treacherously seized, and before the Spanish Government could react, the troops of generals Moncey, Duhesme and Mouton were in possession of all the towns guarding the Pyrenean passes. Tens of thousands of reinforcements poured over the mountains and soon no less than 118,000 French soldiers were spreading all over northern Spain.

The Spanish army was in no condition to oppose the invaders. It was hopelessly disorganised, badly led and seriously ill-equipped. Of the infantry, not a single line regiment was up to strength, whilst of nearly 15,000 cavalry only 9,000 actually possessed horses. Spain's finest body of men, over 15,000 strong, was at that time serving with the French occupation forces in northern Germany. These troops had been despatched to the Baltic on the insistence of Napoleon after Godoy's act of infidelity the year before. This move not only ensured continued Spanish cooperation with France it also deprived Spain of its only effective armed force.

There was nothing it seemed to stand in Napoleon's way and in a few short weeks the entire Iberian Peninsula had been conquered with barely a shot fired in anger. The thrones of both Portugal and Spain had been vacated and Napoleon was at liberty to choose their next occupants. In Madrid, however, events were no longer running quite so smoothly. The mob, already on the verge of insurrection due to the disappearance of the senior royals, particularly the popular young Ferdinand, rioted upon the news that the remainder of the royal family was to be rounded up and deported to France. The wild crowd rushed into the streets, slaughtering every Frenchman it could find.

Three hours later the blood-drenched streets were silent. Hundreds of French and Spaniards alike lay dead and mutilated in the alleyways and gutters. At every street corner a French cannon kept the peace. Martial law was imposed, and scores of supposed ringleaders were shot. But rather than quench the spreading fire of insurrection, these brutal reprisals merely fanned the flames. All over the country local councils, or 'juntas' were formed, and provincial armies were raised. The Peninsular War had begun.[4]

The suddenness of the French invasion had left the Spaniards totally unprepared. No amount of patriotic fervour could make up for the lack of weapons and ammunition. So it was, that in the first week of June, the patriots turned to their old enemy, Britain, for assistance. Lieutenant General Sir Hew Dalrymple, the Governor of Gibraltar, was approached by the Junta of Seville and, at the same time, a delegation from the Asturias sailed to London to beg for arms and money.

The long conflict between Britain and Spain was ended, and on 4 July 1808, peace was officially declared. Yet, despite the Spaniards' desperate appeal for help, the British cabinet was soon to find increasing difficulty in assisting the rebels. Although Royal Navy cruisers, in anticipation of instructions from the Admiralty, were rousing the Spanish patriots along the coasts of Biscay and Valencia, the arrogant and self-interested regional juntas refused to permit British troops to land in their territories and they accepted the first shipments of gold bullion without allowing the British any real say in its distribution. There were, however, reports reaching London of outbreaks of violence in Portugal. The naturally indolent Portuguese had been stirred into revolt by Junot's barbaric rule and indiscriminate plundering by his troops. Junot now only controlled the area around Lisbon and a number of vital fortresses. These disturbances in Portugal offered the British army the opportunity it needed to gain a foothold in the Peninsula. A landing in Portugal would divert French pressure without insulting Spanish pride.

Lord Castlereagh, the Secretary of State for War, was hurriedly marshalling all the available British forces. Although the British Army in 1808 numbered around 200,000 men, most of these troops were dispersed around the world garrisoning the far-flung outposts of the empire. Of the remainder, a number were always retained at home for reasons of national security, leaving only a fraction of the total manpower disposable for field operations.

The largest force under arms was that of Lieutenant General Sir John Moore stationed off the coast of Sweden. Moore's mission to Scandinavia was to assist the Swedes in repelling the anticipated invasion from Russia. The Swedish king, Gustav, however, wanted to throw Moore's 10,000 men at the entire Russian army in a ridiculous offensive operation. Sir John refused to co-operate in such a suicidal venture and was placed under house-arrest by the mad king.

At Cork in southern Ireland, a further 9,500 troops under Sir Arthur Wellesley had assembled for an amphibious operation against Spanish possessions in South America. With the declaration of peace between Britain and Spain, Wellesley's men were temporarily redundant. Another 5,000 men were in transports at Gibraltar, whilst Major General Beresford commanded 3,000 soldiers in Madeira. Lastly, Sir Brent Spencer was in Sicily with around 4,500 men. With favourable winds these units could be united off the coasts of Portugal in a matter of weeks.

While ministers debated which of these generals should lead the expedition to Portugal, Britain's finest weapon, the Royal Navy, was being wielded with great dexterity. The Spanish army of the Marquis de la Romana that was still serving dutifully, though, reluctantly, under the French in the Baltic, was spirited away by a British fleet and repatriated on the northern coast of Spain on 27 August.

Meanwhile the first British troops had reached Portugal, being those under the command of Sir Arthur Wellesley and Brent Spencer, who began disembarking in Mondego Bay on 1 August 1808. Upon landing Wellesley made contact with the local Portuguese commander Lieutenant General Bernardim Freire, who immediately made Wellesley aware of the difficulties of campaigning in the Iberian Peninsula. Freire agreed to cooperate with the British but only if Wellesley undertook to feed his entire force of 6,000 men. As Wellesley was dependent upon the Royal Navy for his own supplies he could not accept such a proposition and when he began his march on the Portuguese capital he was accompanied by less than 2,000 Portuguese light troops.

As soon as he heard of the landing of the British troops Junot sent a corps of 4,000 men under General Henri Delaborde to delay Wellesley's advance. Delaborde took up a defensive position upon a narrow hill to the south of the old walled town of Obidos adjacent to the main highway to Lisbon. Wellesley tried to encircle Delaborde's corps but the French general withdrew in good order to a more extensive range of heights behind the village of Roliça. Wellesley repeated his earlier manoeuvre and again Delaborde held his ground until the last possible moment before disengaging.

Delaborde had done his job well. By nightfall, Wellesley had advanced just seven miles in twenty-four hours, allowing Junot to march up from Lisbon with the bulk of his army, intending to attack the British and drive them back to their ships before any more troops could be landed. He was too late. Two brigades of reinforcements had already arrived and were preparing to disembark at Maçeira Bay.

Wellesley moved along the coast to cover the disembarkation and he deployed his small force along the semi-circle of hills above the village of Vimeiro that encompasses the bay. Without hesitation Junot marched out to attack Wellesley but was repulsed at all points. As the French disengaged, Wellesley ordered an immediate advance but with the reinforcements came a more senior officer, Sir Harry Burrard, who 'did not think it advisable to move off the ground in pursuit of the enemy.' Junot therefore made good his escape.

The following day Burrard was himself superseded by Sir Hew Dalrymple from Gibraltar, who supported Burrard's cautious decision. Wellesley was now relegated to the role of a divisional commander.

Junot, meanwhile, had come to a quick decision. With no possibility of help reaching him from Spain or France, the French commander requested an armistice in order to negotiate a deal that would allow his army to evacuate Portugal without further bloodshed. Dalrymple jumped at the chance of liberating Portugal without any more fighting and agreed, much to Wellesley's dismay, on a cessation of hostilities. Under the terms of the subsequent Convention of Cintra, the French were allowed to retain their weapons and much of the plunder that they had looted from the Portuguese. To make matters worse, the French troops were to be repatriated in British ships and, upon their return, were free to take up arms once again. At this, Wellesley returned to England in disgust. What was particularly galling to Wellesley was that yet more reinforcements had arrived under Sir John Moore who had managed to escape from Sweden, giving the British a considerable numerical superiority over the French forces in Portugal. Junot should have been crushed or forced to surrender unconditionally, not permitted to sail freely away.

Nevertheless, the Portuguese fortresses were handed over intact to the British. This included the key border fortresses of Elvas and

Almeida which guarded the main routes into Spain. The principle objective of Britain's intervention in the conflict in Iberia was to assist the Spaniards in repelling the French invaders, and with these fortresses in his hands Dalrymple could start to plan a move into Spain.

Time, though, was of the essence and the morning after the signing of the convention, Wellesley wrote that, 'I do not know what Sir Hew proposes to do, but if I were in his situation I would have 20,000 men in Madrid in less than a month from this day.'[5]

Dalrymple, though, could not march off into Spain until the French had cleared Portugal, and this process was not completed until the end of September.

While he was waiting for the French to be evacuated Dalrymple devoted his time in Lisbon to establishing some form of interim government in the absence of the prince regent and his court. The only positive military moves he made was to send two brigades under Sir John Hope towards Elvas and a single regiment to garrison Almeida. He declared that he was waiting until Moore's recently arrived corps was fully integrated into the new command structure that Dalrymple busied himself compiling.

Matters, however, were going to take a sudden and surprising turn. When the details of the Convention of Cintra were published in London there was widespread public outrage and ministerial embarrassment. Dalrymple was recalled, to be put before a Board of Inquiry to explain his conduct. But ministers were intent on continuing operations in Iberia in support of the Spaniards and while Dalrymple awaited the start of the inquiry, command of the force destined to advance into Spain was placed in the hands of Lieutenant General Moore.

Even more dramatic events were taking place beyond the Portuguese border. The uprising in Iberia had taken Napoleon by surprise, but he was determined to crush the insurrection before it escalated into a major war. Planning operations from Bayonne, he ordered his troops in Spain to march upon the major towns and the principle centres of insurrection. From his distant headquarters, though, Napoleon had no real understanding of the extent of the rebellion, and his generals found themselves opposed by such strong forces that they were unable to quell the insurgency.

Despite this, and the fact that almost every district was now in open revolt, Napoleon still believed that this unexpected show of Spanish nationalism would soon die on the bayonets of the French grenadiers. But he failed to appreciate the depth of the emotions that the invasion had aroused. His brother Joseph had been persuaded to relinquish his Neapolitan throne and accept the far more prestigious one of Spain. Yet, within days of arriving in his new capital, the 'intrusive' King of Spain was compelled to evacuate Madrid.

This was because General Pierre Dupont, conducting operations in the south of Spain, had been forced to withdraw from Cordoba in the face of mounting resistance. Unwilling to concede failure, Dupont lingered indecisively in the heart of Andalusia, while the Spanish forces and armed peasantry, emboldened by his inactivity, cut off his line of retreat to Madrid. At last realising his predicament, Dupont desperately tried to force his way through the passes of the surrounding mountains. The Spaniards, though, had been allowed too much time to consolidate their positions and despite five successive attacks the French were unable to dislodge them.

Dupont sought an armistice. Two days of tenacious negotiations resulted in the Convention of Bailén and the surrender of Dupont's entire force. The French laid down their arms on the promise that they would be repatriated, yet few of the 18,000 men saw their homeland again. Shipped off to the Balearic Isles or left to rot in prison hulks, many died of disease, even more of starvation.

For the first time in nearly a decade a French army had been defeated, and Napoleon was furious. Never, he wrote, was there 'ever anything since the world was created so senseless, so stupid'.[6]

The repercussions were felt throughout Europe, giving new hope and inspiration to the subjugated nations. King Joseph, already becoming disillusioned with the attitude of his new subjects, immediately abandoned Madrid and retired northwards with all speed. Though he was told by Napoleon to hold the line of the River Douro, Joseph did not stop until his last man had crossed the Ebro.

Napoleon was stunned with Joseph's withdrawal. 'To re-cross both rivers,' he raged, 'is tantamount to evacuating Spain!' With the news reaching Napoleon that Junot had also been beaten, the situation in Iberia was spinning out of control. The Emperor knew that he had to act swiftly or lose the Peninsula completely.

Napoleon may have been guilty originally of under-estimating the ability of the Spaniards to resist his armies; 'The whole of the Spanish forces are not capable of beating twenty-five thousand French in a reasonable position,' he had once asserted. Now, though, he was under no such illusions. Apart from the troops already in Spain he was transferring 100,000 of his best men from their cantonments in Germany, and the Emperor was going with them in person. But before he could commit himself to a campaign beyond the distant Pyrenees, Napoleon had to take steps to ensure the integrity of his northern and eastern borders of his empire. Prussia's military capabilities had been forcibly restricted by Napoleon after its disastrous defeats of 1806, but Austria, to the east, was still a force to be reckoned with. Beyond these two lay the restless might of Holy Russia. After Tilsit Napoleon had boasted that with Alexander as his ally he could achieve anything; now was the time to test the czar's loyalty.

At Erfurt in eastern Germany the two great men sat down to another Tilsit-style summit. This time it was Alexander who held all the trump cards. Napoleon desperately needed Russia's military muscle to bully Austria into acquiescence and a high price he would have to pay for it. After two weeks of intensive wrangling, Alexander consented to 'denounce Austria, and make common cause with France.'

For that vague commitment, Napoleon had to stand aside whilst Russia grabbed more large areas of the Balkans. The Csar's strength and influence was increasing, and he would one day be strong enough to challenge Napoleon again. For now, though, it was a deal Napoleon had to accept, and as soon as he was assured of Russian support, his troops were on the move. In specially-designed carriages the Imperial Guard was sped across Europe to join in the heavy columns converging upon Bayonne.

South of the border the situation was changing rapidly. Weeks of inactivity by Joseph had given the various Spanish juntas the opportunity of combining their forces and forming some kind of unified strategy. The self-appointed principal body, the Central Junta, formulated a grandiose scheme to encircle and trap the

13

entire French army, and tens of thousands of regular troops and peasants were already moving around the flanks of the French encampments along the Ebro. By this time, though, the first of the French reinforcements had arrived, and before Napoleon even reached the front line the first of the Spanish armies was on the run.

The scene was now set for one of the most dramatic episodes of the Peninsular War.

Chapter 2

Blind Confidence

It was on 6 October 1808 that a ship reached Lisbon with despatches from London that were dated 25 and 26 September. Included in the despatches was a letter to Sir John Moore from Lord Castlereagh outlining the Government's objectives:

> His Majesty having determined to employ a corps of his troops, of not less than 30,000 infantry and 5,000 cavalry, in the North of Spain, to co-operate with the Spanish armies in the expulsion of the French from that kingdom, has been graciously pleased to entrust to you the Command in Chief of this Force. The Officer commanding His Majesty's forces in Portugal [Burrard] is directed to detach, under your orders, a corps of 20,000 infantry, together with the Eighteenth and King's German Regiment of Light Dragoons, now at Lisbon, and a due proportion of artillery; to be joined by a corps of above 10,000 men which are now assembling at Falmouth; the detail of which you will receive herewith enclosed, be assembled and equipped to take the field. It has been determined to assemble this force in the North of Spain, as the quarter where they can be most speedily brought together, and that to which the exertions of the Enemy appear at present to be principally directed.[1]

The force assembling at Falmouth, and other ports, was under the command of Sir David Baird, with instructions to sail to the port of Corunna on Spain's north-western coast. Moore was told that he could move his force from Lisbon to meet up with Baird either by land or sea, whichever he felt was most suitable, though he was told that the cavalry must travel by land because of the hazards of a journey along the coast as winter was approaching as well as all the usual difficulties and discomforts experienced in transporting horses by sea.

Moore was thrilled at the prospect of commanding an army of at least 35,000 men, writing in his diary that: 'There has been no such command since Marlborough for a British officer. How they came to pitch upon me I cannot say, for they have given sufficient proof of not being partial to me.' Who Moore meant by 'they', was British cabinet ministers for it was certainly the case that the outspoken Moore had often clashed with the Government. Yet Glasgow-born Moore had established a formidable reputation as a trainer and leader of men.

It was in 1802 that Moore was made the officer commanding the forces in the Southern District of England, during the height of the French invasion scare. With his base at the newly-formed camp at Shorncliffe Camp near Folkestone, Moore promoted the tactics and philosophy that led to the development of light infantry in the British Army. A Rifle Corps of trained marksmen had already been established but Moore, with the backing of the Commander-in-Chief, the Duke of York, wanted to create battalions of infantry that could operate both as traditional line infantry and as open order skirmishers as circumstances dictated. His objective was to create, as one historian has described it, 'the thinking fighting man'.[2] Moore himself told the Duke of York that 'The service of light infantry does not so much require men of stature as it requires them to be intelligent, handy, and active.'[3]

Moore's own regiment, the 52nd Foot, was, predictably, the first to be trained in this multi-functional role, able to fight both in close battalion formation and as open-order skirmishers. In January 1803 the regiment was re-designated the 52nd Light Infantry and it was quickly acknowledged as being one of the finest in the Army and a blueprint for the future. Moore was able to retain the highest levels of discipline without having to resort to corporal punishment. Moore was considerate to his men and they in return rewarded him with their obedience and loyalty. Whether such ideals could be extended to an army almost 40,000-strong remained to be seen.

Without hesitation Moore chose not to move his army by sea, saying that 'a march, well constructed, will do this army much good'. Not everyone agreed, including Moore's Adjutant General,

Sir Henry Clinton, who believed that the best plan would be to transport the British forces to the northern Spanish coast where they could, in cooperation with the Spanish armies, strike at the exposed French right flank. Moore's Quartermaster General, Colonel George Murray, took a slightly different view, declaring that: 'I am inclined to think, that carrying our force into the Asturias would be the best thing we could do'. Murray wrote that if he had a voice in affairs he, 'would propose to begin without loss of time our arrangements for pushing one corps after another by the Tagus and, and also by Almeida, towards the province of Leon; and look to sending round a corps of 10,000 or 12,000 men by the Asturias by sea.'[4]

Significantly, even Sir Arthur Wellesley, before his departure from Portugal, had told Castlereagh that: 'The only effective plan of operations in which the British troops can be employed … is upon the flank and rear of the enemy's advance towards Madrid, by an issue from the Asturias'. He advocated shipping the troops round to Santander or Gijon from where the army could descend into the León plain. 'To secure the Asturias as soon as possible,' Wellesley reiterated, 'is your first object in Spain'.[5]

However, it was the case that what little arrangements had been made by Dalrymple for extending operations into Spain, and continued by Burrard, upon whom command of the army had fallen after Dalrymple's departure, had been with the intention of marching into that country, not sailing around the coast.[6] This, Moore communicated to Castlereagh: 'It is my intention as it was that of Sir Harry Burrard, to move with the troops from this [place] on Almeida and Ciudad Rodrigo'.[7]

Moore now had to start to prepare for his move into northern Spain, but he found his new army in no fit condition to undertake operations. Even though as far back as 2 September after news had reached London of the defeat of Junot at Vimiero (and before ministers learnt of the shocking details of the Convention of Cintra) Hew Dalrymple had been told that 'the immediate employment of your disposable forces in the north of Spain [was] of the utmost importance to the common cause,' little in this respect had been done.[8]

In fact, according to Andrew Leith Hay, aide-de-camp to his uncle, Major General James Leith, who was the head of a delegation sent into the Asturias to assess the military situation on behalf of the

British Government, the British army was already too late to play an effective part in the operations being planned by the Spaniards: 'if an army was to be sent into Spain as an auxiliary force, essentially to benefit the cause, it ought to have been concentrated, and advanced to the line of operations, by the 1st of October.'

But, in the expectation that they would not be committed to an offensive until the spring, the British troops had already begun to establish winter quarters throughout Portugal. Consequently, the army was widely dispersed and utterly unprepared for campaigning. This Moore explained to Castlereagh: 'The great object at present is to get the troops out of Portugal before the rains set in; but, at this instant, the army is without equipment of any kind, either for the carriage of the light baggage of regiments, artillery stores. Commissariat stores, or other appendages of an army; and not a magazine is formed in any of the routes by which we are to march.'

One thing that Dalrymple had done was send one of his officers, Major General Lord William Bentinck, to Madrid to liaise with the Central (or Supreme) Junta. From the Spaniards Dalrymple hoped that he would be informed of his allies' intentions and the role that the British army could take in support of the Spanish forces. With no knowledge of the country, he expected to receive a list of routes that would be suitable for his army to take in order to be able to join the Spaniards and how he could obtain supplies en route. Yet, according to Sir Charles Oman, he obtained only 'a quantity of vague and generally useless suggestions, some of which argued an astonishing ignorance of military affairs.'[9] The result was that Sir Hew's time in Lisbon was wasted in pointless and prolonged correspondence with Madrid, so that when Moore assumed command not a single measure had been decided upon. 'The arrangement for supplies should have been made and the information respecting roads should have been got,' Moore complained in a letter to Bentinck, 'but when I got the command nothing of this sort had been done. They [ministers] talk of going into Spain as of going into Hyde Park; nobody seemed aware of what an arduous task it was.'[10]

In all fairness to Dalrymple and Burrard, the uprising in Spain had taken everyone by surprise and the British force sent to Portugal had been cobbled together hurriedly and it was not equipped for extended operations of any nature. Castlereagh was fully aware of this and in his letter to Moore he had acknowledged that, 'it will require considerable arrangements before a force of this magnitude can be enabled to take the field.' Yet Moore had to move quickly both before both winter and the French army held northern Spain in their respective grips.

As a consequence, Castlereagh advised Moore to 'concert with the Commissary General (Mr. Erskine), who will be attached to the service of your army, the best means of assembling an adequate supply of horses and mules for rendering your army moveable. And that this may be effected with more dispatch, it may be advisable to draw your supplies from different parts of Spain.' A Deputy Commissary had therefore been sent with an officer of the Wagon Train to the Asturias to obtain as many draught animals as could be found.[11]

Food would also have to be found en route but when the Spanish Commissary General was told how much meat the British army would need, he replied that such consumption would mean that in three months all of the oxen in the country and most of the pigs would be consumed!

Moore's other problem was finance. The British Treasury was as ill-prepared for the Government's involvement in Iberia as was the British Army and was 'embarrassed' with the amount of silver coin it had available. What money it did have to distribute had been given to the Central Junta. The Government hoped that Moore would be able to obtain money on the spot by drawing bills on the Treasury. Portugal, however, was virtually bankrupt as Prince John and the aristocrats that had sailed to Brazil had taken with them around half of the coined money in the country. Much of the rest of the silver and gold coin had been hidden when Junot invaded and with the Portuguese facing an uncertain future this coin remained in its hiding places. This left nothing but copper coin and depreciated paper money in circulation.[12]

Moore's military chest amounted to just £25,000, which would not even cover the cost of hiring transport. The lieutenant general expressed his concern about finance to Castlereagh: 'Nothing but abundance of money, and prompt payments will compensate, when we begin to move … It is my intention to make the troops find their own meat, and to call on the Commissary for bread and wine and forage only. This would be attended with many good effects, besides easing the Commissariat. The troops would be satisfied with less meat and gradually learn to live upon what the country produced in greatest abundance; but to adopt this plan I must be certain of money to pay them which at present I am not.'[13]

The problem was that it was not simply a case of the Government sending out money. In Portugal and Spain, the merchants and bullock owners demanded payment in Mexican silver dollars. The Treasury could only obtain these through a convoluted process involving a Spanish Government agency and two British firms. It would take time, therefore, for the Treasury to be able to provide Moore with the money he needed.

To make the financial situation even worse for the army in Portugal, the money officers received an allowance for 'bat, baggage and forage' had been subjected to income tax. The Treasury, desperate to raise more money, saw this allowance as a form of untaxed income that officers were receiving, not realising that this money was for regiments on campaign to pay for transport.[14] Moore also learnt that Baird's force would be landing at Corunna without money. 'Money and shoes are the two articles we shall be principally in want of,' Moore reminded Castlereagh. In the end money would prove worthless and shoes priceless, as the troops retreated to Corunna.

Adding to Moore's burden was the large number of women and children with the army. The regulation number of wives permitted to be 'on the strength' of a company on active service was six per company. When the troops sailed for Portugal this number had been greatly exceeded. In a bid to ease the pressure on the army's provisions, Moore issued the following General Order on 10 October:

> As in the course of the long march which the army is about to undertake and where no carts will be allowed, the women would unavoidably be exposed to the greatest hardship and distress, commanding officers are, therefore, desired to use their endeavours to prevent as many as possible, particularly those having young children, or such as are not stout, or equal to fatigue, from following the army. Those who remain will be left with the heavy luggage of the regiments. An officer will be charged to draw their rations, and they will be sent to England

by the first good opportunity; and when landed, they will receive the same allowance which they would have been entitled to, if they had not embarked, to enable them to reach their homes'[15]

Few women took up this offer, preferring to stay with their menfolk. It was a decision that many would regret.

Assuming that Moore could overcome his logistical difficulties, he needed a campaign plan. He had been told by Castlereagh that the force was to operate in the north of Spain, and that he should, 'take the necessary measures for opening a communication with the Spanish authorities for the purposes of framing the plan of campaign, on which it might be advisable that the respective armies should act in concert.' This, of course, was stating the obvious, but Castlereagh provided a little more detail of his vision for the operations of Moore's army: 'It will be for you to consider on what points in Galicia, or on the borders of Leon, the troops can be most advantageously assembled and equipped for service, from whence they may move forward as early as circumstances shall permit.'[16]

Moore dismissed this 'plausible verbose nonsense' as 'a sort of gibberish which men in office use and fancy themselves military men.' He quite correctly saw that, 'It does not appear that our Ministers are in communication with the leading men in Spain, or are acquainted with their means or designs. Without a knowledge of these, and a perfect concert with the Spaniards, I cannot see how it is possible to determine where or how we are to act.'[17]

Nevertheless, a rough plan was already forming in Moore's mind: 'It is my intention to forward from this [Lisbon] to Almeida as much ammunition and artillery stores as I can; and to form there also a depot of provisions and other stores. Whatever comes with Sir David Baird, and from England, may be landed, or remain on board a ship at Corunna, to be forwarded from thence to such place, in that line, as may hereafter be judged most fit.'

That plan was soon to change. Moore found that Dalrymple had not even ascertained which roads were suitable for the army or if any of the routes out of Lisbon to the Spanish border, other than that the main highway through Elvas and Badajoz to Madrid, was suitable for the passage of artillery. In all fairness to Dalrymple, who had never commanded an army in the field and had not expected to have to carry the war into Spain, he had not been provided with any maps nor received any information regarding the location of the Spanish armies he was supposed to act in concert with.[18]

When Dalrymple was ordered back to London, Burrard had done his best to organise the move into Spain before handing over that responsibility to Moore. His plan, based on what information he could glean, was for one large column of infantry to march by Coimbra, Almeida and Ciudad Rodrigo; another column to move by the 'middle road' through Abrantes and Castello Branco; while the cavalry and artillery were to join Hope's division at Elvas and advance into Spain by that road, universally described as the best in Portugal.

Remarkably, there was little help from the Portuguese, with no one in Lisbon seeming able to offer much advice about their own country. The only thing that all the Portuguese officers were certain about was that artillery could not be transported over the mountains which form the northern boundary between Spain and Portugal. Even Captain Delaney and other officers on the Quartermaster-General's staff, who had inspected the mountain roads of Beira, confirmed the Portuguese intelligence. Unhappy with the reports he had received, Moore instructed Captain William Maynard Gomm, an assistant quartermaster general who had joined Moore's staff, to see for himself and report his findings:

> I yesterday received instructions to proceed this morning on the road towards Almeida; a division of the army marches in this direction, and they are not at all satisfied with the accounts given them of this route. The high-road is through Leyria and Coimbra, turning the chain of the Estrellas by the left, but this road is too long to be undertaken by us at present, and we expect to meet serious obstacles in the road we propose following. My directions are, therefore, to discover what means there are on the road for the quartering of troops, so that they may be under cover after each day's march; and how far the country is practicable for the passage of artillery. The French [under Junot] came with one column in this direction, but their artillery was very light.[19]

Gomm would not be able to report back before the army marched. Moore, though, was determined to move by whatever route, and just three days after receiving his instructions from Castlereagh, he posted a General Order:

> Lisbon, 9th October, 1808.
>
> The Troops under Lieut.-General Sir John Moore will hold themselves in readiness to move on the shortest notice.
>
> Lieut.-General trusts that the General Officers will lose no time in ascertaining that the Regiments under their command are in good order, and complete in every equipment to enable them to keep the field.
>
> Lieut.-General Sir John Moore will take an early opportunity of inspecting the several corps of the army.
>
> All the heavy baggage will be left in Lisbon, and directions will be given hereafter respecting it.
>
> The General Officers will communicate with the Commanding Officers of corps, upon the situation and fitness of the stores for their heavy baggage, and report thereupon for the information of Lieut.-General Sir J. Moore.
>
> Directions will be given with respect to the sick. The Lieut. General sees with much concern the great number of this description, and that it daily increases. The General assures the troops, that it is owing to their own intemperance, that so many are rendered incapable of marching against the Enemy: and having stated this, he feels confident that he need say no more to British soldiers to insure their sobriety.

After the heady success at Vimerio, the troops had endured weeks of inactivity, and too much local wine was not the only problem for the men in their large camp at Queluz, as one officer explained: 'What with the great heat, the cold nights, the eating of fruit and the drinking of young wine, the health of the army became so much impaired that typhus and dysentery broke out and spread rapidly, affecting even the inhabitants of villages lying close to the camp. The pestilential stench of our slaughter-house refuse, also contributed somewhat to the trouble; while, in addition, a huge hospital was installed in one of the wings of the castle, not far behind and below our stores depot, and separated from it only by a long ditch which was used as a latrine by the dysentery patients, and was not 500 yards away. Infection was bound to occur.'[20]

By all accounts the prospect of action 'brightened the spirits of the army'. But ordering the army to move was far easier than making it happen. For Moore soon discovered that Burrard had been entirely correct and that he could not move his entire force along any single route. He had been told that he could not take his artillery directly to Almeida and, as no magazines had been formed in advance, the countryside along the highway through Elvas simply could not support his entire force. Based on this information, Moore saw that he would have to split up his army, a move that worried him greatly, as he told Bentinck, 'you may believe that it is not without regret that I separate the army by the corps which Hope marches on Madrid and Valladolid, but there is no help for it. It was the opinion of General Castaños and the Spanish officers that we should enter Spain by Almeida and Ciudad Rodrigo; the troops were distributed accordingly, and it was only when too late we found that direction would not do for artillery and cavalry; and as it is, we must hope that the French will be kept on the other side of the Ebro until our junction.'[21]

The eventual division of the army that Moore settled upon was:

a) By Coimbra and Celorico

Beresford's Brigade (1st Battalion 9th Foot; 2nd Battalion 43rd Light Infantry; 2nd Battalion 52nd Light Infantry).

Fane's Brigade (1st Battalion 38th Foot; 1st Battalion 79th Foot; four companies 2nd Battalion 95th Rifles).

Five companies 5th Battalion 60th Foot (Rifles).

b) By Abrantes and Guarda

Bentinck's Brigade (1st Battalion 4th Foot; 1st Battalion 28th Foot; 1st Battalion 42nd Foot; four companies 2nd Battalion 95th Rifles)

Hill's Brigade (1st Battalion 5th Foot; 1st Battalion 32nd Foot; 1st Battalion 91st Foot).

c) By Elvas and Alacantara

Anstruther's Brigade (20th Foot; 1st Battalion 52nd Light Infantry; five companies 1st Battalion 95th Rifles).

Alten's Brigade (1st and 2nd battalions Light Infantry of the King's German Legion, one battery of artillery i.e. Captain Wilmot's brigade of light 6-pounders).

d) By Elvas and Talavera

Hope's Division (18th Light Dragoons (Hussars)); 3rd Light Dragoons King's German Legion; 2nd Foot, 1st Battalion 36th Foot; 1st Battalion 71st (Highland) Light Infantry; 1st Battalion 92nd Foot; six batteries of artillery.

The force under Sir David Baird that was to join Moore had embarked at Harwich, Portsmouth, Ramsgate and Cork throughout September and October. By 13 October, most of these troops had reached Corunna, but the cavalry of the 10th and 15th Light Dragoons (Hussars), had been the last to be embarked and were still in transit.

Sir John Hope, whose division was already encamped on the road to Elvas, had anticipated a move along the highway to Badajoz and Madrid, and had already sen this engineers and commissaries forward to improve the road and establish food stores along the route. Reports from reconnaissance parties indicated that the road was paved and well-travelled but would be unable to support his corps if it moved in one large mass. So he divided his troops into ten equal units and sent them off at the rate of one per day. The artillery led the way, followed by the infantry and then the cavalry. A number of infantry battalions were mixed in with the artillery units so they could help the cannons cross difficult terrain.[22]

With most of the army's wagons following the route through Elvas, 'The army ran the risk of finding itself in front of the enemy with no more ammunition than the men carried in their pouches,' wrote a clearly anxious Moore, 'but had I waited until everything was forwarded the troops would not have been in Spain until the spring, and I trust that the enemy will not find out our wants as soon as they will feel the effects of what we have.'[23]

Despite such worries, the reports that Moore received from Spain painted a highly favourable picture of events across the border. The Spanish Government recommended Burgos as the point of union for the British troops, and Madrid and Valladolid were the places appointed for magazines. The Spanish Central

Junta communicated to Moore, through William Bentinck, that it was expected he would find between 60,000 and 70,000 men assembled in the Asturias and Galicia under la Romana and General Joachim Blake who was the Captain-General of Galicia. In addition to these bodies was the main Spanish force, under General the Marquis de Castaños, which was stationed further to the east in the centre of the country. The prospects of a heavy blow being struck against the French forces that had retreated beyond the Ebro, if the Spaniards were to be believed, therefore seemed very good.

Lord Bentinck in Madrid was far less sanguine. The Spaniard might well be full of ardour and enthusiasm, but their 'armies' were hastily-assembled, ill-equipped and disorganised – and worst of all, overconfident and unappreciative of their enemy. 'I am every moment more and more convinced,' Bentinck wrote in a dispatch at the beginning of October, 'that a blind confidence in their own strength, and natural slowness, are the rocks upon which this good ship runs the risk of being wrecked.' Bentinck was showing great perspicacity, for at this stage the allies had no idea that Napoleon was leading his *Grande Armée* towards the Pyrenees, or of the great disaster that was about to unfold.[24]

Napoleon, his personal reputation at stake, was waiting for the Spaniards to reveal their hand before he struck. After considerable wrangling, the Spaniards came up with a plan of operations which was intended to envelop the French on the Ebro and cut their communications with France. A strong force (the Army of Estremadura under the Count of Belvedere) would present itself in front of the French to hold their attention, while Blake moved towards Bilbao along the Biscay coast, and Castaños with the force under José Palafox the Captain-General of Aragon, marched north-westwards to Pamplona. The problem with this scheme was that the two main Spanish forces would be so far apart that there could be no effective communication between them and the isolated centre would be able to offer little resistance if the French decided to take the offensive and march on Madrid.

Moore saw the weakness of the Spanish arrangements. 'The positions of the Spanish armies, I have never been able to understand,' Moore wrote in his diary, 'They are separated, one in

Biscay, the other in Aragon, on the two flanks of the French, leaving the whole country of Spain exposed to their incursion, and leaving the British army exposed to be attacked before it is united.'

Even if large reinforcements were not already gathering on the Ebro, the idea that 80,000 or so Spaniards, divided into two wings separated by 200 miles, with no strong covering force to hold their centre, could hope to surround 65,000 French was entirely preposterous.[25] What this plan actually meant was that Napoleon would be able to attack and crush each wing in turn before pushing through the weak centre. The Spaniards really could not have presented Napoleon with an easier route to victory.

It would be that Spanish army under the Count of Belvedere in the centre which Moore's force was supposed to join. He just had to hope he would get there in time to be able to play a part before Napoleon struck, as he told Castlereagh: 'It is impossible to be more anxious than I am to get forward; but it is needless to take forward troops without the means to enable them to act; and however light the equipment I have fixed, yet the difficulty of procuring it is very considerable; add to this, a Commissariat extremely zealous, but quite new and inexperienced in the important duties which it now falls to their lot to execute. I am, however, sufficiently aware of the importance of even the name of a British army in Spain, and I am hurrying as much as possible.'[26]

What seems remarkable is that the British Government should want to expose its only field army to such a reckless venture. There would be much criticism of Moore in the weeks to come, but the reality is that he was being sent on an ill-defined operation – 'one so vague and so hazardous'[27] – the success of which was dependent entirely upon the Spaniards.

When Bentinck had pressed Castaños, who had been nominated president of the Central Junta's Military Board, for precise details regarding the part the British army was to play in the coming campaign and how it would be supplied and how, and to whom, Moore should communicate to co-ordinate operations, he received only imprecise answers. The reality was that the Central Junta, whose authority was always in question, exercised little control over the provinces or of their provincial armies. As each general jealously guarded his own position, it meant that no supreme commander-in-chief had been appointed, which is why Castaños could not offer Bentinck a firm operational plan.

Moore, meanwhile, and hoping for the best, continued to devote his energies to providing the transport that would enable his troops to begin their march into Spain, and he wrote in his diary on 14 October: 'The Commissariat had at its head Mr. Erskine, a gentleman of great integrity and honour, and of considerable ability; but neither he nor any of his officers have any experience of what an army of this magnitude requires to put it in motion. Everything is, however, going on with zeal; there is no want of that in an English army; and though the difficulties are considerable, and we have to go through a very impracticable country, I expect to be past the frontier early in November. I have spoken to the general officers, and told those commanding what I expect from them, and, if they are diligent, as I believe they will be, the army will at the end of its march be far better than it is at present.'[28]

Napoleon, meanwhile, had quickly detected the weaknesses of the Spanish plan and waited patiently until the two wings of the Spanish forces had marched beyond the point of no return. One of Napoleon's marshals, however, seeing Blake's 19,000 (not the 60,000 the Madrid Junta had claimed) tramping through Bilbao, could not resist the temptation to attack this isolated force. Marshal François Lefebve fell upon Blake with 21,000 men at Pancorbo. Though Blake was beaten, it was not the decisive blow that Napoleon had intended, and the Emperor was justifiably angry.

There was still a chance that Blake could be trapped if Napoleon moved quickly. So, somewhat prematurely, Napoleon crossed the Ebro and opened his offensive on 7 November.

To the east, marshals Ney and Moncey bided their time as Castaños and Palafox marched ever further north. Being out of communication with the other Spanish forces, they had no idea that they were walking into a trap, and as Napoleon had once famously said 'never interrupt your enemy when he is making a mistake', the two marshals allowed the Spaniards to continue their movement blissfully unaware of what was soon to befall them. It was into this unfolding disaster that Moore was about to march.

None of this was known to Moore, who had also been misled about the size and capacity of the Spanish forces. Notwithstanding the extensive correspondence that he carried on with Madrid, he could obtain no certain accounts of the numbers or condition of the Spanish forces, before the arrival of Napoleon. The true state of the wretchedly equipped and weak Spanish armies was deliberately withheld from not just the British but also the people of the country, 'to prevent its sinking the nation into despair.'[29]

Captain, later Lieutenant General, Samuel Ford Whittingham had been Dalrymple's assistant military secretary but had sought permission to join the Spanish forces as a volunteer. He duly joined Castaños and saw for himself the state of the body under the Marquis: 'The army of Castile was drawn up to receive the General,' Whittingham wrote to Bentinck on 25 October. 'Its strength about 11,000 men. But to form any idea of its composition, it is absolutely necessary to have seen it. It is a complete mass of miserable peasantry, without clothing, without organization, and with few Officers that deserve the name. The General and principal Officers have not the least confidence in their troops; and, what is yet worse, the men have no confidence in themselves. This is not an exaggerated picture; it is a true portrait.'[30] This was the force with which Castañosand Palafox were supposed to engulf the French left wing.

Nevertheless, for his part, Moore had knocked his army into shape and his march to Spain, and into history, had begun.

Chapter 3

Portugal Adieu

On 13 October, the camp at Queluz was broken up and the first regiments started out on the 300-mile trek across difficult and mountainous terrain to Salamanca in Spain. A force of 10,000 men was retained at Lisbon under Harry Burrard, and then Lieutenant General Sir John Craddock when Burrard, like Dalrymple before him, was summoned to face the Board of Inquiry into the Convention of Cintra,

Moore's troops moved off by regiments in succession along the different routes that had been selected. Spirits were high at the prospect of action, 'and an army in better heart, finer condition, or more gallantly commanded were ever produced by any nation upon earth,' wrote young Lieutenant Blakeney who had just been appointed to the Light Company of the 28th (North Gloucestershire) Regiment.' George Napier agreed, 'A more glorious set of fellows never was seen.'[1]

Robert Kerr Porter, an artist friend of Moore's who had accompanied him to Spain, had a somewhat different opinion of the departing troops: 'In faith, I must confess, that unless military necessity obliges, I know of no set of men more indolent in putting themselves in motion than those belonging to the army.'[2] Nevertheless, Moore was able to inform Castlereagh on 18 October that, 'The greatest part of the troops are in motion; in the course of this week all will, I hope, be clear of Lisbon. As soon as they are placed on their different routes, and I have concluded the arrangements here, I shall leave the conduct of the marches to the Generals conducting the different columns, and shall proceed myself direct to Almeida, to determine their further movement.'[3]

Just over a week later, Moore wrote in his journal of 27 October that: 'All the troops are out of Lisbon except two regiments, which will march tomorrow and the next day, and, having finished every arrangement, I left Lisbon this morning, meaning to follow this road to Abrantes, and then to be guided by the information I received.'[4]

It is clear that, because of the urgent necessity to deliver his troops into Spain at the soonest possible time, Moore was embarking on a very hazardous enterprise with so little information either of the routes along which his troops were travelling or of the military situation ahead of him. He was also only able to travel with the light baggage of the troops, what he described as a 'scant' supply of medicines, and the barest minimum of ammunition. He hoped that the Commissariat would be able to establish a depot at Almeida, the Portuguese fortress on the north-eastern border with Spain.

Moore was taking an enormous risk in marching into a war zone with the flimsiest of arrangements. His greatest danger was that of being caught with his army divided. Hope had set off on the highway to Madrid via Badajoz with the cavalry and most of the artillery, a total of approximately 6,000 men, or around a quarter of the force directly under Moore's command. Moore described this route as 'a great round,' but said that 'there is no help for it; the road turns to the left a short distance from Madrid, and leads upon Espinar, from whence it can be directed on Valladolid and Burgos, or whatever other place may be judged hereafter best for the assembling of the army.'

As we have already learned, the main elements of the reinforcements from England under Baird had arrived off Corunna on the same day that the first regiments started out from Lisbon, 13 October. Moore intended that the whole of the troops coming from Portugal should unite at Salamanca; and that Baird and Baird and Hope join them there or, as we have seen, at Valladolid or Burgos. According to Moore's military secretary, John Colborne, Moore expected Baird to arrive at Salamanca in early November. With his army joined, Colborne declared, 'it was more probable that the army would incline towards Madrid than any other point'.[5] Moore, though, could make no fixed plans at this early stage of the campaign with the military situation in Spain so unclear.

Moore wrote to Baird upon the latter's arrival at Corunna, explaining that when he had taken over command of the army from Burrard nothing had been done to prepare any of the regiments for offensive operations in Spain:

> It was left to my option to march through Spain and Portugal, or to embark and join you at Corunna by sea – for many reasons I have preferred the march. There is much to do in the way of preparation; mules must be purchased for the light baggage of officers, and for the carriage of such stores as are indispensable; and provisions must be forwarded on the line by which the troops are to march.
>
> In this country (Portugal) the roads are abominable, and the means of carriage very limited. There are many other difficulties to encounter, with which I shall not trouble you, yet in spite of them I do not despair to have the army completely equipped and passed the frontier of Portugal before the wet season sets in.[6]

The troops duly set off on their respective routes. Marching with Beresford's Brigade was an 'old' 52nd man, Lieutenant, later Captain, John Dobbs:

> Our first day's march was a short one, but the weight each man had to carry was tremendous in addition to heavy knapsacks; there were their muskets and accoutrements, seventy rounds of ammunition, a blanket, a mess kettle, and wooden canteen. They and their officers had three days' provisions.[7]

Sir Richard Henegan was with the Commissariat in Portugal and, with the title of Ordnance Commissary in the Field Train, was given the task of moving the army's reserve ammunition. This consisted of 2,500,000 rounds of ball cartridges and a large supply of round shot, canister and shell for the artillery. He has left us this description of just how monumental a task he had to undertake: 'The stores were to be conveyed, in the first instance, by water from Lisbon to Abrantes, in fifteen boats, provided by the [Portuguese] Regency, of about forty tons each, and such was the clumsy negligence, or want of proper information, on the part of the authorities, that instead of reaching Abrantes, it was found impracticable to ascend the Tagus in large boats beyond Santarem, not half the distance'. The large boats actually grounded in the shallow water. The only thing that Henegen could do was commandeer every small boat that passed by. 'It was a cruel necessity to stop the peasants as they plied backwards and forwards with fruit and other perishable articles, forcing them to discharge their little cargoes on the banks of the river, for the purpose of re-loading their boats with our heavy stores; but in this manner, we laid strong hands on one hundred and ninety-eight small craft, into which, after tedious labour, the transfer of the ordnance stores was effected … and we proceeded onwards to Abrantes.'

The 32nd Regiment had been detailed to act as escort for the reserve ammunition and, after all the exertion of transferring the stores when the boats reached Abrantes, the whole lot had to be loaded onto bullock carts. Then, over 'rugged mountains and wretched roads' the ragged convoy had to negotiate the difficult defile at Villa Velha, where a flying-bridge had been thrown over the Tagus. It took eleven days for the reserve ammunition to reach Castello Branco, exposed throughout to an incessant, drenching rain. 'Should any of the gallant fellows of the 32nd be still alive,' Henegan commented after the war, 'they will not have forgotten this breaking into the hardships of a soldier's life.'[8]

A young engineer, Ensign Boothby, had been sent ahead of Hope's division to inspect the roads and countryside ahead of the main body. He described part of the route, leading to Penaparda as a 'bleak, rocky, wretched road, with a black hill on one side, and a precipice on the other, both lost in the impenetrable clouds, and what one could see of them covered with the stumps of heath, which, having been burnt, were quite black, and this, added to the excessive cold, made me feel as if I were travelling on the bare outside of the world.'[9]

For John Dobbs of the 52nd, that first march was a 'distressing' one as they had not a drop of water from dawn to dusk. 'The consequence was, that the men fell out by hundreds, but even this had some advantage, as they marked the road for those in the rear.'[10]

Water might have been scarce, but not every liquid. Assistant Commissary Schaumann was smoking cigars and talking politics with Lieutenant Colonel Hinde and other officers of the

32nd Regiment in a house in Villa Velha, when the sergeant-major walked in, saluted and said: 'Colonel, I come to inform you, sir, that the whole regiment, including the guard and picket is dead drunk; many of the men are lying like dead … just now, when I inspected the guard, I found the corporal with all his men stretched out on the floor dead drunk.' The men had discovered ten casks full of strong brandy.[11]

In the second week of November the troops reached the Portuguese frontier. Rifleman Benjamin Harris of the 95th Rifles recalled the journey from Lisbon consisted of long, tiring marches: 'I do not know how many miles we traversed ere we reached Almeida, which I was told was the last town in Portugal,' Harris later wrote, 'some of my companions said we had come five hundred miles since we had left Lisbon. We now passed to the left and bade adieu to Portugal for ever. We had fought and conquered, and felt elated accordingly. Spain was before us, and every man in the Rifles seemed only anxious to get a rap at the French again.'[12]

Robert Porter riding with Hope's division was similarly excited at the prospect of a glorious campaign: 'We do not merely carry our own strength, but are to join hosts of determined patriots ready to fight or to die in defence of their injured land. How can we then, with such advantages, doubt of marking our track with victories; and, at the close, plant the united colours of England and of Spain upon the farthest promontory of the Pyrennees!'[13]

It may be recalled that Moore had been told by the Portuguese that the road to the frontier at Almeida was entirely unsuitable for artillery, but, as he discovered, this was not the case at all. 'The road, except in a few places within a short distance of Gavido, was good and fit for artillery,' Moore wrote on 5 November. His officers then learned that there was a perfectly good road that bypassed the narrow defiles near Gavido. 'I now find I could have brought the artillery by this road; but the difficulty of obtaining correct information was such, that this road was only discovered stage to stage by our own officers.' Moore, it now seemed, had separated his army unnecessarily. As has been pointed out by one historian, it should have occurred to Moore that on the ramparts of the border fortress of Almeida, the second strongest in Portugal, were guns far heavier than the field pieces of the British army. They had to have reached Almeida from the arsenal at Lisbon by road. Equally, Junot had invaded Portugal through Ciudad Rodrigo and Almeida and his subordinate, General Louis Loison, operated around the border with his artillery in supressing a rebellion in the province of Beira.[14]

Moore realised that he had been negligent and that if he was attacked before his army was united he could not use the state of the roads as an excuse. He admitted this to Hope in a letter from Almeida on 8 November: 'If anything adverse happens, I have not necessity to plead: the road we are now travelling is practicable for artillery: the brigade under Wilmot has already reached Guarda, and as far as I have already seen the road presents few obstacles, and those easily surmounted.'[15]

Such introspection was generated by the reports he had received from Bentinck and Charles Stuart, which gave him depressing accounts of Spanish affairs. He was seriously concerned that he had committed a terrible blunder dividing his army as he had done. He told Castlereagh, on the other hand, that Wilmot's brigade of artillery only reached Salamanca 'with infinite difficulty' along 'the worst roads I ever saw'[16]. Blakeney described in some detail the problems Wilmot's brigade experienced getting through the pass of Villa Velha: 'The first gun conveyed across had two drag-ropes attached, and to resist its rapidity while being trailed downhill these ropes were held by as many soldiers as the short and frequent turning of this zigzag would permit; yet their resistance was scarcely sufficient to preserve the guns from rolling over the precipice.'[17]

The reality probably lies somewhere between the two, in that it might just have been possible for the artillery to accompany the main body, though with great difficulty and much delay. Equally, while Moore had failed to ascertain the true condition of the roads leading to Almeida, he had very little time in which to do this after taking over command of the army, as he was impelled to move over the mountains to the frontier before the onset of the autumnal rains. The absolute necessity of this was made apparent as soon as the columns began to ascend the mountains beyond Castello Branco in early November. Adam Neale wrote that when the column reached Guarda on 15 November, 'It rained incessantly during the two days we were there, and the atmosphere was so foggy, that we could scarcely see from one side of the street to the other.' Robert Blakeney had similar memories: 'On the day upon which we marched into Guarda the 5th Regiment lost five men and the 28th two men, who actually perished on the road in consequence of heavy rain which incessantly fell the whole day. A person who has never been out of England can scarcely imagine its violence.'[18]

Nevertheless, if the information given to Moore by the Secretary of State was correct, the risk Moore had taken in dividing his army was not great. According to Castlereagh, the assembling and mobilisation of Moore's army was designed to take place on the borders of Galicia and Leon, where its flanks would be secured by the troops of Romana and Blake and by the Asturian levies, in all 60,000 or 70,000 men, over and above the Spanish troops opposed to the front and right of the French. In such circumstances the danger the division of his army posed would be, according to Sir John Fortescue, 'so small as to be negligible'[19].

It must also be remembered that Moore had the option of moving his troops by sea. He was told that the cavalry must travel by land, but he was given the choice of land or sea for the rest of his force. If he had moved them by sea, the troops could have landed at Gijon and easily joined hands with Baird's corps. This would have just left the quick-moving cavalry to march north, possibly along the route through Almeida taken by the infantry. Moore's entire force could have been united days if not weeks earlier. This was the opinion of General Sarrazin, who pointed out that if the British force had been assembled in November it would have been in a position to perform the task for which it was intended – to support the Spanish armies which, at that date, were still unbeaten.[20]

Though back in the UK, Sir Arthur Wellesley continued to take a keen interest in Moore's movements. As well as reiterating his belief that Sir John should have moved his army by sea, with his usual foresight, Wellesley told Castlereagh that Moore would soon find himself in trouble. 'From all I have seen and heard of the Spanish armies I am very well convinced that if they are not already defeated and dispersed, they will be before long.'[21] If Moore had remained in touch with the coast rather than marching inland, should he find the Spanish armies defeated, a re-embarkation could be undertaken without undue difficulty.

Be all that as it may, Hope was still a long way off, perhaps further that Moore had expected by the middle of November. He sought to remedy this by asking Hope to send out officers to see if they could find a suitable road that would save his division from marching all the way round Madrid.

As for the force under Baird, its arrival at Corunna had been noted by Henry Crabb Robinson, who became *The Times'* first war correspondent: 'In the morning, when I was over my books, I was startled by the report of cannon, and, running to the ramparts, beheld more than 150 vessels, transports, sailing in a double row before a gentle breeze. It was a striking spectacle, and I felt proud of it. But I remarked that the sight was rather mortifying than gratifying to the pride of some of the Spanish gentry, who were looking on, and who might feel humiliated that their country needed such aid.'[22]

Crabb Robinson was all too correct in his observations as no one had given Baird permission to land his troops and the local junta was either unwilling or unable to do so. While Baird was given a tremendous reception by the Spaniards, the troops remained bobbing at anchor on the transports in the Corunna roads.

Moore stayed at Almeida on 9 and 10 November, writing letters to Madrid and trying to glean information about the situation in Spain. What he did learn from Stuart and Bentinck was that the Central Junta was inefficient, and the Spanish armies were weak, untrained and ill-equipped.[23] He also learnt that the French had already received a reinforcement of 27,000 men with more to follow. 'The Supreme Junta begin to be alarmed, and to do that from fear which they should have done three months ago from prudence and good sense,' Moore wrote in his journal. 'They have not, however, yet appointed a Commander-in-chief, though, from General Castaños being appointed the person with whom I am to correspond, it looks as if he was considered as the officer in whom they placed most confidence.' He then made the following prophesy: 'Some change must take place, or affairs cannot prosper.'[24]

Though ill-informed and as yet still unaware of the true state of the Spanish armies with which he was supposed to act, Moore continued on into Spain, leaving Brigadier General Anstruther with the 6th Regiment to hold Almeida, and therefore safeguard his line of retreat back into Portugal should the situation change dramatically. Moore had chosen to place the 6th Regiment in Almeida because, 'their conduct has been bad, and their officers have been shamefully negligent.' One of their men had been court martialled for 'marauding and robbing' and sentenced to death. Moore saw the crime as that of 'deliberate villainy' and announced that, 'He must therefore suffer the awful punishment to which he has been condemned.'[25]The man was shot to reinforce Moore's stern reminder that: 'The army is sent by England to aid and support the Spanish nation, not to plunder its inhabitants.'[25]

The 6th Regiment was, consequently, to be left behind: 'I spoke to them with great severity,' Moore wrote, 'and told them I should not take them into Spain; they were unworthy of it.'

Moore left Almeida on 11 November: 'I proceeded to Ciudad Rodrigo, six leagues over an open country,' he wrote in his diary. 'A small rivulet divides the two countries … the country is open and the river passable everywhere. Ciudad Rodrigo is an ancient walled town. The Governor met us two miles off, and I was saluted from the ramparts by a discharge of artillery, taken to the house of the richest gentleman of the town, well entertained.' Moore was suitably impressed with his reception and he declared that: 'No change, whether in the face of the country, in men and manners, can be greater than that immediately perceptible upon entering Spain from Portugal. The advantage is entirely on the side of Spain and of the Spaniards.'[26]

Robert Blakeney agreed: 'Pleasure we experienced at the wonderful contrast between the people whom we had just quitted and our present hosts, entirely in favour of the latter; and although we did not understand their language, yet it fell so melodiously on the ear that I for one could never after suffer the Portuguese dialect.'[27]

On 13 November Moore rode the twenty-seven miles from Ciudad Rodrigo to Salamanca where he hoped, by the beginning of December, to have concentrated his forces and then be in a position to strike at the French in combination with the Spanish armies. Unfortunately, this scheme was already looking highly impracticable. The day he arrived, a 'dishevelled' courier reached Moore's headquarters with the news that 'the French, after beating the army of Estremadura, are advanced to Burgos. Gen. Blake's army in Biscay has been defeated, dispersed, and its officers and soldiers are flying in every direction; and the armies of Castaños and Palafox, on the Ebro and Alagon, are at too great a distance to render me the smallest assistance. Under such circumstances the junction of this Army becomes exceedingly precarious, and requires to be conducted with much circumspection.' In a long letter to Bentick, Moore wrote: 'The moment is a critical one – my own situation particularly so – I have never seen it otherwise; but I have pushed into Spain at all hazards; – this was the order of my government and it was the will of the people of England.'[28]

What had actually happened was that Soult's II Corps, leading the way towards Madrid, had encountered the Army of Estremadura posted in front of Burgos on 10 November. Regarded as 'the flower of the Spanish armies', the Count of Belvedere's force consisted of some 11,000 infantry and 1,200 cavalry, all equipped with British-supplied arms and accoutrements, along with a similar number of levies. The Spaniards were slaughtered. Almost 3,000 were left dead on the ground and the rest were scattered. Except for a few thousand miserable fugitives whom Blake was later able to rally at Reynosa, the entire Estremadura army fled, spreading confusion and dismay throughout the neighbouring provinces.[29]

By that evening Napoleon was in Burgos. The following day his cavalry swept southwards unopposed. Napoleon knew he could now concentrate on crushing the other Spanish armies, and that afternoon Soult was sent to Reynosa to surround the remnants of Blake's 12,000 men of the Army of Galicia whilst Marshal Ney cut Castaños off from Madrid, leaving just the weak Spanish Army of the Centre to defend the Spanish capital. Moore assembled the Salamanca junta and told them of the information he had received and told them that with the French so close he would no longer be able to concentrate his army as he had hoped and would have no choice but to return to Portugal.

Moore also learnt of the problems Baird was experiencing at Corunna: 'I am sorry to say, from Sir David Baird, I hear nothing but complaints of the Junta of Corunna, who afford him no assistance,' he wrote to William Bentinck on the day he entered Salamanca. 'They promise everything, but give nothing; and after waiting day after day for carts, which they had promised to procure for the carriage of stores, his Commissary was at last obliged to contract for them at an exorbitant price, and then got them. This is really a sort of conduct quite intolerable to troops that the Spanish Government have asked for, and for whose advance they are daily pressing.'[30]

Money was also becoming a pressing problem, writing on 19 November to the newly-appointed Ambassador to the Central Junta in Madrid, Mr Hookham Frere, who had arrived in Spain exactly a month earlier:

> A Courier from Madrid brought me this morning letters from Mr. Stuart and Lord William Bentinck of the 17th: the former inclosed [sic] an order from the Supreme Junta of Ciudad Rodrigo, to place 20,000 dollars at my disposition, to be repaid hereafter. The Junta of this town are endeavouring to get money for us. Nothing can exceed the attention of the Marquis Cinalbo, the President; the Clergy, with Dr Curtis at their head, exert themselves; and even a Convent of Nuns have promised five thousand pounds; – all this shews great good will. The funds, however, which it can raise, are small, and very inadequate to our wants. I trust that you will be able to supply us more amply from Madrid, until those from England arrive. A King's messenger brought me, on the night of the 17th, a Letter from Lord Castlereagh of the 2nd, in which he informs me, that two millions of dollars are upon their passage to Corunna; but his Lordship adds, that the difficulty of procuring silver is such, in England, that I must not look for a further supply for some months, and he impresses the necessity of taking every means of obtaining money upon the spot. The expected arrival of the above sum from England, must not, therefore, lessen your endeavours to get what you can for us at Madrid.[31]

The urgent need for money merely added to Moore's increasing woes. After all the great expectations he had just a few weeks earlier, Moore was now thoroughly downcast, writing on the 26th to one of his brothers of his disappointment: 'Upon entering Spain, I have found affairs in a very different state from what I expected, or from what they are thought to be in England. I am in a scrape from which God knows how I am to extricate myself.'

What Moore also said in this letter was that the concentration point of the British forces should have been at Seville rather than Salamanca. Moore had been instructed to operate in the north of Spain, but this had resulted in the French being able to attack the Spaniards before he could unite with Baird. Had the concentration point been in the south of Spain, as Moore now realised, Baird's corps could have been shipped round to Cadiz rather than Corunna, and Moore could have marched *with all his artillery* along the highway from Lisbon, though Badajoz, and on to Seville. This alternative course of action will be considered later, the merits of which will become apparent as this story unfolds.

The other aspect to this was that the British army had arrived in theatre far too late to be of any practical use to the Spanish armies, as Leith Hay, who had travelled 900 miles across Spain before joining Moore's army, wrote: 'One month earlier, it might have produced the most powerful as well as most beneficial effect; but the time was past. A body of really good troops, co-operating with the Spanish armies, and vigorously attacking the French before they became reinforced, might have totally changed the aspect of affairs; but what great impression was to be expected from 30,000 British taking the field against the enormous strength of the enemy, particularly after the total discomfiture of every Spanish force with which they were destined to act.'[32]

Meanwhile, the troops that had marched from Lisbon were arriving at Salamanca untroubled by the burdens that their commander was under and oblivious to the successive defeats that had been inflicted upon their Spanish allies. 'On and on we toiled,' recalled Rifleman Harris, 'till we reached Salamanca. I love to remember the appearance of that army as we moved along at this time. It was a glorious sight to see our colours spread in these fields. The men seemed invincible; nothing, I thought, could have beaten them.'[33]

Major Patterson marched with the 50th Regiment and was delighted with the reception the army received from the Spaniards:

> Not only before we entered the gates of Salamanca, but previous to our entry into every other town or city, the inhabitants came out in crowds to meet the troops; men, women, and children, shaking

hands with and embracing officers and soldiers, while, as they escorted them, the air was rent with their loud and enthusiastic acclamations – '*Viva los Ingleses!*' '*Mueran los Francesa!*' issued from every quarter.

At Salamanca, the city guard turned out, with a non-military display of court dresses, rather soiled, of different reigns and fashions, and armed with various weapons … They felt themselves highly honoured and much gratified on being relieved by a British guard, to whom the city keys were with all due ceremony confided.[34]

The first, favourable, impression that troops had of the Spaniards very soon began to evaporate, however. 'What a difference between the friendly, hospitable Portuguese and these disobliging Spaniards,' remarked one officer. 'Everyone here is grave, monosyllabic and gloomy.'

John Dobbs' first contact with the Spaniards was also a disappointment: 'In the first village we had a sample of Spanish welcome; we were told that we were not wanted, that they could fight their own battles without our help.'[35]

Another officer of the 50th (West Kent) Regiment was also unimpressed with the Spaniards and doubted that they could ever achieve anything on their own: 'I hope I am not a prophet, but if the British troops don't save Spain, I think the Spaniards can't, for so vain are they that already they talk of invading France, forgetting that the best general and 300,000 of the second best troops in the world are to be conquered first.'[36]

Adam Neal, writing on 26 November, was astonished at the apparent indifference of the locals to the war that was developing all around them:

> Since my arrival here, I have witnessed so much apparent apathy and indifference, that I feel the most serious apprehension of the result. Indeed I cannot help, at times, asking myself if I am really in the midst of Spain. The beings I see muffled up in long cloaks, sauntering here in listless indolence under the piazzas, are so different from the bold impassioned race, which the heated imagination had been contemplating … you would imagine the country was in a state of profound peace; no energy, no bustle, no alacrity.[37]

A large proportion of those French troops, having compelled Blake's force to abandon all its baggage and heavy equipment and run for the hills of Galicia, met the combined armies of Castaños and Palafox at Tudela. The inevitable French victory opened the road to Madrid. But a disturbing feature of the war in the Peninsula was already becoming a factor in what would become a bitter and ruthless war – the actions of the guerrillas.

The French generals were having considerable difficulty keeping their men fed, and despite strict orders to the contrary, officers were unable to prevent widespread looting and pillage. Soon hundreds, possibly thousands of angry Spaniards, took to the mountains and began to wage a savage guerrilla war on the invaders' lines of communication. No isolated French detachment was safe, and most couriers had to be provided with a strong escort. The deeper Napoleon penetrated into Spain the longer, and more vulnerable, became his communications.

Napoleon needed to bring the war to a rapid conclusion. He paused at Aranda to await the result of the Battle of Tudela on 23 November and for his troops to concentrate. Then, on 28 November, the advance on the Spanish capital commenced, and 130,000 men began their march to Madrid.[38]

Moore was, as yet, unaware of the disaster that had befallen Castaños and Palafox and he conducted his affairs, we are told, 'with order, and without procrastination'. James Carrick Moore, the general's brother, described Moore's routine at Salamanca: 'He always rose between three and four in the morning, lighted his fire and candle by a lamp which was placed in his room, and employed himself in writing till eight o'clock, when the officers of the family were assembled for breakfast. After breakfast he received the General Officers, and all persons with whom he had business; and the necessary orders were issued. His pen was frequently in his hand in the forenoon also; for he wrote all his letters himself. He always rode before dinner for an hour or two, either to view the troops, or to reconnoitre the country. His table was plentiful, and the company varied from fourteen to twenty officers. He was a very plain and moderate eater, and seldom drank more than three or four glasses of wine, conversing with his officers with great frankness and cheerfulness. His portfolio was usually opened again before he went to bed; but, unless kept up by business, he never sat up later than ten o'clock.'[39]

The organised and disciplined British general was already becoming severely disillusioned with the disorganised Spaniards, as he told Castlereagh on 24 November: 'The enthusiasm of which we heard so much nowhere appears … I am at this moment in no communication with any of their generals. I am ignorant of their plans or of those of their Government … I cannot calculate the power of a whole people determined and enthusiastic, if persons are brought forward with ability to direct it, but at present nothing of this kind appears, and yet I see no other chance Spain has of resistance. We are here by ourselves, left to manage the best way we can, without communication with any other army; no knowledge of the strength or positions of the Enemy, but what we can pick up in a country where we are strangers, and in complete ignorance of the plans or wishes of the Spanish Government.'[40]

Moore must have reflected at this time about his decision to march into Spain without his cavalry to scout ahead of the army to watch for the approach of the enemy. If the French were to drive upon Salamanca Moore would have little warning and no time to respond. He admitted this, though not quite in so many words, in a private letter to Castlereagh on 24 November: 'I certainly thought I was perfectly safe in assembling the army at Salamanca, but if I had had sooner a conception of the weakness of the Spanish armies, the defenceless state of the country, the apathy of the people, and the selfish imbecility of the Government, I should certainly have been in no haste to enter Spain.'[41]Moore's position was extremely precarious, and it was about to get even more so.

The terrible news of the Battle of Tudela had also reached Madrid and the Central Junta had begun to organise the defence of the capital. The forces available to it were put under the command of General Eguia. This force comprised of General Benito San Juan's 12,000 men who were principally from the Army of Andalusia and remnants of other armies, plus the survivors, some 8,000 or so, of the wrecked Army of Estremadura. These troops were sent to block the passes of the Sierra de Guadarrama through which the two main roads from the north travelled to Madrid.

Of these two routes, Napoleon chose to force the pass defended by San Juan's contingent, the Somosierra Pass. Napoleon arrived at the foot of the pass on 29 November and, after a preliminary attack led by General Ann Savary was easily driven off by the Spaniards, the Emperor knew that breaking through the mountains would be a major undertaking.

The following morning his troops climbed up the 4,500-foot, steep-sided pass until the Spanish position came into view. The infantry of General François Ruffin's division formed up for the attack as described in the 'Thirteenth Bulletin of the Army of Spain' published for the consumption of the French public, and reproduced the *The Times* of 19 December:

> The Enemy thought themselves unattackable in that position. They were entrenched in the narrow passage called Puerto with 16 pieces of cannon. The 9th light infantry marched upon the right, the 96th upon the causeway, and the 24th followed by the side of the heights on the left. General Senarmont, with six pieces of artillery, advanced by the causeway; the action commenced by the firing of musketry and cannon. A charge made by General Montbrun, at the head of the Polish light horse, decided the affair; it was a most brilliant one, and this regiment covered itself with glory, and proved it was worthy to form a part of the Imperial Guard. Cannons, flags, muskets, soldiers, all were taken, or cut to pieces.

What actually happened was that, unaccountably, Napoleon suddenly snapped. Instead of conducting a conventional, co-ordinated attack, Napoleon ordered his escort squadron of the Imperial Guard, the 3rd Squadron *1er Régiment des chevaux-légers (polonais)* to 'Take that position for me – at the gallop!'[42]

The tiny force of seven officers and eighty men charged the Spanish position, not once but twice. Galloping into the face of sixteen cannon backed by well-disposed infantry, the Poles were slaughtered.

Common sense then prevailed and a properly organised assault was mounted that eventually forced the pass. The Poles were to have their revenge as the other two squadrons plus the *Chasseurs à*

Cheval de la Garde Impériale leapt amongst the Spanish gunners at the critical moment in the fight, slashing and stabbing without restraint. Soon, San Juan and the rest of his men were making for Madrid as fast as they could run. Nothing then stood between Napoleon and the Spanish capital.

Chapter 4

'The Fate of Spain'

David Baird had received a grand welcome when he arrived at Coruna on 13 October but, as we have seen, had been denied permission for his troops to land. This was in part because Galicia had been almost stripped of its mules and carts by the earlier passage of Blake's army, and it was suggested by the provincial junta that he should take his men up to Santander or possibly Gijon where such a large body of troops might find suitable transport and provisions.

Baird absolutely refused to countenance such proposals and so was told by the Galicians that he would have to wait until the matter was referred to the Central Junta. Ten crucial days were lost before permission was received from Madrid to disembark his troops. Even then he was told by the local authorities that he could only send his men forward into the interior in detachments of 2,000 at a time with a considerable interval between them, as the resources of the country could not support more than this. This would mean even more time would be lost before Baird and Moore could be united.

Baird wrote to Moore about his predicament:

> Instead of arrangements being made for our reception, as I was led to expect would be the case, the provincial government was not only unprepared to receive us, but appears disinclined to afford us any active assistance. As we brought no money with us, I have been compelled to endeavour to obtain a supply, and I am in expectation of procuring five thousand pounds. I am afraid we shall find great difficulty in fulfilling that part of my instructions

which relates to the purchase of horses and mules, as they appear to be extremely scarce in this province.[1]

Moore could hardly believe the attitude of the Galician authorities. Was not the British army there to help liberate the country? Moore may have thought that the British were there to save Spain, but the 'credulous' Spaniards did not believe that they needed any help from these outsiders. They, 'were accustomed in the streets and in their houses to assemble, and whilst one read the *Madrid* or *Corunna Gazette*, which contained more of invention than matter of fact, the rest laid down the positions for their nominal armies, generally amounting to 200,000 men and the French army which they never admitted to exceed 50,000 was always being surrounded and annihilated. If the British officers attempted to describe the true state they were disbelieved and the Spaniards would only admit as fact such intelligence as was acceptable and in their own favour.'[2]

Henry Crabb Robinson of *The Times*, submitted his second report from Corunna, which was published on 31October:

> In a former letter, I barely told you that our numerous fleet of transports was safely moored in the fine harbour of Corunna. It will perhaps mortify you to hear that the reception of troops was not quite so enthusiastic as our notion of our importance led us to expect. There were no shoutings [*sic*] or illuminations, but a very sober, civil sort of a welcome … In one respect I was almost pleased to remark the indifference of our reception – they do not want us, thought I … and God grant that they may not find themselves mistaken.

As Baird had explained to Moore, he arrived at Corunna with virtually no money and little in the way of a military train. Moore sent him £8,000 in dollars that he could ill-afford to spare but this was wholly inadequate to hire even the few mules and carts that were available at the enormously inflated prices the muleteers were demanding.

As it happened Hookham Frere, as mentioned earlier, arrived on 19 October to act on behalf of the British Government. Frere had been set no easy task by Foreign Secretary George Canning, being instructed to create a peace treaty between Britain and Spain but at the same time to encourage a more liberal approach to Spain's dealings with its colonies that Britain might be able to take commercial advantage of. Regarding the British forces in Spain, Frere was to inform the Central Junta that Moore's army was to be employed in one body and not weakened by detachments to various Spanish armies.

Frere had brought with him £410,000 in coin for the Spanish authorities but none for Britain's own troops. There was a general distrust of paper money in Spain and few would accept the British Treasury bills with which Baird was expected to use to supply the army with its needs. Baird was only able to raise £5,000 or £6,000 in dollars in exchange for bills.[3]

William Napier of the 43rd Regiment, wrote angrily of the ludicrous situation the British Government had placed Baird in, complaining that millions of dollars were being 'lavished' on the Spaniards while the British army was penniless:

> The penury of the English general obliged him to borrow from the funds in Mr. Frere's hands. Thus assisted, the troops were put in motion; but, wanting all the equipments essential to an army, they were forced to march by half battalions, conveying their scanty stores on country cars, hired from day to day; nor was that meagre assistance obtained but at a great expense and by compliance with a vulgar mercenary spirit predominant among the authorities of Gallicia. The Junta frequently promised to procure the carriages, but did not; the commissioners had to offer an exorbitant remuneration; the cars were then forthcoming, and the procrastination of the Government proved to be a concerted plan to defraud the military chest.[4]

In addition to this, the most immediate financial problem facing Baird was that his troops were in arrears of pay, which had to be made good upon landing in Spain. Baird managed to persuade Frere to hand over £40,000 and the Junta of Galicia lent him 92,000 dollars, of what was effectively British money. After struggling even to find two carriages for himself and his staff, Frere set off for Madrid towards the end of October. None of this boded well for the future.

On 8 November, the first elements of the cavalry arm of Baird's corps, the 7th and 10th Light Dragoons (Hussars), arrived at Corunna, along with two troops of horse artillery and the army's Waggon Train. (The third cavalry regiment assigned to Baird, the 15th Light Dragoons, had been delayed by adverse weather, but reached Corunna a few days later.)

Then, the following day, 9 November, the frigate *Tigre* arrived from the UK with 500,000 dollars. This was the first instalment of the 2 million dollars which Castlereagh had promised Moore the army should have, and it was supposed to be shared between Lisbon and Corunna. But as Baird still had precious little cash, he kept it all. This placed Moore in a real quandary. 'I am without a shilling of money to pay the army their subsistence,' Moore told Castlereagh, 'and I am in daily apprehension that, from the want of it, our supplies will be stopped. The 500,000 dollars your Lordship mentions, Sir David Baird considered as sent to him; he detained them, and has nearly expended them. The money which it is possible to procure at Madrid and in other towns of Spain is quite trifling, and it is impossible to describe the embarrassment we are thrown into from the want of this essential article.'[5]

The money in question finally enabled Baird to begin providing his troops with transport, despite prices having reached 'famine' levels. Also on the 9th, ships arrived with a three-month supply of oats and hay for the horses. The disembarkation of the cavalry could then begin.

'The first day's disembarkation of the 7th [Hussars] was truly deplorable;' wrote Hussey Vivian in his memoirs, 'it rained in torrents; and from the transports not being able to haul up to the quays, the horses were slung into the water and most of them obliged to swim on shore. The poor men, most miserably soaked, having no place to go to but an open shed—many of them having lost their appointments and necessaries, and no man having a dry article to put on. Add to all this the easy rate at which the men obtained wine, and consequent drunkenness, and the misery and confusion of the scene may be imagined!

'Fortunately, the following days were very fine, and the regiment had an opportunity of getting into some sort of order; but still, from the distance to which it was necessary for them to go for procuring forage, &c., nothing could possibly be more harassing than the duty of the soldier, who had scarcely an instant to himself from morning till night.'[6]

It was the horses, though, that came off worst from the haphazard disembarkation, having had to swim around a quarter of a mile to reach the shore. 'The horses after 7 weeks confinement on a ship then plunged into the sea to be swum ashore in a state of fever, have of course suffered severely, especially their feet,' Lady Elizabeth Holland wrote in her journal, 'besides the change of food from oats and hay to chopped straw and maize has affected their health.'[7]

'So much for our first day …' wrote Major Edward Hodge of the 7th Hussars. 'How easy it would have been for the disembarkation to have been deferred one [more] day and a Quarter M[aste]r and two men per troop sent ashore to prepare. Then all would have been well, instead of a fine Regt. murdered.'[8]

Baird's infantry had begun landing from the transports on 26 October to start out on the 300-mile march to join Moore at Salamanca. But with the troops only permitted to march in small detachments, it was not until 4 November that the last of the infantry regiments were disembarked, and many days later before the final men moved out. Only being allowed to march in such small detachments Baird's corps was soon spread all along the road to Astorga. 'We began our march on the 28th of October, that is just the beginning of the rainy season,' wrote Lieutenant John Brumwell. 'We had nothing but torrents of rain for a considerable time. On our march from Corunna to Astorga there was nothing particular. The main road was tolerably good, considering we had so much rain. The country was uncommonly barren, and the inhabitants the most miserable set of creatures I ever saw.'[9] Little could the men have known that they would travel this road again – in the opposite direction and in conditions far worse than they experienced on that first march of the campaign and far worse than they could ever have imagined.

Baird himself was still at Corunna on 11 November, writing to Frere about the ludicrous situation his corps was in:

> I propose setting out to-morrow or next day, for the purpose of approaching sir John Moore, now, I understand, advancing towards

Salamanca. Indeed, the expediency of an early junction becomes every day more apparent, as, from the large reinforcements which are pouring in, to the French army in Navarre, it might become doubtful (in the event of their pushing rapidly forward into the plains of Castile and Leon) whether, if it was much longer delayed, it could be effected at all. Under such circumstances, the continued indifference and inattention to our wants, which we experience from the Galician junta, is particularly mortifying, and strongly proves the necessity, that the central government should depute some person of consequence to accompany the army, with power to procure from the local authorities, not only of this province, but of any others we may pass through on our advance, such aid and assistance as the country can afford, and may be necessary to enable us to move. From the want of such an arrangement, we have been compelled to make contracts for provisions and forage at a most exorbitant rate; and the British government is thus subjected to a loss, which might be prevented by our being furnished upon the same terms as the Spanish troops.[10]

While Baird was on his way to Salamanca, Moore, as we have learnt, had been informed that a large French force had reached Burgos, having brushed aside part of the Army of Estremadura. He warned Baird of this approach by the enemy, which could seriously jeopardise his junction with Moore:

In what force they are, or whether their intention is to advance farther, I know not. If they advance whilst we are assembling, they will embarrass us … I wish, as soon as you have ascertained that they can be subsisted, that you would push on your corps to Benevente. I shall probably, by the time they reach that, order them to continue on to Zamora, and ultimately, we may be able to have the whole assembled in Zamora, Toro, and this place [Salamanca].

In all this, however, you must be guided by the information you receive of the enemy. Were they to advance immediately, whilst the regiments on this side were moving forward in succession, I should have no option but to fall back, in which case also you must get back to Astorga, and prepare, if pressed, to get back into Galicia.[11]

Moore then told Baird that once he had been joined by Hope, he would try and march to join Baird, rather than just remain waiting at Salamanca. Moore must again have regretted his decision to separate himself from his artillery, for he was stuck at Salamanca until Hope's corps arrived. This is evident from a letter he wrote to Castlereagh from Salamanca around this time:

> This army is certainly too much adventured, and risks to be brought into action before it is united, and before its stores, ammunition, &c. are brought forward to enable it to act … I certainly thought I was perfectly safe in assembling the army at Salamanca: but if I had had sooner a conception of the weakness of the Spanish armies, the defenceless state of the country, the apparent apathy of the people, and the selfish imbecility of the Government, I should certainly have been in no haste to enter Spain, or to have approached the scene of action, until the army was united, and every preparatory arrangement made for its advance.[12]

Baird, meanwhile, reached Astorga, roughly halfway between Corunna and Salamanca, on 19 November. On the 22th, while still at Astorga, he learnt that Blake's army had been utterly routed at Espinosa and that the French had entered Valladolid with their cavalry reaching Benavente, which was less than fifty miles to the south-east on the very road to Salamanca that Baird was expecting to take. None of this information had been forthcoming from any of the Spanish juntas, Baird's only source of intelligence being from Colonel Thomas Graham and other British officers. A worried Baird wrote to Moore of his concerns:

> In all probability Castanos and Palafox may by this time have met with the same reverse as Blake; in which case the Spaniards could have no force deserving the denomination of an army in the field.
>
> As it could never be intended by the British Government that our army should engage in the defence of this Country unaided and unsupported by any Spanish force, I confess, my dear Sir John, I begin to be at a loss to discover an object at this moment in Spain: it being very evident that the Spaniards are not at this moment in a situation to be capable of assembling a force

competent to offer any serious resistance to the progress of the French arms.

Moore had already reached a similar conclusion, writing in the same vein to Hookham Frere in Madrid:

> If things are to continue in this state, the ruin of the Spanish cause and the defeat of their armies is inevitable, and it will become my duty to consider alone the safety of the British Army, and take steps to withdraw it from a situation where, without the possibility of doing good, it is exposed to defeat.[13]

Moore also expressed his concerns to Lady Hestor Stanhope on 23 November, who had asked if her young half-brother James could join Moore as an aide-de-camp:

> I am within four marches of the French, with only one third of my force; and as the Spaniards have been dispersed in all quarters, our junction with the other two thirds is very precarious; and when we all join we shall be very inferior to the enemy … We are in a scrape; but I trust we shall have the spirit to get out of it. You must, however, be prepared to hear very bad news.[14]

He then added, prophetically, 'If I can extricate myself and those with me from the present difficulties and can beat the French I shall return to you with satisfaction, but if not, it will be better that I should never quit Spain.'

But Moore had been instructed to help the Spaniards as much as he was able and he felt he could not abandon them without making some attempt at supporting them, especially in light of all the money and resources Britain had already committed to the struggle in the Peninsula. 'I see my situation as clearly as any one, that nothing can be worse,' he wrote in his journal, 'for I have no Spanish army to give me the least assistance, only the Marquis Romana is endeavouring to assemble the fugitives from Blake's army at Leon. Yet I am determined to form the junction of this army, and to try our fortune. We have no business here as things are but, being here, it would never do to abandon the Spaniards without a struggle.'[15]

Baird urged his men to march as quickly as possible but, according to Hussey Vivian, rushing the troops forward was a case of 'more haste less speed', with large numbers of horses becoming lame after their long confinement on the transports (thirty-seven days) coupled with the long distances they were immediately expected to make. Of the 7th Hussars alone, twelve horses had been lost on disembarkation, seventeen became lame at Corunna, eighteen at Betanzos, two, three and four at Salquiero, Bahamonde, and Guitirez, and at Lugo another thirty-one were left behind. Even those still plodding along with the army were in poor condition due to the 'miserable' quality of forage and were scarcely fit for active service – and the campaign had hardly begun.[16]

Vivian was already angry with the treatment the army had received at the hands of the Spaniards and he complained bitterly in his journal about the condition of the troops, little realising the horrors to come in the weeks ahead:

> To attempt to describe our sufferings and privations, of men and horses, is beyond my power. No description can be at all adequate to it. It surely would have been reasonable, before the army started from Corunna, for Sir D. Baird to have said: 'We are come to assist you, and before I move a single man I must have so many mules and so many bullock carts attached to each regiment.' Whether this was done, I know not, but at all events I do know that we were without the proper assistance; and daily (whilst we were without the means of carrying our camp kettles except on our troop horses, and actually without tents) did we meet whole droves of mules carrying sardines, the value of the whole cargo of which was not that of a single troop horse.[17]

Yet disturbing reports had been received at Salamanca of the French sweeping through northern Spain. When the leading elements of Baird's corps reached Trebadildos on 23 November, an officer of the 2nd (Royal North British) Dragoons riding up from Blake's defeated army, declared that a considerable French force was collecting at Ampudia a few miles to the south-east of Benevente. This confirmed the earlier reports Baird had received, and, if this was true, then the French could easily place themselves astride Baird's route to Salamanca. Vivian also wrote in his diary that a report had been received that a French column was making its way through the mountains to Ferrol in an attempt to cut Baird's corps off from the coast. Baird decided on an immediate retreat and turned his army round to head back for Corunna.

Moore, however, doubted that the French were so near, and he ordered Baird to continue to try and reach Salamanca. So, Baird's men turned round again and recommenced their march to join Moore, but valuable time had been lost.

Such confusing reports did not help Moore, who was becoming increasingly worried about the entire strategic situation. On 27 November, he wrote again expressing his concerns in a letter to Hookham Frere in Madrid:

> Madrid is threatened – the French have destroyed one army, have passed the Ebro, and are advancing in superior numbers against another, which, from its composition and strength, promises no resistance, but must either retire, or be overwhelmed. No other armed force exists in this country. I perceive no enthusiasm, or any determined spirit amongst the people.
>
> The French Cavalry, even in parties so weak as eleven or twelve men, enter the villages in Leon and the neighbouring provinces, and raise contributions without opposition.
>
> This is a state of things quite different from that conceived by the British Government, when they determined to send troops to the assistance of Spain. It was not expected that these were to cope alone with the whole force of France; but as auxiliaries, to aid a people who were believed to be enthusiastic, determined, and prepared for resistance.

Moore then went on to explain the various courses of action he might have to take when Hope and Baird joined him. If Castaños had been beaten by then he would march directly to Madrid 'and throw myself into the heart of Spain, and thus run all risks, and share the fortunes of the Spanish Nation', or retreat into Portugal and remain on the defensive there until an opportunity arose for him to be able to return and help the Spaniards. If he did march deeper into Spain he would be moving ever further away from his resources and, because of the insufficient transport available and the need to travel quickly, he would not be able to take much with him. If he did march to Madrid and then find that the French were in overwhelming strength, he might find himself cut off from Portugal, in which case he would have to try and escape to the south to Cadiz or Gibraltar, both of which were considered virtually impregnable. It would then be up to the British Government to decide whether to bring Moore's army back to the UK or employ it elsewhere in the Peninsula.

Interestingly, Moore then sought Frere's opinion on the course of action he should take. Stating that he wished to throw no responsibility off his own shoulders, he, nevertheless wanted Frere to put his views on record. If anything went wrong, Moore could argue that he was only following the advice of the Government's representative:

> The question is not purely a military one. It belongs at least as much to you, as to me, to decide it … the question is, What would that [the British] Cabinet direct, were they upon the spot to determine? It is of much importance this should be thoroughly considered; it is comparatively of very little, on whom shall rest the greatest share of responsibility. I am willing to take the whole, or a part, but I am anxious to know your opinion.[18]

When Frere replied a few days later (30 November), he wrote: 'I would venture to recommend retaining the position of Astorga. A retreat from that place to Corunna would (as far as an unmilitary man may be allowed to judge of a country which he has travelled over) be less difficult than through Portugal to Lisbon.'[19]

Moore now had the approval he sought. He expected that there was little his army could do to help the Spanish cause and that he would be compelled to retreat having achieved nothing. At least, though, he had told his political masters of the situation and a retreat to Corunna had been recommended. If such a withdrawal became necessary, there was nothing the British Government could do other than publicly support him. Moore, though, was careful in his use of the word 'retreat' in his official correspondence, as it implied that he had been outmanoeuvred or beaten.

Moore's military secretary, Major John Colborne, shared his commander's gloomy prognosis, which he communicated in letters dated 26 and 27 November: 'We have been here about a week, collecting our force. Owing to the badness of the roads, the cavalry and artillery were obliged to march by a different route, and we are very much separated ... We have 14,000 men at Salamanca, 4,000 at Escorial, and Sir David Baird at Astorga. The French are at Valladolid, and they have beat General Blake, dispersed his army, and have defeated the Estremadura army. I am afraid they will attack us before we are united. They have about 80,000 men in Spain, or more ... Since my last letter a third army has been defeated, the Aragoneese. I fear we shall not be able to unite. The Spaniards are a fine people, but have fallen into bad hands, not a person fit to direct them. I rather think we must retire on Portugal. We expect to be attacked in our turn. Nothing can be more unfortunate.'[20]

With the junction of the British forces uncertain and the military situation changing daily, there was a possibility that Baird might yet have to move quickly back to Corunna. Consequently, all the stores not essential to Baird's corps, which might slow his progress, were to be disposed of. This event, recorded on 24 November at Astorga, was watched by Captain Adam Wall of the Royal Artillery:

> Here a transaction occurred which was ill-judged indeed (whether orders had been issued or not I cannot say); but prior to the moving of the troops from the town of Astorga, the stores were destroyed. This occasioned such a scene of confusion as I believe was never witnessed before; – the streets flooded with rum, casks of beef and pork, and bags of biscuits strewed in every street, the troops conveying the rum in camp kettles, and drinking it to horrid excess.[21]

The following day a drum-head court-martial was assembled to punish those who had disgraced themselves, but such scenes, both of destruction of valuable commodities and of drunken excess, would be repeated in the desperate days to come.

More serious matters, however, were occupying the attention of Moore, who wrote the following to Baird on 28 November:

> I have received this evening dispatches from Mr. Stuart at Madrid, announcing the defeat and dispersion of Castanos's army. The French in Spain are estimated at 80,000 men, and 30,000

are expected in the course of a week. It certainly was much my wish to have run great risks in aid of the people of Spain; but, after this second proof of how little they are able to do for themselves, the only two armies they had having made so little stand, I see no right to expect from them much greater exertions; at any rate we should be overwhelmed before they could be prepared. I see no chance of our being able to form a junction; as certainly at Burgos the French have a corps which will now move forward.'[22]

Castaños had indeed been beaten by Marshal Lannes' III Corps, suffering the loss of around 7,000 killed, wounded, missing or captured, almost a quarter of the Spanish force engaged. Castaños' army broke into two, as it retreated from the battlefield. This was certainly terrible news, as Moore confided to his journal: 'This renders my junction with Baird's [corps] so hazardous that I dare not attempt it, but even were it made, what chance has this army, now that all those of Spain are beaten, to stand against the force which must be brought against it? … As long as Castanos' army remained there was hope, but I now see none. I therefore determined to withdraw the army.'[23] Moore, consequently, informed Baird of the momentous decision he had taken:

> I have, therefore, determined to retreat upon Portugal with the corps I have here; and, if possible, with Hope's corps, if by forced marches he can join me. I wish you to fall back on Corunna; send back immediately your stores, under such part of your force as you judge proper.

Moore explained to Baird that he planned to fall back only as far as the Portuguese border, hoping to cover Lisbon for as long as possible. Moore could not consider holding the frontier, however, without Hope's division with its cavalry and artillery. If Baird was to turn back immediately for Corunna, there would be no British forces to the north to hold back the French and Moore might be attacked before Hope could reach Salamanca. Baird was therefore told to hold on where he was for a little longer but to watch for the approach of the enemy and make sure he retired safely upon Corunna. Once back at Corunna he was to sail for the Tagus, where further orders would be waiting for him. Baird was also instructed to send any other transports to Lisbon that might be at Corunna as he believed the British would be forced to evacuate the Peninsula. 'For,' he explained, 'when the French have Spain, Portugal cannot be defended.'[24]

In fact, Baird had not heard from Moore for some days before this message had been sent and had presumed that communications with Salamanca had already been cut. Baird, consequently, decided that he must retreat to Corunna. Then Major Temple, aide-de-camp to Lord Paget, having been sent on the 26th with despatches to Sir John, and having passed by Benavente and Zamora to Salamanca, returned on the night of the 29th to Astorga without having met with any interruption. Baird, once again, ordered his men forward.

It is not hard to imagine the confused state of mind that Baird and Moore found themselves in. They were in a supposedly friendly country where they had expected to be fighting alongside their allies but were adrift alone in an alien land devoid of any reliable information.

The British had been placed in an impossible situation and on that same day, 29 November, Moore explained his predicament to Lord Castlereagh, telling him that if he stayed any longer in Spain his army would be sacrificed without in any way benefitting the Spaniards, and suggesting to the foreign secretary that he and Baird should sail for Cadiz. His most immediate concern was with Hope's corps and in a letter on the 28th he conceded that: 'I have determined to give up and retire. A junction with Baird is out of the question, and with you, perhaps problematical … This is a cruel determination for me to make – I mean to retreat: but I hope you will think the circumstances such as demand it.' Nevertheless, he told Hope to push on by forced marches by Peñaranda or Alba de Tormes to try and reach Salamanca.[25] If this seemed too difficult, he was to march directly to Ciudad Rodrigo on the Portuguese border and meet Moore there. Even this might not be possible in the rapidly deteriorating situation which the British army faced and so Moore told Hope that if a junction with Moore became too dangerous he was at liberty to re-trace his steps back to Lisbon. The only important objective now was to save the army.

Moore's decision to divide his army had placed him in a situation where he could not advance to meet Baird without distancing himself even further from Hope and, likewise, if he moved to join up with Hope, he would be marching away from Baird. At a time when stories of fresh disasters befalling the Spanish armies were being received every day, and of French troops massing in northern Spain, Moore had to sit impotently in Salamanca, when, if he had moved the bulk of his army by sea, his army would already have been united.

Hope had intended to march by Adanero to Arrivola and from there to Masrigal, Penaranda, Huerto and on to Salamanca. When he learnt of the collapse of the Spanish armies, he 'prudently' altered his route to travel further to the west and further away from the enemy's probable avenue of advance towards the Spanish capital. The main body of the cavalry was posted to the rear of Hope's column with patrols sent far to the east. 'Thus,' wrote Brigadier-General Charles Stewart, later Marquis of Londonderry, who commanded Hope's cavalry, 'were the rear and the right flanks of the division perfectly secured; and it was rendered impracticable for the enemy to harass its movements, without sufficient time being gained to provide against emergency.'[26]

As Charles Stewart noted, Hope's column had travelled a considerable distance through Spain without encountering the enemy. That all changed on the night of 29 November. 'It might be about midnight,' Stewart wrote, 'when the videttes furnished by the picket at Arrivola, gave an alarm that the French were coming on. The troopers mounted and made ready, and in a few minutes found themselves attacked by a strong party of cavalry; concerning the nature of which, whether it were the advanced-guard of a corps, or a mere patrol, they were, unavoidably, ignorant.'

Having located the enemy, the patrol had accomplished its task and, as the patrol's duty was not to become embroiled in a fight but to continue to watch the enemy's movements, it was unable to determine whether or not this body of French cavalry was part of a larger force. The videttes therefore withdrew but were not pursued and so they fell back only half a mile or so from Arrivola, reporting their encounter to Stewart.

Hope continued to march on towards Salamanca but, with the enemy so close, he ordered his infantry the following night, the 30th, to lie down in squares so that they would be able to form up quickly if the French cavalry burst through Stewart's pickets, 'and in that position we remained all night,' complained a soldier of the 71st Regiment. 'It was one of the severest nights of cold I ever endured in my life. At that time we wore our hair, formed into a club at the back of our heads. Mine was frozen to the ground in the morning; when I attempted to rise, my limbs refused to support me for some time. I felt the most excruciating pains over all my body, before the blood began to circulate.'[27]

Hope drove his men on at astonishing speed to try and reach Salamanca before the French could intervene, forcing his men to march a remarkable forty-seven miles in the course of just thirty-six hours. The pace, however, took its toll, for six of the guns – the equivalent of a full battery – had to be abandoned because the artillery horses collapsed from fatigue. The guns were buried so that they could not be found and taken by the enemy.

Moore now had to tell the officers under his command at Salamanca of his decision to withdraw. He knew this would not be easy, as his men were keen to fight, so he addressed them in a firm manner, telling them that: 'he had not called them together to request their counsel, or to induce them to commit themselves by giving any opinion upon the subject. He took the responsibility entirely upon himself; and he only required that they would immediately prepare for carrying it into effect.'

This information was not well received by Moore's men and the first rumblings of discontent were heard in the ranks, as Archibald Alison recorded: 'This determination excited the utmost dissatisfaction in the troops. Officers and men loudly and openly murmured against such a resolution, and declared it would be better to sacrifice half the army than retire from so fair a field without striking a blow for the Allies, who had staked their all in the common cause.'[28]

Hussey Vivian with Baird's corps took the news particularly badly:

> From the Spanish armies we could expect no regular movements, no systematic assistance; but energy on our part would have created energy on theirs; and the probability is that although in the junction we might have suffered much, yet from the losses of the enemy, and from their attention having been drawn off from

the Spanish armies, it would have occasioned a very considerable turn in their affairs, and, in all probability, a favourable one. At all events, anything is better than the horrible disgrace that must attend a retreat such as we are about to make.[29]

It was easy for Vivian to make such comments, as he did not have responsibility for the army which Moore had been told, above all other considerations, he had to preserve. William Napier saw the situation far more practically: 'The English general [Moore was actually a Scot] was prepared to confront any danger and to execute any enterprise which held out a chance of utility, but he also remembered that the best blood of England was committed to his charge, that not an English army, but the very heart, the pith of military power of his country was in his keeping. ... The object of succouring the Spaniards called for great, but not useless sacrifices.'[30]

Unhappily, the regiments began to prepare for the retreat, with the heavy baggage under an escort of the 5th Battalion, 60th Regiment, moving off immediately to get a head-start rather than dragging along in the rear. The one piece of good news was that Hope's forced marches had brought his column within a short distance of Salamanca and nothing now could prevent his junction with Moore.

On 1 December, Moore wrote to Charles Stuart at Madrid, explaining the reality of the situation to him:

> The Enemy do not, at present, seem to have anything but cavalry on this side of Valladolid; they certainly have a division at Burgos, and the thirty thousand from France will be there shortly; and they will detach from the army which has defeated Castanos, and may have done so already, unless they first choose to enter Madrid. It is from the Centre and South that an effort should be looked for: in this quarter the business is up, and the people without enthusiasm think they have nothing left for it, but to submit ... The armies, you see, are also without enthusiasm, or even common obstinacy – they do not stand – and the individuals we see passing as fugitives are not ashamed, nor are they thought ill of by the people, nor indignation excited.

What Moore also explained to Charles Stuart was that he was almost completely out of funds to keep the army supplied. 'But such is our want of money,' he wrote, 'that if it can be got at a hundred per cent, we must have it; do therefore, if possible, send me some at any rate.' All that Moore was really asking for was some of the money that had been given so generously to the Spaniards – money for which there was, so far at least, no obvious return.

Though coin may not have found its way to Moore from Madrid, two senior Spanish generals did, reaching Salamanca on 2 December. Brigadier Don Agustin Bueno and Don Bentua Escalante, Captain-General of the Armies of Grenada, arrived at Moore's headquarters bearing a letter from Don Martin de Garay, the secretary of the Central Junta. The purpose of their journey was to: 'decide on the operations and other points that may occur. So that the troops of his Britannic Majesty may act in concert with ours; and, in accelerating their combined movements.' Here at last was what Moore had been wanting all along. Even though he described them as 'two weak old men, or rather women, with whom it was impossible for me to concert any military operations', at last there was a chance of being able to operate in conjunction with the Spaniards as had been expected from the outset.

Once again, just as Moore was about to retreat, he was encouraged to persist with his expedition. One can only wonder at the mental and emotional conflict Moore was experiencing at this moment. Repeatedly he had been urged to help the Spaniards only to be disappointed, believing that he was placing his army in extreme danger in defence of what was clearly a lost cause.

This time the two generals said that: 'General San Juan, with 20,000 brave Spaniards, was in possession of the pass of Somosierra; which he had fortified so strongly as to render the approach to Madrid impracticable.' Unfortunately, Moore knew this to be the usual vain boast. He called into the room Colonel Thomas Graham who had just brought the latest news that Napoleon had broken through the Sierra de Guadarrama and San Juan's men had been dispersed. There was nothing the two Spanish officers could do to dissuade Moore. He had heard it all before. He was going to retreat and save his army as soon as Hope reached Salamanca.

For his part, Hope had already met General Tomas Morla, Spain's Secretary of War, at Talavera, seventy-five miles to the south-west of Madrid. Morla begged Hope to send his troops to Madrid to help defend the city. Hope, naturally, refused to commit his forces without knowing the situation first hand, so he went to Madrid to see the state of affairs for himself. He was unimpressed with what he saw, writing to Moore on 20 November: 'It is perfectly evident that they [the Central Junta] are altogether without a plan as to their future military operations, either in the case of success or misfortune.'[31] As a result, Hope rejected Morla's request, being more concerned with pushing on as hard as he could for Salamanca, knowing that there was every likelihood that Napoleon could well intervene and cut him off from Moore.

As it transpired, Brigadier-General Charles Stewart at the head of Hope's cavalry, reached Salamanca at around midday on 5 December. Moore told Stewart of his decision to retreat, explaining his reasons in great depth. He 'warmly' condemned the Spanish government, Stewart recalled, 'and enlarged upon the absence of all right understanding among, as well as upon the absurdity of their military movements, which had subjected them all to be beaten in detail.'

Stewart expressed his regret but did not press the matter with his commander-in-chief. Yet he soon became aware of the sentiments of the other soldiers in Salamanca who were universally opposed to withdrawing and who were openly vocal in their condemnation of Moore's judgement. 'Seldom do men, situated as we were, venture to speak out so boldly against the measures of their chief,' Stewart wrote. 'But murmurings and remonstrances were useless; the die was cast, and it could not be recalled.'[32]

Lord Paget was one man who, through his social as well as military status, was prepared to challenge Moore, even suggesting that he should lead his cavalry in a mad Quixotic adventure rather than meekly retreat. 'I really am ashamed of our conduct in Spain. There has been much indecision, and at length the decision come to has been a bad one. What an ignominious thing it is to go off and embark!' he wrote in a letter to his father dated 3 December, which continued:

> I have sent in a proposal to endeavour to march to the right by Orense, and so into Portugal, with the most effective part of

the cavalry; and I have even determined to take with me four guns, although it is stated to be impossible; but we have so often been taught by the French that nothing is impossible that I have resolved to try it. The roads will be desperate, and there are several rivers to pass. But as I shall be without infantry, and as the enemy might push a small corps of light infantry across Portugal (and a very small corps would be a desperate annoyance to us), and might even stop our march without a few shrapnel shells to assist us, I shall force through all the difficulties that may occur for the artillery, and, by hook or by crook, get them on … It will be the finest operation in the world – a rapid march over an immense plain (a perfect sea which has been overrun by the enemy's cavalry), with a compact body of British cavalry and artillery, ready and willing to fall upon almost anything, in its own way, that presents itself.[33]

Of course, Moore could not permit Paget to ride off with the cavalry and this request was denied. Meanwhile, after driving San Juan's men from the Somosierra pass, Napoleon's advanced cavalry had reached the outskirts of Madrid. On 2 and 3 December, the Madridese rejected the Emperor's demands for their surrender, declaring that they would sooner bury themselves under the ruins of their houses and perish to a man than permit French troops to enter their city.

Reports of the determination of the Spaniards to fight to the last to defend their nation's capital reached Salamanca on the 5th, soon after Stewart's arrival. 'In the short space of forty-eight hours they had unpaved the streets and loaded the balconies and flat roofs of their houses with the stones to be hurled on the heads of the assailants,' it was reported. 'A huge trench was already drawn round the entire circumference of the city; numerous outworks were begun; and men and women of all ranks and classes were labouring incessantly for their completion … all were united in one enthusiastic resolution to conquer or perish.'[34]

Surprisingly, Moore seems to have actually given this some credibility. Despite everything that had happened in the previous few weeks, of every unfilled unfilled promise and every false boast, Moore genuinely appears to have swallowed this latest manifestation of Spanish bombast, if not whole, then at least in part in part. From immovable determination upon withdrawal in the morning, by evening he was writing to Castlereagh to tell him that he had decided to remain a little longer at Salamanca to wait on the turn of events, and had ordered Baird, who had fallen back to Villa Franca, to suspend his march until further advised. 'This is the first instance of enthusiasm shown,' Moore wrote in his diary, 'there is a chance that the example may be followed and the people be roused, in which case there is still a chance that this country may be saved. Upon this chance I have stopped Baird's retreat, and have taken measures to form our junction whilst the French are wholly occupied with Madrid. We are bound not to abandon the cause as long as there is hope.'[35] Baird had to order his poor, bewildered men, who had repeatedly marched and counter-marched, to turn round yet again.

The reality is that Moore simply did not know what to do. 'We are here by ourselves, left to manage the best way we can, without communication with any other army; no knowledge of the strength, or position of the Enemy, but what we can pick up in a country where we are strangers, and in complete ignorance of the plans or wishes of the Spanish Government,' he complained to Castlereagh. 'In this state of things, it is difficult for me to form any plan for myself, beyond the assembling of the Army.'

Moore then wrote to Hookham Frere in a similar vein, hoping the British representative could influence the Central Junta:

> I am in no communication with any of the Spanish armies, nor am I made acquainted with the plans either of the Government, or of the Generals. Castanos, with whom I was put in correspondence, is dismissed from his command, at the moment I expected to hear from him; and Romana, with whom I suppose I now ought to correspond, is absent.
>
> In the meantime, the French, whose numbers I cannot learn, are only four day's march distant from my army, which is only assembling. No channel of information has been opened for me, and I have not been long enough in the country to procure one for myself. I give you this information, and I wish I could go myself to Aranjuez or Madrid, to make a representation of it for, in truth, if things remain in this situation, the ruin of the Spanish cause, and the defeat of their armies, is inevitable; and it will become my duty only to consider the safety of the British Army, and to

take measures to withdraw it from a situation where, without the possibility of being useful, it is exposed to certain defeat.[36]

Yet he was in Spain to fight. His men wanted to fight, his government expected him to fight and the Spaniards needed him to fight. There was no point in his army being in Spain if it was not going to strike a blow at the French. It was likely that the Madridese would prove no more resilient than the other Spanish forces had done but if they did fight to the last and reports reached London of brave civilians battling the enemy in the streets of the Spanish capital while the British army, entirely unmolested, sat idly by, Moore would have great difficulty defending his inaction. It would also be an enormous embarrassment to the government and it would mean that partisans in other counties under French domination would be discouraged from taking up arms for they could not rely upon help from Britain. A letter, dated 2 December, which arrived at Salamanca on the 5th, was presented to Moore from Thomas Morla and the Prince of Castelfranco, who were deputies of the Central Junta entrusted with the defence of Madrid, begging him to either join the forces defending Madrid, or to fall upon the French from the rear.

While Moore was considering this appeal, another letter arrived, this time from Hookham Frere at Talavera confirming the determination in Madrid to resist:[37] 'I have no hesitation,' he told Moore, 'in taking upon myself any degree of responsibility which may attach itself to this advice; as I consider the fate of Spain as depending absolutely for the present upon the decision which you may adopt.' The bearer of the letter was Colonel Charmilly who described how everyone in Madrid was in arms and had joined with the troops who had fallen back on the capital. He confirmed that the streets had been barricaded, batteries had been erected and that peasants from around the countryside were flocking into the city.

Moore made no comment in the presence of Charmilly, a person Moore knew and whom he despised, but went into his private quarters to consider how he should respond. He was now being pressed from the representatives of both governments to make some move to help Madrid. He could hardly refuse, but however determined the Spaniards might be the fact remained that they no longer had an effective army as every force sent against the French had been beaten and Madrid would inevitably fall sooner or later. The most that the British army could do was distract the French to buy a little more time for the Spaniards to strengthen their defences or to gather more men to garrison them.

Still, Moore had to do something, and if he was going to pounce on the French rear he needed his full force. He therefore wrote that same day to Baird:

> The City of Madrid have taken up arms, have refused to capitulate to the French, are barricading their streets, and say they are determined to suffer everything rather than submit. This arrests the French; and people who are sanguine entertain great hopes from it – I own, myself, I fear this spirit has arisen too late; and the French are now too strong to be resisted in this manner. There is, however, no saying; and I feel myself the more obliged to give it a trial, as Mr. Frere has made a formal representation, which I received this evening. I must beg, therefore, you will suspend your march until you hear from me again, and make arrangements for your return to Astorga, should it be necessary. – All this appears very strange and unsteady; but, if the spirit of enthusiasm does arise in Spain, and the people will be martyrs, there is no saying, in that case, what our force may do.[38]

Moore, we can only presume, must have spent a restless night. He had told Baird merely to suspend his march while he considered the course of action he should take. The next morning, having reached a decision, he wrote to Baird again:

> The people of Madrid, it is said, are enthusiastic and desperate; and certainly at this moment do resist the French—the good which may result from this it is impossible to say; I can neither trust to it, nor can I altogether despise it. If the flame catches elsewhere, and becomes at all general, the best results may be expected; if confined to Madrid, that town will be sacrificed, and all will be as bad, or worse than ever. In short, what is passing at Madrid may be decisive of the fate of Spain; and we must be at hand to aid and to take advantage of whatever happens. The wishes of our Country, and our duty, demand this of us, with whatever risk it may be attended. I mean to proceed bridle in

hand; for, if the bubble bursts, and Madrid falls, we shall have a run for it.

Yet the information presented to Moore by Frere and Charmilly, and upon which he had based his decision, was already out of date. With his offer of surrender having been rejected, Napoleon acted swiftly. After a preliminary artillery bombardment followed by a successful assault upon the Retiro heights that dominated the city, the heroic zeal of the citizens soon evaporated. The Central Junta escaped down the highway to Badajoz and the Spanish capital was once again in French hands. The date was 4 December. The bubble was about to burst.

Chapter 5

In Fortune's Way

Moore desperately hoped that the reports from Madrid marked a turning point in the war in the Iberian Peninsula. Even Thomas Graham, when passing through Madrid to reach Salamanca, was impressed with the seemingly genuinely-felt resolution of the Madridese to resist the invader. He saw men and women working day and even at night under the glare of flambeaux, to dig a defensive ditch around the city, strengthened by outworks. He confirmed that the townsfolk had torn stones from the cobbled streets and piled them on balconies and flat roofs to hurl down at their enemies. Equally, Brigadier-General Charles Stewart, commanding Hope's cavalry, had ridden on to Madrid as Hope's column passed close by the Spanish capital on its way to join Moore at Salamanca, and had seen that the men and women of Madrid were all 'united in one enthusiastic resolution to conquer or perish'.

But Moore was acutely aware that the enthusiasm of the Spaniards in the capital, and the fine words from Morla and Frere, might be no more than the usual overly optimistic and wholly inaccurate presentation of a situation that was already beyond redemption.

Therefore, after ordering Baird to halt his withdrawal to Corunna and concentrate his infantry at Benavente, he told him to be prepared to continue his retreat at a moment's notice. He advised him to establish a magazine at Villafranca, Astorga and one other place further back along the road to Corunna. These were to be stocked with salt meat, biscuit, rum or wines, and forage brought up from the coast, 'for though we may do something here, we must always look to a retreat.' He also asked Baird to send two cavalry regiments to Zamora along with a brigade of horse artillery. Moore was particularly anxious that Baird's cavalry watched out for French patrols, because it was information about the movements of Napoleon's men that would determine Moore's next step. As it was highly likely that at any moment the British army would have to make a dash to the coast, Moore wrote to Craddock at Lisbon, asking him to send the fleet of transports then at Lisbon round to Vigo. From Benavente there were two roads leading to the coast – to Corunna and to Vigo – and that which led to Vigo was the shorter of the two. If Moore was forced to make a rush to the coast with the enemy at his heels, the road to Vigo might prove to be the quickest.

The next morning, 6 December, unaware of Moore's change of plan, Colonel Charmilly presented the British commander with another letter from Frere that he had brought with him but had withheld:

> In the event, which I did not wish to presuppose, of your continuing the determination already announced to me of retiring with the army under your command, I have to request that Colonel Charmilly, who is the bearer of this, and whose intelligence has been already referred to, may be previously examined before a Council of War.

As before, Moore held his tongue in Charmilly's presence, though he must have been absolutely furious. Here was Frere telling Moore to ask his officers what course of action he should take! The action Moore did take was to have Charmilly dismissed from his headquarters and sent packing back to Madrid, with Frere's representative believing that he had failed in his mission.

Nevertheless, Frere was the king's minister and Moore could not simply ignore him. So he replied, explaining that he had stopped his preparations for withdrawal just in case the Spaniards did defy Napoleon at Madrid. But, he added, 'There has been no example of any such resistance in any other part of Spain; and, though I hope this will produce it, I have neither seen nor heard of much enthusiasm elsewhere. Their armies are devoid of both; and, though I trust it will prove otherwise, I cannot but consider it as doubtful, whether the people of Madrid will continue firm when they come to be pressed. If they yield, the whole is gone.'[1]

Nevertheless, Moore was in Iberia to fight and he planned to march to Zamora to link up with Baird at Benevente and also, hopefully, with la Romana who commanded the only Spanish force still in being, as he told Baird on the 8th. 'Madrid still holds out … as long as there is a chance, we must not abandon this country. The conduct of Madrid has given us a little time, and we must endeavour to profit by it. My first object must be to unite with you, and thus connect myself with the Marquis Romana.'[2] Moore then wrote to Romana who was at Léon, 160 miles away, offering to join forces with him and to undertake with him 'such operations as we may judge best for the support of Madrid, and the defeat of the Enemy.'

With this considerable Anglo-Spanish force he aimed to strike at the French line of communication at Burgos. Moore, though was careful not to raise the Secretary at State for War's expectations too high: 'Your Lordship may depend upon it, that I never shall abandon the cause as long as it holds out a chance of succeeding; but you must be sensible that the ground may be in an instant cut from under me: Madrid may fall and I may be left to contend with very superior numbers indeed.'

Moore's biggest problem was that he had no real idea of what was happening beyond Salamanca. It could be argued that he was too reliant upon the Spaniards for information instead of finding out for himself. At Lisbon he had not taken the opportunity to send officers out to investigate the roads leading to the border and once again he wasted many days at Salamanca listening to the contradictory reports that came his way.

Moore did send a few officers out to gather information, but it is surprising that Moore did not have a considerable number of officers scouring the countryside to locate the French forces. Instead of sitting at Salamanca in a state of perpetual anxiety, which caused him to repeatedly change his mind, he could have been well informed, or at least much better informed, of the events that were taking place in northern Spain.

One of those officers sent to discover the current state of affairs was Thomas Graham who went to Madrid on 6 December to try and find out what was happening in the capital, but the words he used in his diary describing this, was that he sent Graham to 'let me know exactly what is passing: for we find the greatest difficulty to get people to bring us information.' This shows that Moore was not taking measures to find out information for himself and was merely relying upon information being brought to him.

The next entry in his diary further exemplifies the error he made in being dependent upon others for information: 'Colonel Graham returned on the 9th without getting into Madrid, which capitulated on the 3rd. The people will not give up their arms, but they say they have been betrayed by the Duke of Castelfranco and by Monsieur de Morla. It was those two who wrote to me on the 2nd to ask my assistance, and next day it appears that they capitulated!'[3]

Napoleon, naturally, wanted the Spanish people to accept his brother as the country's legitimate ruler and to turn against the British, and, having learned that Hope's division had passed within thirty miles of Madrid only a few days before, he used a proclamation issued from the Spanish capital on 5 December to denounce the Spaniards' new ally:

> The conduct of the English is shameful! Since 20 November there have been 6,000 of them near Escorial; they have spent several days there … Their soldiers are superb and well disciplined. They have inspired inconceivable confidence in the Spaniards. Some hoped that this division would march to Somosierra; others that they would come to defend the capital of so dear an ally. But they all misunderstood the English … They have retreated … They are only willing to spill blood for their own immediate and selfish ends. Expect nothing from their egotism![4]

Nevertheless, Moore's worst fears had been realised. Despite all the boasting and bravado, Madrid had fallen as easily as the Spanish armies had been defeated. Yet it was said that the Madridese had not yet given up their arms and genuinely felt betrayed by their leaders. Further hope had come Moore's way two days earlier in the form of a message from the Junta of Toledo in central Spain, which had; 'signified to General Eredia, the Commandant of this Capital, that it is their intention to reunite here the dispersed armies; and to take the proper measures to enable him to defend this City to the last extremity. The Junta is besides in communication with

Aranjuez, and other points of union; and have the satisfaction to assure your Excellency that they are resolved to die in defence of their country.'

There was in this a hint that in some parts of Spain there was a determination to resist the invaders. What was also evident was that Napoleon had no idea where the British army was, as there was no sign of his troops anywhere near Salamanca – cavalry patrols had ascertained that there were no French within forty-five miles. Maybe, just maybe, if he struck across Napoleon's lines of communication it would come as such a shock to the Emperor that it would divert him from his subjugation of the rest of Spain just long enough for the Spaniards to coordinate their resistance.

He wrote back to Toledo that; 'the determination you express to die for your country, do you and the City of Toledo the greatest honour. If similar sentiments animate the rest of Spain, and the Spaniards will adhere faithfully to each other, there can be no doubt of your ultimate success, whatever temporary advantages the French may perhaps gain … The British army, like the British nation, is desirous of rendering every assistance to the Spanish cause, and you may depend upon its best exertions. I am uniting the different corps of the army, and preparing to act. The Marquis of Romana is at Leon, collecting the army that was with General Blake in Biscay; and, in concert with him, whatever is possible on this side shall be done.'

Moore followed this up by telling Castlereagh what he actually intended to do. Whilst making it clear that he could not believe 'that real enthusiasm is spread over any considerable portion of Spain,' he acknowledged that there was 'a chance; and whilst there is that, I think myself bound to run all risks to support it.'

He explained:

> I am now differently situated … I have been joined by General Hope, the artillery, and all the cavalry (Lord Paget with 3 Regiments is at Toro); and my junction with Sir David Baird is secure, though I have not heard from him since I ordered him to return to Astorga.
>
> Madrid, though it has capitulated, must still engage a considerable part of the Enemy's force. Saragossa[5] is also

a considerable diversion; and the collections forming in the South cannot be neglected; all his force cannot thus be directed against me.

Though he had been told by Baird that the corps under the Marquis de la Romana was in poor shape he still planned join up with it at Léon and with the combined force fall on the French lines of communications. This was a dangerous and bold move but, as he had said to Castlereagh, the unrest across Spain would tie down much of Napoleon's force, giving Moore an opportunity to strike a significant blow in support of the Spanish resistance. 'I must take my chance,' he wrote. 'I shall be in Fortune's way; if she smiles, we may do some good; if not, we shall still, I hope, have the merit of having done all we could. The army, for its number, is excellent; and is, I am confident, quite determined to do its duty.' But with the French now in the Peninsula in very large numbers there was little prospect of British forces being able to remain for long in either Spain or Portugal, so Moore suggested to Castlereagh that it would be prudent to keep sufficient transport ships at Lisbon and Corunna/Vigo to re-embark the army.[6]

Baird, on the other hand, suggested an alternative strategy, writing to Moore from Villafranca on 8 December:

It has frequently occurred to me that, in the event of our being obliged to adopt defensive measures, it might be more advantageous for the combined British army to cover Galicia and part of Leon, than, by my proceeding to join you at Salamanca, to abandon the defence of these provinces. The Asturias might be occupied by the troops of the marquis de la Romana, and if you judged it proper, by a flank movement, to join us in the neighbourhood of Astorga, I entertain a confident belief that, by occupying the strong ground behind it, we should be able to cover the country in our rear, and might wait until it is seen what efforts the Spanish nation is disposed and determined to make in defence of the national independence. The royal road from Coruna to this place and Astorga is remarkably good, although mountainous; and, with the sea open to us, we should be able to receive with facility such reinforcements and supplies as the British government might deem it proper to send. I do not think much difficulty would be experienced for a few months, from a want of provisions. The country abounds with cattle: bread, indeed, would be required; but flour might be obtained from England; and, in the meantime, Galicia would have an opportunity of arming under our protection; and our presence in Spain would furnish a rallying point, and act as a stimulus to the Spaniards.[7]

Back in London, there was increasing alarm about the situation in Spain, having received so many disconcerting despatches from Moore and Baird. Foreign Minister, George Canning, had at last realised that the British Government had been misled about the state of affairs in Spain, and he was worried that Britain was about to lose its army. On 10 December, he wrote the following to Frere:

You will recollect that the army which has been appropriated by his majesty to the defence of Spain and Portugal is not merely a considerable part of the disposable force of the country: it is, in fact, the British army. The country has no other force disposable: It may, by a great effort, reinforce the army for an adequate purpose, but another army it has not to send.

You are already apprised, by my former despatch (enclosing a copy of General Moore's instructions) that the British army must be kept together under its own commander; must act as one body for some distinct object, and on some settled plan. It will decline no difficulty, it will shrink from no danger; when, through that difficulty and danger, the commander is enabled to see his way to some definite purpose: but, in order to do this, it will be necessary that such purpose should have been previously arranged, and that the British army should not again be left, as that of sir John Moore and sir David Baird have recently been, in the heart of Spain, without one word of information except such as they could pick up from common rumour of the events passing around them.[8]

Moore certainly had no intention of shrinking from danger, now that he had a definite purpose, and he planned to move off as soon as he could get his troops on the road and be at Valladolid by the 16th. Moore had also just received a letter from Craddock who had gone up to Corunna where he had deposited half of the money that had been shipped out to help Moore. The other half was being retained at Lisbon.

On the morning of the 11th, the first troops set off from Salamanca in two columns. They marched or rode 'across the bleak, almost treeless plain,' wrote Thomas Graham's biographer, 'the scene was vibrant with noise and outwardly bright with expectation. Waggons went creaking by under the weight of ammunition. Batmen and servants led spare mules and horses, while donkeys trotted past under such women and children as still accompanied the regiments. Mules by the hundred lumbered along with heavy loads of baggage, or strutted behind marching troops whose bayonets were glittering in the wintry sunlight.'[9]

The risk that Moore was taking was not lost on Andrew Leith Hay: 'Sir John Moore had no friendly corps to protect his flanks – no reinforcements to expect. He commanded an army, brilliant in appearance, yet weak in numerical strength; but upon that, and that alone, was dependence to be placed for the successful result of a very bold advance against a superior enemy.'[10]

One of the columns aimed for Toro where Lord Paget and most of the cavalry were waiting, the other took a more easterly route to Tordesilla. The objective of the cavalry was to provide a screen on the army's right flank to conceal and safeguard the movements of the main body, and so on 12 December, Paget moved from Toro to Tordesillas while Stewart reached the village of Rueda, where he had learned the previous day that a detachment of French cavalry with some infantry were quartered. The next day, the 12th, Stewart sent his aide-de-camp into the village disguised as a peasant. The aide returned with information on the numbers and disposition of the enemy troops. The French, it appeared, had no idea that there were any British forces near them and Stewart decided he would try and take them by surprise. 'With this intention,' he wrote, 'a squadron proceeded against them on the night of the 12th; and, having made good our entrance unobserved, we soon threw them into confusion. The greater number were sabred on the spot, many were taken.'[11]

Some, only a few, managed to escape, taking news of the presence of the British army to General Franceschi at Valladolid. The clash at Rueda had not been necessary. It achieved nothing of any consequence other than prematurely alerting the enemy.

This, of course, changed the whole game. Until this time, having seen nothing of the British, Napoleon had assumed that Moore had returned to Portugal, and in due course he would send forces to re-capture that country. Napoleon was excited with this news: 'Moore is the only general now fit to contend with me,' he declared. 'I shall advance against him in person.'[12]

Moore, meanwhile, left Salamanca on the 13th with the last of the troops, having replied on the 12th to Baird's suggestion of defending Galicia rather than risking an offensive action against an enemy the strength of whose forces were unknown:

> I am much obliged to you for your opinion on the Galicias and Vigo; and it is that which now probably I shall follow, should such a measure become necessary.
> I am therefore most anxious that magazines should be formed on that communication. I have written home to direct that all transports, &c. should call at Coruna, and go to Vigo, unless otherwise directed. Coruna must be the place for all supplies from England.[13]

Adopting such a policy, though, was only if Moore's daring bid to cut Napoleon's communications failed or became operationally impossible. For now, he was on the march to cause as much trouble to the French as he could in conjunction with la Romana or any other Spanish armies. Moore did in fact receive a reply from the Marquis on the 14th, but the letter only stated that he understood Moore's reasons for considering a retreat, but mentioned nothing about any forward movements together, in case the letter was intercepted. Coincidentally, that very same day, an intercepted packet of French despatches was handed to Moore at Alaejos. It was to prove to be one of, if not the, most important interceptions of the Peninsular War. A French officer had ridden into the village of Valdestillos near Segovia where, apparently, he acted in an 'insolent manner' to the villagers, in particular the postmaster. As he was alone in an occupied country this was not a smart move. The insult to the postmaster was repaid and the officer was set upon and murdered. When the peasants stripped the body they found the packet of letters which were offered to Captain John

Waters, (who would later become one of Wellington's 'Exploring Officers') who had been sent by Moore to try and gather intelligence on French movements. Waters purchased the letters for twenty dollars. Rarely can a British official have spent public money so wisely.[14]

The packet had been sent by Marshal Berthier, Napoleon's chief of staff, from Chamartin, Napoleon's headquarters near Madrid, to Marshal Soult, the Duke of Dalmatia, in charge of the French II Corps stationed at Saldana.

The main letter to Soult informed him that the regiments under General de Belle and Franceschi would be placed under his command which, along with the divisions of generals Merle and Mouton already with him, would give him a force that 'nothing can resist'.

With that force, Soult was told to 'Take possession of Léon, drive back the enemy into Galicia, make yourself master of Benavente and Zamora. You can have no English in your front, for some of their regiments came to the Escurial and Salamanca, and every thing evinces that they are in full retreat. Our advanced guard is this day at Talavera de la Reyna, upon the road to Badajoz, which it will reach soon. You clearly perceive that this movement must compel the English to hasten immediately to Lisbon, if they are not gone there already. The moment, Marshal, you are sure that the English have retreated, of which there is every presumption, move forward with rapidity. There are no Spaniards who can resist your two divisions.' Soult was told to occupy Valladolid and Zamora, andwas then given a free hand.'To conclude, the Emperor thinks that you can do what you please, as soon as the English retire to Lisbon.'[15]

At last Moore had very specific information about the location and movements of the French. The letter was dated 10 December and so the details were fresh and certain to be fairly accurate. Instead of all the guessing and false facts that had hitherto ruled Moore's decision-making, he now had solid information. The man who had seemed so indecisive and had repeatedly vacillated between advancing and retreating, now became the firm commander – he now knew exactly what he was going to do. He was going to attack Soult.

The French marshal was about 100 miles to the north with no more than around 18,000 men. Moore commanded approximately 25,000 infantry and 2,450 cavalry, along with 1,297 artillerymen manning sixty-six guns. If he could catch Soult unawares he might bring about the greatest British victory in mainland Europe since the Battle of Blenheim. 'But was it probable that we should succeed in this?' Asked Charles Stewart. 'Still not a man in the army desponded, but all felt their spirits rise as the prospect of meeting the enemy became more decided.'[16] An excited Captain Boothby wrote in his journal that: 'Sir John dines with General Paget – and Battle is the word!'[17]

Speed now was essential to catch Soult before he could be reinforced or before other French troops moved unwittingly behind Moore cutting off his avenue of retreat back to Portugal. Moore wrote to Baird to tell him about the intercepted despatches and to inform him of his change of plan. Baird was told to move on Benavente as soon as possible, whilst Moore's main body would march to Toro, 'from whence, either by a forward or flank movement, the two corps can be joined.' Moore also sent a rider to Frere at Badajoz, where the Spanish Government had fled after the French capture of Madrid, giving him the same information.

Moore had been informed that Napoleon was moving with a large body of troops towards Badajoz with the intention of re-conquering Portugal. This meant that Moore would have enough time to defeat Soult and then withdraw to the coast at Corunna or Vigo before Napoleon was able to respond and turn northwards – providing Moore acted quickly. Moore was under no illusions about what he could achieve, telling Castlereagh that: 'it is evident how the business must terminate. For, even if I beat Soult, unless the victory has the effect to rouse the Spaniards … it will be attended with no other advantage than the character it will attach to the British arms.' That, though, was enough justification for the men of Moore's army.

Yet, just as Moore was about to take this bold and daring step, he received what can only be called an offensive letter from Hookham Frere, written in the belief that the British army was heading for the coast and abandoning the Spaniards. He warned Moore of the consequences of 'adopting, upon a supposed military necessity, a measure which must be followed by immediate if not final ruin to our Ally, and by indelible disgrace to the Country with whose resources you are entrusted'.

Frere's tone then became even more insulting: 'if the British army had been sent abroad for the express purpose of doing the utmost possible mischief to the Spanish cause, with the single exception of not firing a shot against their troops, they would, according to the measures now announced as about to be pursued, have completely fulfilled their purpose.' Moore did not reply.

The army now set off with purpose, despite the wintry conditions. 'On 14 December we advanced to a place called Toro,' wrote a soldier of the 71st Highland Light Infantry. 'The roads were bad; the weather very severe; all around was covered with snow. Our fatigue was dreadful, and our sufferings almost more than we could endure.'[18]

Even at this early stage of the march, many were already falling out of the columns: 'Every movable article, being in front, had so cut up the roads … or any opening through the woods, that we were not only mid-leg, but knee-deep in mud,' Sergeant Douglas of the 1st Royal Scots wrote in his diary. 'On the 2nd day's march from Salamanca, a woman a little to the right of the column had sunk under the hardships and expired, but her infant was still alive; and a little further on the left a Portuguese soldier, worn with hunger and fatigue, had also sunk in the mud and was totally unable to extricate himself.'[19]

Captain Alexander Gordon of the 15th Hussars also maintained a journal throughout the campaign:

> December 14th. The Light Brigade of Sir John Moore's army passed through Morales at one o'clock, and we received orders soon afterwards to march to Tordesillas, five leagues distant. We did not arrive there until eight o'clock, and the roads were so slippery, owing to the severity of the frost, that we could scarcely keep our horses on their legs.[20]

This was echoed by another Scot, Ensign William Gavin, in his diary, dated the 16th, 'Marched to Toro; the weather dreadful, the whole face of the country covered with snow. In this town the troops committed dreadful deprevations.'[21]

The march continued through Villapando and Valderos and, on 20th December, the army reached Majorga where it was joined by the Brigade of Guards and General Manningham's brigade of Baird's corps. At last Moore's command was together. He now re-organised his army, presumably in what he considered the most suitable for the expected coming battle. In this re-shuffle, Baird was given command of the 1st Division, Hope took the 2nd Division, the 3rd was under Fraser, with Edward Paget taking command of the Reserve. The two light brigades were led by brigadier-generals Karl Alten and Robert Craufurd. Lord Paget took command of the cavalry, its two brigades being those of John Slade and Charles Stewart. Any lingering hope that Moore would receive help from the Marquis de la Romana's army was quashed when a report was received from Lieutenant Colonel Symes, dated Léon, 14 December:

> In the morning I waited on the Marquis, and pressed him, as far as I could with propriety, on the subject of joining Sir John Moore; to which he evaded giving any more than general assurances … [he] regretted his want of cavalry; expressed a wish to procure 2,000 English muskets, and shoes for his army. When I asked him for 100 draft mules for General Baird's army, he replied, it was impossible; he had not one to spare … I attended the review. The troops were drawn up in three columns; each might, perhaps, consist of 2,500 men … Their movements from column into line were very confusedly performed, and the Officers were comparatively inferior to the men; there was only one brigade of artillery in the field; and I doubt whether there is any more in Leon. The guns were drawn by mules. On the whole, from what I have been able to observe, since I came here, and from the tenor of my conversations with the Marquis, I am disposed to doubt his inclination of moving in a forward direction to join Sir John Moore. I suspect he rather looks to secure his retreat into Galicia.

Paget's cavalry, leading the way, approached the abbey of Melgar Abxo on the 20th, where they learnt that a brigade of Soult's light cavalry, under General César Alexandre Debelle, had its headquarters at Sahagun just nine miles away. With the French still unaware of Moore's movements, Paget saw the chance of taking Debelle's men by surprise. At 23.00 hours, the 10th and 15th Hussars were assembled as quietly as possible. 'The night was dark as the grave, the ground covered with snow,' wrote an officer of the 15th, 'and so slippery that we were obliged to lead our horses out of the village; under all these circumstances it was one o'clock before we were formed, told off, and ready to march.'[22] As no bugles were sounded, some hussars were still asleep when the party moved off and they missed the regiment's finest hour.

Paget's plan was that the 15th Hussars would march west of the River Cea and attack Sahagun from that direction while the 10th, with a detachment (two guns) of horse artillery, moved directly upon the town. The French would be trapped. Paget hoped to capture the entire enemy force which was estimated to be around 700-strong. Watches were synchronised with the attack to take place at exactly 06.30 hours on the morning of the 21st.

After the hussars had covered about six miles, the 15th was sent off on its flank march, leaving the 10th and the artillery to approach Sahagun slowly. Unfortunately Slade, with the 10th, took far longer than expected to reach Sahagun and the 15th encountered Debelle's outpost long before the 10th were in position. Realising that unless he acted immediately all surprise would be lost, Paget attacked the French picket and cut down and captured all except for one man who, unfortunately for the hussars, escaped to raise the alarm in Sahagun.

Debelle had two regiments in the town, the 8th Dragoons and the 1st Provincial Chasseurs à Cheval. The men had slept fully accoutred and they were quickly mounted and under arms. By the time Paget's force reached the town, the French were formed in close column of squadrons on the outskirts of the town, facing the road to Carrion. There was still no sign of Slade and the rest of the brigade. Very soon Debelle would realise that he was faced by only a single regiment and would be certain to charge and break through the 15th. Paget had no choice but to attack while the French were still uncertain of what they faced. His objective was not merely to defeat the French cavalry but to prevent any of them escaping to warn Soult that the British were almost upon him. For this Paget formed the hussars into column of divisions so that they could move quickly in the hope that he could outpace the French and then swing round in front of them and cut off their means of escape. 'As soon as we came in sight of them [the French cavalry] we … took an oblique direction at a gallop in order to gain their flank,' wrote an officer of the 15th, 'and after having gone a few hundred yards parallel to each other we both halted & wheeled into line; they then gave three cheers and waved their swords in the air, which we answered in the same way, our trumpets then sounded a charge which Lord Paget led at the head of the right squadron, and in a moment we were in their ranks.'[23]

In the march to Sahagun, the men had become almost paralysed with cold and for fear of losing his grip of his sword, Sergeant Major Tale of the 15th, 'twisted the buff [sword] knot to an extent that became painful; but this proved a bootless precaution, for on wheeling into line for the charge, the temperature of the blood mounted at once from below zero to the boiling point'.[24]

Captain Gordon of the 15th also left an account of this little battle in the snow:

> The attack was made just before daybreak, when our hands were so benumbed with the intense cold that we could scarcely feel the reins or hold our swords. The ground was laid out in vineyards intersected by deep ditches and covered with snow … The French were well posted, having a ditch in their front, which they expected to check the impetus of our charge; in this, however, they were deceived … The mêlée lasted about ten minutes, the enemy always endeavouring to gain the Carrion road … having rode together nearly a mile, pell-mell, cutting and slashing at each other, it appeared to me indispensable that order should be re-established, as the men were quite wild and the horses almost blown; therefore, seeing no superior officer near me, I pressed through the throng until I overtook and halted those who were farthest advanced in pursuit.[25]

'We attacked them again,' wrote Lord Paget. 'They again fired, by which they killed two and wounded one horse. They stood firm, we broke them, killed several, wounded twenty and took prisoners, one officer, 100 men and fifty horses. *We* are in the greatest favour.'

With the detachment of the Royal Horse Artillery was 2nd Captain Richard Brogue: 'Marched with the 10th (Light Dragoons/ Hussars) and 4 guns at one o'clock this morning, a deep snow on the ground. Reached Sahagun, where we knew the French had a position, by half past six, when we found they had news of our approach, & were drawn up (700 cavalry) ready to receive us. The 15th (Light) Dragoons (Hussars) met them first & 400 of them charged them. We came up at the time they were dispersing and assisted in taking them.'

In fact, more than twenty of Debelle's men were killed and many others wounded. A total of some 170 Frenchmen were taken prisoner including two colonels. It was a resounding victory and if Slade would have shown a little more dynamism it is not impossible that both French regiments would have been captured in their entirety. According to Sir Charles Oman, the action at Sahagun was 'perhaps' the most brilliant exploit of the British cavalry in the whole six years of the Peninsular War.[26]

Paget also wrote of the battle to his brother Arthur: 'The March & the attack were beautiful, nothing could exceed it, but the pursuit was sadly disorderly. I gave the Regiment a good scolding for it after the affair was over, & the answer they gave me was three cheers, & a request that I would accept as a token of their regard the two best Officers' Horses that were taken.'[27]

This was all very well, but Moore needed to know the exact position of Soult's corps and that task was given to Major Edwin Griffith of the 15th Hussars:

> On the 22nd of December we were detached to the villages in front of Sahagun which was soon after occupied by the infantry, and Sir John Moore established his Headquarters there on the same day.
>
> On the morning of the 23rd Colonel [James] Bathurst, Deputy Quarter Master General, arrived at Villabrin where I was quartered with my troop and ordered us to accompany him on a reconnoitring party; we proceeded in the direction of Carrion and Saldana, which we came in sight of at sunset; at the latter Marshal Soult was stationed. Having ascertained the exact position of the

French army, Colonel Bathurst returned full speed to Sir John Moore, who told me at parting meant to make an attack upon it at daybreak. I was directed to remain till the rest of the cavalry came up.[28]

Moore was now within striking distance of II Corps, but the French cavalry that managed to escape from Sahagun took the news to Soult of the proximity of British army. Though the survivors could give the Duke of Dalmatia no information regarding the British infantry, it had to be assumed that Moore's main column was close behind its cavalry. Soult's first move was, therefore, to concentrate his own force as quickly as possible behind the River Carrion, placing pickets at the fords and bridges. He withdrew a detachment that had been posted at Guardo to join the 7,000 he had at Saldana and the 5,000 in the town of Carrion. He also sent his aides-de-camp to Burgos and Palencia to find any regiments they could. They were able to divert General Lorges' dragoon division and General Delaborde's infantry division of Junot's VIII Corps (returning to the Peninsula after its evacuation from Portugal) which were found marching from Burgos down to Madrid.

Until these could reach Carrion, Soult was in danger, but Moore did not press home his advantage with the kind of energy that might have been expected in such circumstances. He was now within striking distance of the partially-formed II Corps and possibly on the verge of a momentous victory. Quite understandably he wanted to give his men a little rest before throwing them into battle. But, inexplicably, he let his men relax for around forty-eight hours. 'I march this night to Carrion,' Moore therefore told Frere on the 23rd, 'and the next day to Saldana, to attack the corps under Marshal Soult.' He was a day too late.

Chapter 6

Risking too Much

Moore was under no illusions as to the enormous risk he was taking. News of the contact that the cavalry had with the French at Rueda had been relayed to Madrid and just as Moore saw an opportunity to catch Soult isolated, so Napoleon had realised that a similar chance of trapping the British army had suddenly presented itself. Moore knew that he had just a few days to defeat Soult and then try and escape to the coast before Napoleon could react. 'The movement I am making is of the most dangerous kind,' he told Frere, 'not only risk to be surrounded every moment by superior forces, but to have my communication intercepted with the Galicias. I wish it to be apparent to the whole world, as it is to every individual of the army, that we have done every thing in our power in support of the Spanish cause; and that we do not abandon it, until long after the Spaniards had abandoned us.'

Lord Paget was even more vociferous in his condemnation of Britain's allies:

> Such ignorance, such deceit, such pusillanimity, such cruelty, was never both united. There is not one army that has fought at all. There is not one general who has exerted himself, there is not one province that has made any sacrifice whatever … We are treated like enemies. The houses are shut against us; we are roving about the country in search of Quixotic adventures to save our own honour, whilst there is not a Spaniard who does not skulk or shirk within himself at the very name of a Frenchman.[1]

On the evening of the 23rd, the army began its advance towards Soult's position between Carrion and Saldana in two columns, covered by the 10th and 15th Hussars on the left, the 18th Hussars and the 3rd Hussars King's German Legion on the right, with the 7th Hussars out in front. Baird led the left column, consisting of his own division and the 1st Light Brigade and three brigades of artillery, and Hope the right column with his and Fraser's division and two brigades of artillery, the intention being that Baird would ford the river north of the only bridge that led to the town of Carrion, while Hope would ford the river south of the bridge. If Hope and Baird could not find suitable fords, Hope would capture the bridge – which was certain to be held by the French – and Baird would follow once Hope's men were across the river.

The prospect of action once again lifted the spirits of the troops. 'The cheering effect which this notification produced throughout the brigade was conspicuous,' recalled Major Rautenberg of the King's German Legion. 'The sick and baggage had been ordered to be left behind at Villada, but of the thirty-two men of the brigade who might have taken advantage of this order, twenty-four reported themselves to be fit to march.'[2]

The Light Brigade, which included Rifleman Harris, set off before the rest of the infantry: 'War is a sad blunter of the feelings of men,' he wrote. 'We felt eager to be at it again. Nay, I am afraid we longed for blood as the cheer of our comrades sounded in our ears; and yet, amidst all this, softer feelings occasionally filled the breasts of those gallant fellows even whilst they were thirsting for a sight of the enemy.'[3] Those softer feeling were aroused because one of the riflemen had looked at the snow through which they marched and reminded his fellow soldiers that it was after midnight which meant that it was the 24th of December, Christmas Eve, and that on the day of 'goodwill to all men' they were due to fight and kill.[3]

The men were told to keep as quiet as possible on the march towards Carrion, the tread of their boots being further muffled by the deep snow through which they moved. But the recollection that it was Christmas even prompted the men to talk quietly of home, 'and scenes upon that night in other days in old England,' remembered Harris, 'shedding tears as they spoke of the relatives and friends never to be seen by them again.'[4]

If the men of Moore's army were contemplating the battle to come, their commander-in-chief was having doubts. He had received a letter from the Marquis de la Romana, dated Léon 22 December, which read:

> A confidential person whom I had placed on the river Duero has written to me, on the 18th instant, that he is assured that the Enemy's troops posted at the Escurial [in Madrid] are moving in this direction. He adds, that if the person who gave him this intelligence should not arrive the same day, he would go himself to Villacastin, twelve leagues from Madrid, to watch the two roads; the one of which leads to Zamora, and the other to Segovia. I hasten to give this information to your Excellency, that you may judge what measures are requisite to be taken.

If this information was accurate it meant that a large part of Napoleon's force was heading north, not in the direction of Badajoz and the main road to Lisbon as Moore had believed. This would place the Emperor many days' march closer to Carrion than Moore had calculated upon. Once again Moore was wracked with uncertainty, but this time the situation was far more critical. Continuing with his move against Soult might well result in a glorious victory. But if Napoleon fell upon the British rear while it was engaged with II Corps, Moore's entire force might be slaughtered or captured.

Other snippets of information began to be received at Moore's headquarters throughout the course of the day. One was that a strong reinforcement of French troops had just arrived at Carrion and that a large quantity of provisions and forage were being prepared in the villages in front of that town. This possibly indicated that the French were making ready for the arrival of large numbers of troops. Then a courier arrived from Estremadura saying that a French corps that was heading into the south of Spain had been halted. This was followed by several other messengers bringing reports that confirmed that a large body of French troops was heading north from Madrid.

Moore simply could not ignore this mounting body of evidence. With, no doubt, the heaviest of hearts the British commander decided that he would have to cancel his orders for the advance on Carrion and head for the coast. The Royal Artillery's Lieutenant Colonel George Cookson was with Hope's Division when the order to retreat was received:

> The column had been marching slowly on till about 12 at night when a despatch arrived from General Sir J Moore. I was with Sir J Hope at the head of the column at the time. He asked me for a light which I instantly brought him one from the guns. The General read the dispatch and said 'we are to retreat, halt your guns and desire the word to be quietly passed to the rear of the column'. He then gave orders that three guns of the horse artillery, a squadron of cavalry and a light brigade of infantry should remain upon the ground all night and to push some patrols near to Carrion.[5]

After the excitement of being given command of the largest field army Britain had assembled for a generation and the weeks of eager expectation of a glorious encounter with the enemy, Moore had to turn and run having accomplished, it seemed, certainly to his men, practically nothing.

He replied to Romana in a letter that evening:

> Your Excellency knows, my object in marching in this direction was to endeavour to free you from a troublesome neighbour, and to strike a blow at a corps of the Enemy, whilst it was still imagined that the British troops had retreated into Portugal. I was aware of the risk I ran, if I should be discovered, and the Enemy push on a corps between me and my communication. My movement has, in some degree, answered its object, as it has drawn the Enemy from other projects, and will give the South more time to prepare. With such a force as mine, I can pretend to do no more. It would only be losing this army to Spain and to England, to persevere in my march on Soult; who, if posted strongly, might wait, or, if not, would retire and draw me on until the corps from Madrid got behind me: in short, single-handed, I cannot pretend to contend with the superior numbers the French can bring against me.[6]

Moore, though, had not given up all hope on maintaining his army in the field, informing the Marquis de la Romana that he intended only to retire as far as Astorga: 'There I shall stand;

as my retreat thence, if necessary, will be secure. I shall be in the way to receive the supplies and the reinforcements which I expect from England. At the worst, I can maintain myself, and, with your Excellency's aid, defend the Galicias, and give time for the formation of the armies. of the South, and that which you command to be prepared, when a joint effort may be made, which can alone be efficacious.' He added that: 'you may rest assured that I shall not retreat a foot beyond what is necessary to secure my supplies from being intercepted; and that I desire nothing more than to meet the Enemy upon anything like equal terms.'

Though he had presented Romana with a positive view of the situation, his diary entry for the 24th seems to show that he had little belief in his allies, or that he really had no intention of remaining in Spain:

> I gave up the march on Carrion, which had never been undertaken with any other view but that of attracting the enemy's attention from the armies assembling in the south, and in the hope of being able to strike a blow at a weak corps whilst it was still thought the British army was retreating into Portugal. For this, I was aware that I risked infinitely too much; but something, I thought, was to be risked for the honour of the service and to make it apparent that we stuck to the Spaniards long after they themselves had given up their cause as lost.[7]

Moore issued orders cancelling the move to Carrion and the men were told to return to their quarters pending further instructions. 'If we can steal two marches upon the French we shall be quiet; if we are followed close, I must close [up] and stop and offer battle. At this season of the year, in a country without fuel, it is impossible to bivouac; the villages are small, which obliges us to march thus by corps in succession. Our retreat, therefore, becomes much more difficult.' They were to be the last words Moore entered in his diary.

'It would be no easy matter to describe the effect which this un-looked-for event produced on the army,' wrote Stewart concerning the cancelling of the attack upon Soult. 'Troops, who had panted to meet the enemy, and who, but an hour ago, were full of life and confidence, suddenly appeared like men whose hopes were withered. Few complained, but all retired to their quarters in a state of sullen silence, which indicted, more powerfully perhaps than words, the mortification under which they laboured.'[8]

Major Edwin Griffith had remained with his troop close to Carrion after the departure of Colonel Bathurst waiting for the rest of the army:

> The ground was covered with snow, and the cold most intense; it was as much as ever we could do to keep the men from falling asleep. Twelve o'clock came and nothing appeared; at length a few minutes before one, the sound of our advancing army was distinctly heard, but no part of it ever reached us: a halt was sounded and orders were soon after given for the *whole* to return to their respective quarters.; thus instead of reaping fresh laurels on the plains of [the] Carrion, the dawn of the 24th beheld us more dead than alive re-entering our miserable villages.[9]

The men were devastated when they received the orders to return to their quarters. Anthony Hamilton of the 43rd put the feelings of the men into words:

> When the resolution of their General was made known to the army, it was received by all ranks with more than murmurs of dissatisfaction and disgust. The British army had suffered no disaster; it had never been brought into contact with the enemy; and all felt that to retreat with untried prowess from the scene of contest would fix a tarnish on our arms, and, by diminishing the confidence of the Spanish nation in our zeal and devotion to their cause, would proportionally contribute to strengthen and consolidate the power of the usurper. All lamented the order for retreat – all felt that it must cast a blight on that cause which they were prepared to defend by the outpouring of their blood.[10]

Sergeant Surtees of the 95th said that he appreciated the reasons for Moore's decision to abandon the attack upon Soult, but saw the impact the news had upon the troops:

> This was most distressing information, for never was an army more eager to come in contact with the enemy than ours was at

this moment, and never was there a fairer prospect of success, had things remained as they were; but now, instead of honour and glory being acquired, by, showing the French what British troops could do in the field, it was evident nothing remained but to commence a retrograde movement, the worst and most unpleasant, in a British soldier's view, of any other.[11]

'How great was our disappointment!' wrote Robert Porter:

No advance has taken place, though at the hour appointed the whole of our force were under arms. Even our right column had began its march, and all the rest, in high spirits, were impatiently counting the moments until the word should be given for their starting also. An order was issued; but, oh! My friend, to what purpose! We were to go back to our quarters! … The effect this sudden and extraordinary alteration of intention had upon the troops is indescribable. A minute before, and every heart beat high with a resistless courage that longed to rush into the battle. Victory seemed to wave them from the hills. Already they heard the shout of their country on the news of this glorious day; and with eager-trembling of unloosed hounds in sight of their prey, they impatiently awaited the order of release which was to send them like bolts upon their enemies.

Think then what was our blank, when at this moment of high-wrought enthusiasm, the *order* was declared that all must return to their quarters! Every countenance was changed; the proud glow on their cheek was lost in fearful paleness; the strongly-braced arm sunk listlessly to the side; a few murmurs were heard, and the army of England was no more. Its spirit had fled.[12]

The Highlanders of the 42nd Regiment were told by Baird to go back to their quarters, and: 'for several moments the men stood transfixed, and at length their disappointment broke out into a murmur, and every countenance lost its high-wrought anxiety. Indeed, the effect of this counter-order on our soldiers was the most extraordinary, and from the greatest pitch of exultation and courage at once a solemn gloom prevailed throughout our ranks,' wrote Captain James Sterling. 'Nothing was heard on every side but the clang of firelocks thrown down in despair, which before they guarded as their dearest treasure.'[13]

Colonel Hussey Vivian, though fully conscious of the reasons why the retreat had been ordered, believed that Moore should have continued with his great enterprise and struck at Soult. The army was in Spain to fight, not run away:

> It is true Ministers were deceived as to the state of the Spanish armies; it is true that there appeared a great want of energy in the people; it is true there was a want of cordiality and assistance towards us; but still, having come into the country as friends to their assistance, having, in allprobability, in some measure been the cause of their starting their own efforts by leading them to expect great things from us, having most certainly occasioned Buonaparte's having sent a larger force than he otherwise would have sent, calculating upon merely a Spanish army – I say, under all these circumstances, I freely own it was my humble opinion that we should have risked everything rather than retreat.[14]

The men returned to the quarters they had abandoned a few hours earlier, but remained enranked, no-one being permitted to put down his weapon or lie down, but to be ready to move off again as soon as orders were issued. Those next orders that Moore gave his now dispirited troops were for a retreat. Accordingly, Lieutenant General Mackenzie Fraser with the 3rd Division, followed by Hope's 2nd Division, set off in the direction of Valderos and Majorga on the 24th. Baird, with the 1st Division, moved towards Valencia de Don Juan where there was supposed to be a ferry over the Esla. The reserve, under Major General Sir Edward Paget, did not leave Sahagun until the morning of the 25th, leaving just the cavalry to hold back the enemy. Before the troops left Sahagun, there was, with reference to our investigation into the loss of the military chest, an intriguing episode, according to a private of the 42nd: 'There being a large sum of money here for paying the army, every private soldier got two dollars. It was as well to give us these dollars, seeing we were obliged to retreat; but it would have been better to have given it all to us, according to our rank, as it was reported to have been destroyed, thrown over rocks, or into rivers on the retreat.'[15]

Behind Edward Paget's Reserve, Lord Paget was told to push his cavalry patrols close to the advanced posts of Soult's corps to cover the retreat, and it was not until the evening of the 25th that the cavalry began its withdrawal. Moore left Sahagun with the cavalry.

Lord Paget was unable to hold back all of the French cavalry, it would seem, as early the following morning, the 26th, the main column, with the British cavalry still some distance in the rear, approached the bridge of Castrogonzalo, amid a dense fog. The stores and baggage were a long time crossing the bridge and, concealed by the fog, a number of French horsemen, who had already begun to 'infest' the army's flanks, managed to cut off and capture some of the baggage. Two of Carthew's guns and Brigadier-General Karl Alten's brigade of the King's German Legion were posted on the bank of the river and drove off the enemy cavalry.[16]

If Moore was to escape he had to cross the River Esla and gain the mountain defile beyond Astorga before Napoleon. He would then be ahead of the French and providing he marched steadily for the coast no enemy force would be able to block his route to safety. From Sahagun to the Esla was nearly fifty miles and the Galician defile another thirty. Beyond that was 150 miles of mountain road to Corunna, the whole passage of which the French would be at his back. Food would be hard to find in the sparsely populated mountains and he could not allow his troops to wander off scavenging. Already his troops were voicing their disapproval of his conduct and morale was slipping. Yet, if discipline was not maintained, the whole army could fall apart in the trying conditions it was about to face, and then there would be disaster.

Moore explained his predicament to Castlereagh on 28 December. His despatch reveals that he no longer had any intention of remaining in the Peninsula, regardless of what he had told Romana:

> The roads are very bad, and the means of carriage scanty. If I am pressed I must lose some of them; and I may be forced to fight a battle. This, however, I shall endeavour to avoid; for, certainly, in the present state of things, it is more Buonaparte's game than mine. It is said that he comes himself with 10,000 of his guards. The force moving against us cannot be less than 50,000 men: we shall, when at Astorga, be about 27,000. The Marquis la Romana

came forward to Mansilla with 6,000 to co-operate with me in the attack on Soult: I therefore conclude that he cannot have above 8,000 fit for action. The country about Astorga offers no advantage to an inferior army; I shall, therefore, not stop there longer than to secure the stores, and shall retreat to Villafranca, where, I understand, there is a position. But, if the French pursue, I must hasten to the coast; for there is a road to Orense which leads more direct to Vigo, and which, of course, renders the position at Villafranca of no avail.[17]

This is an extraordinary communication. Moore had already concluded that he was hopelessly outnumbered and that he was going to run for the coast without stopping. It was as if he had given up and just wanted to take his army back home.

Six days earlier Napoleon had received messages from Franceschi and Soult announcing the presence of the British army, not trying to reach Lisbon as he imagined, but deep in northern Spain. The Emperor saw that he might, just might, be able to trap the British and prevent them escaping to the coast, but first he had to try and guess the direction Moore was moving. 'The manoeuvre of the English is very strange,' he wrote to his brother Joseph, 'it is proved that they have evacuated Salamanca. Probably they have brought their transports round to Ferrol, because they think that the retreat on Lisbon is no longer safe, as we could push on from Talavera by the left bank of the Tagus and shut the mouth of the river … Probably they have evacuated Portugal and transferred their base to Ferrol, because it offers advantages for a safe embarkation.'

Napoleon, then revealed great perspicacity by correctly predicting Moore's probable move against II Corps. 'But while retreating,' he continued, 'they might hope to inflict a check on the corps of Soult, and may not have made up their mind to try it until they had got upon their new line of retreat, and moved to the right bank of the Douro. They may have argued "If the French commit themselves to a march on Lisbon, we can evacuate on Oporto, and while doing so are still on our line of communications with Ferrol."'[18]

In Napoleon's mind, nothing mattered more than inflicting a defeat upon the British and he immediately cancelled all other operations to concentrate his effort on cutting Moore off from the coast. The cavalry of the Imperial Guard and the cavalry of Marshal Ney's corps set out on the 21st for the Guadarrama Pass, followed by Ney's infantry, the rest of the Guard and General Lapisse's division. Other troops were ordered to join Marshal Soult. If Napoleon's divisions could move quickly enough, Moore would find a powerful force in his front and an even stronger one bearing down on his rear.

The advance cavalry crossed the Sierra de Guadarrama despite very bad winter conditions. The next day, as the weather worsened, Napoleon with the rest of his force reached the mountain pass. A staff officer, Lieutenant [later Marshal] Castellanne-Novejan, described the crossing of the Guadarrama in his journal:

> The Emperor wished to pass over the mountain without delay, but the weather was frightful – there was snow in drifts, a fearful wind and an abominable frost. Nevertheless, the Emperor ordered the Dragoons of the Guard to advance. These soldiers, after fighting their way up a quarter of the slope, came back reporting that 'It was impossible to go any further.'[19]

Napoleon was not going to let the weather stop him from destroying the British, as the Baron de Marbot, who was on the staff of Marshal Lannes, described in his memoirs:

> A furious snowstorm, with a fierce wind, made the passage of the mountains almost impracticable. Men and horses were hurled over precipices. The leading battalions had actually begun to retreat; but Napoleon was resolved to overtake the English at all costs. He spoke to the men, and ordered that the members of each section should hold one another by the arm. The cavalry, dismounting, did the same. The staff was formed in similar fashion … we following with locked arms; and so, in spite of wind, snow, and ice, we proceeded, though it took us four hours to reach the top.[20]

Halfway up, the marshals and generals, who wore jackboots, could go no further through the snow. Napoleon, therefore, climbed onto a field gun, straggling the barrel. His staff followed suit, and in that manner, the elite of the French Empire reached the convent at the top of the pass. The passage of the Guadarrama took until late on the 23rd. Those two terrible days saved the British Expeditionary Force.

Napoleon, though, was still confident that he could ensnare Moore's force, reaching Tordesillas on the 26th, having moved over 200 miles of country in just ten days. 'Put it in all the newspapers … If the English are not already in full retreat they are lost,' he told Joseph on the 27th, 'and, if they retire, they will be pursued right up to their embarkation and at least half of them will not get away … Put it in the newspapers and have it spread everywhere that 36,000 Englishmen are surrounded; that I am at Benavente in their rear while Marshal Soult is pressing them from the front.'[21]

Napoleon was wrong. The British army was already slipping beyond the Emperor's grasp, with Moore's columns marching hard for the River Esla. That Moore had made the correct decision was almost immediately apparent as his cavalry were already being pressed by Soult's squadrons.

Paget was determined to parry vigorously every thrust made by the French cavalry with as many squadrons as he could collect to give the impression that he commanded a large body of horsemen in the hope that it would make the French more circumspect.

On the 26th, Paget fell in with two squadrons of the 15th Chasseurs à Cheval at Majorga and he immediately ordered Colonel Leigh, with two squadrons of the 10th Hussars, to attack the French who had halted on the summit of a steep hill. One of Leigh's squadrons was kept in reserve while the other rode briskly up the hill. To ensure his horses were not exhausted before they charged the enemy, Leigh halted for a few minutes to allow his mounts to recover from the climb, even though the hussars were within range of the French carbines. When he judged that his horses were ready, he charged. The chasseurs were completely overthrown, with three of their men being killed and many wounded, with between forty and fifty being taken prisoner. The action at Majorga was described by Lieutenant Colonel Vivian of the 7th Hussars in his memoirs:

> They fell in with the enemy's advance in the street, and, after a little skirmishing, drove them out of the town into the plain

beyond. Here they found a squadron of about 100 formed. Lieut.-Col. Leigh, with a squadron of the 10th, immediately charged and dispersed them, killing, or taking about 80 prisoners. The remainder were taken by a baggage guard of the 7th and the 18th Hussars, who were marching by another route.[22]

The cavalry was now repeatedly in contact with the enemy. On the 27th, the 18th Hussars turned round to drive back the French horsemen six times. Arthur Kennedy described one of these actions in a letter to his mother:

> In the morning at 7 o'clock I observed a picquet of his [Napoleon's] cavalry advancing towards my post. Instantly turned out and gave them chase which they did not relish but on the contrary took to flight, we pursuing them into the town where their main body was nearing us fast when to their no small surprise (I believe) I halted and faced about and charged them, killing, wounding and making prisoners of almost the whole party before the main body came up. Finding that we must inevitably be taken had we delayed a moment longer I made off thinking myself lucky indeed to carry away two mounted dragoons of theirs and to have only eight of our men and an officer wounded and one horse killed.[23]

While the cavalry was daily in action, which kept the morale of the men high, the infantry, with no such excitement, were thoroughly dispirited. A soldier of the 71st explained that many of the troops lost all their 'natural activity and spirits', becoming increasingly angry and frustrated. 'The idea of running away from an enemy we had beat with so much ease at Vimeiro, without even firing a shot, was too galling to their feelings. Each spoke to his fellow, even in common conversation, with bitterness; rage flashing from their eyes, on the most trifling occasions of disagreement.'[24] It was the Spaniards, though, for whom the men felt the most rage:

> The poor Spaniards had little to expect from such men as these, who blamed them for their inactivity. Every one found at home was looked upon as a traitor to his country. 'The British are here to fight for the liberty of Spain, and why is not every Spaniard

under arms and fighting? The cause is not ours; and are we to be the only sufferers?' Such was the common language of the soldiers; and from these feelings pillage and outrage naturally arose.[25]

The consequence of such feelings was that the men did indeed ransack almost every village that they passed through without compunction, and Moore was compelled to issue a General Order on the 27th from Benavente:

> The Commander of the Forces has observed with concern, the extreme bad conduct of the troops at a moment when they are about to come into contact with the Enemy, and when the greatest regularity and the best conduct are the most requisite … The misbehaviour of the troops in the column which marched by Valderas to this place, exceeds what he could have believed of British soldiers. It is disgraceful to the Officers; as it strongly marks their negligence and inattention.

Moore was conscious of the mood of the men and he ended his General Order with these remarks:

> It is impossible for the General to explain to his army the motive for the movement he directs. … When it is proper to fight a battle he will do it; and he will choose the time and place he thinks most fit: in the meantime he begs the Officers and Soldiers of the army to attend diligently to discharge their parts, and to leave to him and to the General Officers the decision of measures which belong to them alone.[26]

If Moore would have devoted some words of explanation for his actions, instead of what many must have seen as quite an insulting address, his subordinates might have responded more positively to his appeal for them to maintain discipline. This was certainly the view of General Sarrazin. Sir John, he wrote:

> Paid too much attention to abuses that are almost unavoidable, and the repression of which ought to be left to subaltern officers, or to the colonels of regiments … His ill-timed severity had other effect than to disgust several officers, while they were

proclaimed to be the authors of the evil, endeavoured to diminish it as far as their power extended. … there are critical moments in war, when the commanders must wink at some improprieties, in order to avoid greater ones. Is there not, indeed, a great deal of inconsistency in punishing marauders, when no provisions are distributed to the soldier?[27]

Moore's rebuke was certainly not well received by the junior officers, who saw their commander as the man who had landed them in this difficult situation, but who then blamed them for the deteriorating state of the army. Their feelings were put into words by the commissary of the 32nd Regiment, A.L.F. Schaumann:

At the very beginning of the retrograde movement disorder, a lack of discipline and subordination must have set in, and this was brought about in the first place through the rapid marches, secondly through deficient victuals, appalling weather and bad roads, and finally through the dejection and sense of ignominy caused by a continuous retreat and the inability to measure oneself with the enemy, complicated by the fact that General Moore maintained throughout the most absolute secrecy and silence regarding the movement. He was very much blamed for this, for it was the wrong time for secrecy, and he ought to have acquainted all officers and men with the necessity for the retreat long before. Even the officers became careless; and no one knew why or the wither of all that was happening. The only thing that everybody believed was that all must now be lost.[28]

These sentiments led to such widespread anxiety that early on the 28th, a 'cowardly' report by just one individual that the enemy was upon them, 'spread like wild fire and made Benavente a scene of confusion, women running and screaming through the streets, soldiers flying to their alarm post, horsemen galloping in all directions … In a very few minutes the whole of our troops were under arms, the flying [horse] artillery was sent into the plain. [Yet] The only enemy that appeared was a thick cloud which drenched us all to the skin.'[29]

In another similar incident, as related by an officer of the Quartermaster's Department, a false alarm deprived the army of every commissary's cart attached to those divisions. 'There were parks of 60 or 70 which had been hired at Salamanca by the commissariat. The drivers being mostly owners and men of some respectability were thought to be sufficiently tied by their own interest, fear however proved stronger than this, in the middle of the row, they mounted their mules and made off, leaving the commissaries to give to anybody who passed to have it, biscuit, rum, shoes, blankets &c.'[30] One can only speculate at how serious a blow it was to the army to lose so many mules. In the days to come enormous quantities of food and other items had to be abandoned for the lack of a means of conveyance. Many of the thousands of men lost over the course of the retreat may well have survived – as indeed might have the military chest – had these mules remained with the army.

One officer declared that the British army was no longer conducting a campaign: 'it is rather a devastation by bandits in uniform … The towns and villages half-burned, the farm animals and mules killed or stolen, all the tools and instruments of the peasantry and artisans used as fuel because it is easier to throw them on the fire than cut down trees, all the churches sacked and profaned; this is all that is left of this Kingdom.'[31]

It was quite different at the rear of the retreating army where the men of Robert Craufurd's light brigade and the cavalry were in almost constant contact with the enemy. Rifleman Harris recalled the first encounter with the French cavalry on the 28th, as the light brigade covered the crossing of the Esla. Craufurd's men were drawn up in a semi-circle around the bridge by the village of Castrogonzalo their rifles and muskets poking out from behind a make-shift wall of broken-down carts, tumbrils and felled trees. When the French cavalry appeared, they were met with a hail of lead that brought the horsemen to an immediate halt. The 95th, 43rd and 52nd held their ground during the night with elements of Paget's cavalry, as the engineers prepared the bridge for demolition:

> Towards morning we moved down towards a small bridge, still
> followed by the enemy, whom, however, we had sharply galled,
> and obliged to be more wary in their efforts. The rain was pouring
> down in torrents this morning, I recollect, and we remained many

hours with our arms ported – standing in this manner, and staring the French cavalry in the face, the water actually running out of the muzzles of our rifles. I do not recollect seeing a single regiment of infantry amongst the French force on this day. It seemed to me to be a tremendous body of cavalry – some said nine or ten thousand strong – commanded, as I heard, by General Lefebvre.

Whilst we stood thus, face to face, I remember the horsemen of the enemy sat watching us very intently, as if waiting for a favourable moment to dash in upon us like beasts of prey; and every now and then their trumpets would ring out a lively strain of music as if to encourage them. As the night drew on, our cavalry moved a little to the front, together with several field-pieces, and succeeded in crossing the bridge; after which we also advanced and threw ourselves into some hilly ground on either side of the road, whilst the 43rd and 52nd lay behind some carts, trunks of trees, and other materials with which they had formed a barrier.[32]

At the same time that Moore wrote his General Order at Benevente, he sent a message to General Brodrick at Corunna asking him to tell Admiral Samuel Hood to prepare for the possible evacuation of the army:

I had advanced to Sahagun in the hope of attacking Marshal Soult, who with 16,000 men was at Saldanha. The real object of my march, however, was to create a diversion in favour of the south of Spain, by attracting the attention of the enemy in his direction. I knew the danger of having my communication with the Gallicias interrupted, but from a wish to do something I took my chance. On the 23rd the army was prepared to march from Sahagun to Carrion, when I received information that reinforcements had arrived from Valencia, and that the French were marching from Madrid on Valladolid or Salamanca. I had no time to lose. I began my retreat on the 24th and arrived here on the 26th. We are continuing our march. I shall leave this with the last of the infantry to-morrow. As yet the enemy's infantry are not up, but are near. Their cavalry is becoming very numerous. It is not my wish to fight a battle. That at present is not our game, which is rather to save this army: to protect and give time to the Spaniards to rally, if they can. I may, however, be compelled to fight one if much pressed. If once I enter the mountains I fear the want of subsistence will compel me to go to the coast. At all events, a re-embarkation is a most probable event.[33]

The British cavalry was continuing to experience repeated success against its French counterparts. Every one of Paget's five regiments had its full share of fighting on the 26th and 27th, yet they were still in perfect order and their discipline was unbroken. As Oman pointed out, since the start of operations from Salamanca they had in twelve days taken no less than 500 prisoners, besides inflicting considerable losses in killed and wounded on the French. They still had one more success before them, before they found themselves condemned to comparative uselessness amongst the mountains of Galicia.'[34]

That final success came on the 29th and was described by Otway who had been made Field Officer of the Outlying Picquet of the 18th Hussars with fifty men under his command, stationed some two miles from Benavente, on the bank of the Esla by the village of Castrogonzalo. The bridge had, by that time, been demolished and the river was flooded due to the heavy rain of the previous days:

> Got on my horse at daybreak – saw the whole of the French cavalry on the other side of the river near a bridge which was rendered impassable by us during the night. I observed their motions, saw them return up the hill and presently discerned [them] opposite a place, where in dry weather there is a ford. They attempted the [crossing] in two places, at length they proceeded swimming the centre of the stream; [I] sent an officer off to give notice.[35]

Sergeant, later Captain, Jean-Roche Coignet of the Grenadiers à Pied de la Garde Imperiale, was amongst those ordered to wade across the river:

> We came to the shore of a river, which we found was extremely rapid, and from which all the bridges had been cut away. We had to ford it, holding on to one another, scarcely daring to raise our feet lest we should be carried away by the rapidity of the current. Our caps were covered in sleet. Imagine the delights

of such a bath in the month of January! [*sic*] When we stepped into this river it came up to our waists. We were ordered to take off our breeches before crossing the two branches of the river, and, when we came out of the water, our legs and thighs were as red as lobsters.[36]

Vivian agreed that crossing the river was a 'most gallant' act. They 'were obliged to ford the river at a place where the water was so deep as to occasion several of the horses to swim, and the current so rapid as to render it impossible they could do it quickly.'[37]

Otway immediately called in a small body of one officer and twenty men that had been posted around a quarter of a mile away and another party of similar strength which was at the broken bridge. Otway also sent his orderly to call up the 10th Hussars.

As the French forded the river, Otway's men fell back, skirmishing with the enemy to delay their advance and give the rest of Paget's cavalry a chance to mount up. About half a mile from the village they were joined by a small picquet of the KGL Hussars.

Otway now had sixty men with him and he halted at a point where some old walls protected both his flanks and he decided he would make a stand. Advancing towards him were approximately 400 men of the Chasseurs à Cheval de la Garde Imperial, Napoleon's most treasured cavalry regiment. As it halted, Otway's mixed force was strengthened by the arrival of Sergeant Major Jeffs and twenty-five men of the 18th Hussars Inlying Picquet and then sixty men of the 10th Hussars who came up on the left. Though still vastly outnumbered, Otway was in a strong position, with his flanks secured and men in reserve. Yet such was the confidence of the British cavalry, rather than simply holding back the enemy until all of Paget's force came up. He decided to attack:

> The enemy halted at this time, one squadron was somewhat in advance of the others, [I] thought it a favourable time to charge – [and] gave the word – the men gave a loud shout & rushed upon the enemy. Their squadron was broken in an instant, tho' composed of Bonaparte's best cavalry, his Imperial Guards. After the charge [I] gave the word to halt but in vain our men continued

to pursue and while dispersed the 2nd squadron of the enemy advanced on our left & took us in flank & rear.

Otway's attack had been watched by thousands of Spaniards under the walls of Benavente, the spectators urging on the British cavalry with cries of *'Viva los Ingleses'*.[38]

At this moment, General Stewart appeared on the scene and rallied the light dragoons and hussars, and then retired slowly in good order further back towards Benavente, where Paget was waiting with the 10th Hussars. He had assessed the situation very astutely and saw an opportunity to take the French by surprise. Keeping the 10th concealed behind some houses, he waited until the chasseurs à cheval were completely in the open. Then he ordered the 10th to charge. As William Napier of the 43rd Regiment wrote, the scene changed instantly:

> The enemy were seen flying at full speed towards the river, the British following close at their heels, until the French squadrons, without breaking their ranks plunged into the stream, and gained the opposite height, where, like experienced soldiers, they wheeled instantly, and seemed inclined to come forward a second time, but a battery of two guns opened upon them, and after a few rounds they retired. During the pursuit in the plain, an officer separating himself from the main body, and making towards another part of the river, being followed, and refusing to stop, he was wounded and brought in a prisoner. It was general Lefebvre Desnouettes.[39]

Lord Paget's artillery arrived just as the French horsemen struggled up the far bank. As the Imperial Guardsmen began to reform, the artillery fired two or three shots into their ranks, and they quickly and ignominiously made off. If the artillery had arrived just a few minutes earlier the chasseurs would have been caught in the water with unimaginable consequences.

According to the Baron de Marbot, Napoleon was the cause of this disaster. Being 'furious' at not having caught Moore, when at Villapanda he heard that the British were only a few leagues ahead, he sent a column of infantry and the chasseurs ahead of the main French force to intercept the retreating rear-guard. But Marbot did not excuse Lefèbvre-Desnoëttes, who he called 'a brave but somewhat imprudent officer':

> On reaching with his cavalry the banks of the Esla, the general could see no enemy, and proposed to reconnoitre the town of Benavente, half a league beyond the stream. This was all right; but a picket would have sufficed, for twenty-five men can see as far as two thousand, and if they fall into an ambush the loss is less serious. General Desnouettes should, therefore, have awaited his infantry before plunging recklessly into the Esla. But without listening to any suggestion, he made the whole regiment of chasseurs ford the river, and advanced towards the town, which he ordered the Mamelukes to search. They found not a soul in the place, a pretty certain sign that the enemy was preparing an ambush. The French general ought in prudence to have drawn back, since he was not in sufficient force to fight a strong rear-guard. Instead of this, Desnouettes pushed steadily forward; but as he was going through the town, four thousand or five thousand English cavalry turned it, covered by the houses in the suburbs, and suddenly charged down upon the chasseurs.[40]

It was during the fight at the Esla that Captain John Dobbs with the Reserve, caught a brief glance of a famous figure: 'On this occasion, for the first and last time, I saw Napoleon I; he had a numerous staff in attendance; but, my brother's glass being a good one, I was able to distinguish him, as he reconnoitred us.'[41]

Hussey Vivian also spotted the Emperor:

> About the middle of the day a general, with a large suite, made his appearance on the hill immediately above us and reconnoitred our position. From the number of attendants, and more especially from there being some Mamelukes of the party, we had every reason to suppose it was Buonaparte himself. The officer commanding the artillery wished rather to have given him a shot. Despising a war of outposts, I declined it. I afterwards rather regretted having done so, when I reflected, if it was Buonaparte and should a shot have been successful, on the benefit that would have resulted to the world in general.[42]

The Emperor wrote to Josephine on 31 December about the capture of Lefèbvre-Desnoëttes: 'Lefèbvre has been captured. He has had a skirmish with 300 Chasseurs. These gallants swam a river, and ended up in the middle of the English cavalry. They killed a number of them, but Lefebvre's horse was wounded, and when he was swimming back, the current carried him to the opposite bank, where he was taken. Console his wife.'[43]

Baird, it may be recalled, was to cross the Esla by the ferry at Valencia de Don Juan. This, though, proved impractical as there was only one small slow boat and it would have taken all day to get the division across the river. However, it was discovered that there was a ford a little further downstream, and there most of the division, with all its baggage, crossed. But as Leith Hay explained, only just: 'It is difficult to conceive a more gloomy scene. The weather continued as bad as possible, and the pouring rain was rendered more galling by a piercingly cold wind. The animals of burden, the followers of the army, with the women and children accompanying a column of 8000 men, added to the confusion. Many were seen struggling in the rapid stream that rolled past, while groups on either bank watched their progress. Nothing could be more comfortless than the appearance of all present; but notwithstanding the overturning of cars, the refractory exertionsof mules, the terror of the women, and vociferation of the Spaniards, the whole reached the right bank of the Esla without any lives being lost, or any serious accidenthaving occurred.'[44]

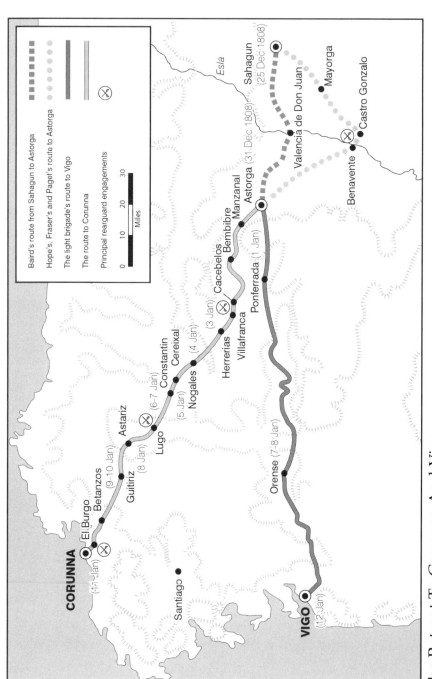

The Retreat To Corunna And Vigo

Chapter 7

Retreat

The army was safely beyond the Esla, and the clash at Benavente, in the words of Robert Southey, 'dampened the ardour' of the French, who then kept a respectful distance between them and the British cavalry. The following day, the 30th, Moore and the leading units reached Astorga, where Baird's column, coming from Valencia, united with the main body.

That same day, Schaumann was asked by the Commissary-General, Sir Robert Hugh Kennedy, to take charge of 'an enormous number' of bullocks along with their drivers. 'Off we marched,' wrote Schaumann, 'and soon reached a stone highway which ran across a marsh. The latter, however, was covered over with tall grass, and looked like a beautiful green meadow. This deceptive appearance misled the poor bullocks, which, having been confined the whole night in empty wooden enclosures … were mad with hunger, and longed to graze. The whole lot, therefore, left the stone highway for the marsh, and before many of them had got very far, and a few were quite close, they began to sink into the mud, some with their heads foremost and their hindquarters high in the air, while others showed only their heads and forelegs.'[1]

Schaumann and the drivers tried to stop the remaining bullocks from leaving the road, but the 'stupid' animals would not obey and ploughed on into the marsh. Just then, a division of infantry appeared, marching up the road. Schaumann begged the soldiers to help, but the men just laughed. Some even drew out their knives and sliced off large steaks of beef from the exposed rumps of the partially submerged, and in most cases still alive, creatures. The sight eventually proved too much for Schaumann, who spurred his horse and trotted off to Astorga. In view of the desperate need for draught animals in the days to come – not least with regard to the military chest, as we shall shortly see – such losses would be severely felt by the army.

Astorga was also where Romana's ragged army was encountered by the British troops. Moore had asked the Spanish general to retreat across the Cantabrian mountains into the Asturias, but the pass at Pajares was blocked by snow, and the Spaniards fell back to Astorga. Charles Stewart was shocked when his saw Romana's troops:

> It is hardly possible to conceive men bearing less resemblance to soldiers, or having a stronger claim upon compassion, than these wretched creatures. They were almost all in a state bordering on nudity – they had no provisions; their arms were, for the most part, useless; and of ammunition, either for musketry or cannon, they were entirely destitute.[2]

Joseph Sinclair of the 71st was equally shocked: 'Here we found the army of General Romana. I can convey no description of it in words. It had more the appearance of a large body of peasants, driven from their homes, famished, and in want of everything, than a regular army. Sickness was making dreadful havoc amongst them.[3]

Vivian was even more scathing in his comments:

> Here we fell in with the Marquis of Romana and his rabble of an army, who were retiring with all the speed they could on Orense, without ever having attempted or offered to make a stand or afford us the least assistance; nor indeed is it possible to conceive how anyone in their senses, who had seen such a force as his was, could have expected to have derived the slightest advantage from their co-operation.[4]

But here at Astorga had been formed one of the magazines that Moore had asked Baird to prepare in anticipation of being forced to retreat, and Romana's men were at last able to find food. The British troops themselves were not a great deal better off and yet they had to witness the large-scale destruction of valuable stores. Baird had also deposited large quantities of camp equipage that had been brought up from Corunna. Such items were considered of no use to a retreating army and they too had to be destroyed to prevent them falling into the hands of the enemy.

Lieutenant Samuel Thorpe was with the 23rd Foot and saw the terrible waste:

[When we] reached Astorga … want of shoes and food, and long marches, had much altered the appearance of the Army; the number of sick and stragglers was immense, and the men generally bare-footed. The commissariat stores in this place had been collecting for many weeks, and now we were under the necessity of destroying the whole to prevent their falling into the hands of the enemy. As we marched through the town, the rum was running down the canals of the streets, and with much difficulty we prevented the men from remaining behind and getting intoxicated; those who had shoes slipped them off their feet, and filling them with rum and mud drank it off at a gulp before Officers could prevent them; others filled their caps for the same purpose.[5]

Surtees of the 95th with the rear-guard, saw the same scene:

We moved into Astorga, where we halted for an hour or two, til the destruction of the magazine was completed, although nothing but rum remained; and here I witnessed such a brutal and swinish eagerness for drink as was quite disgusting. The rum casks were ordered to be staved, and to let the contents run out onto the street, that they might not fall into the hands of the enemy: thus the rum which had cost so much trouble in bringing up all the way from Corunna was about to be lost for ever; a thing most heart-rending to the numerous soldiers looking on, who loved it so dearly. However, they were determined not to lose all, for when the heads of the casks were knocked in, and their contents permitted to run in streams down the gutters, some of those brutes deliberately took off their greasy caps, and laving up the rum and the mud together, drank, or rather ate, the swinish mixture.[6]

To Captain Pierrepoint of the Quartermaster's Department, 'Help yourself was become the mode of distribution, the enemy will soon have what you leave, the motive for it. Thus I have seen shoes which several regiments were in the greatest want of, selling for a shilling in the streets of Astorga; thus I have seen a heap of biscuit which might have served the whole reserve, trampled on by the muddy feet of a hundred stragglers belonging to the preceding divisions.'[7]

The destruction, or abandonment, of a great deal of equipment, had unforeseen consequences for the retreating army. As will be seen later in the retreat, the Royal Engineers were not always successful in their attempts to destroy the road or bridges to try and delay the enemy. While condemned by many as being incompetent, part of the reason why the Engineers failed was because so many tools had been discarded.

Though Moore had let it be known that the army would stand and fight at Astorga, the destruction of the stores was a clear indication that Moore had no intention of engaging the French and was intent only on making for the coast as quickly as he could. Particularly revealing was the destruction of large quantities of ammunition and an entire depot of entrenching tools – exactly the items the army would need if it was to prepare defensive positions to hold back the French.

Further proof that Moore was not going to fight was delivered via a General Order issued from Astorga on the 30th. Though he assured the men that: 'It is very probable that the Army will shortly have to meet the Enemy', it was the next words that must have chilled the already cold bones of his troops: 'The present is a moment when the Army is necessarily called upon to make great efforts, and to submit to privations, the bearing cheerfully with which is a quality not less estimable than valour.'[8]

With the army united and with the addition, albeit unlooked for, of the Spanish force, Romana fully expected Moore to make a stand at Astorga, and it was to his 'utter astonishment' that he learned that Fraser's division had already set off for Villafranca. Romana confronted Moore and, 'represented to him the propriety of facing the enemy where they were, a point from whence they had always a secure retreat by ... passes so strong that a small force might maintain them against any numbers.'[9] He could not believe that Moore was running away. He pointed out that at the city of Ponferrada an artillery park had been established along with hospitals and magazines of corn. The combined armies could hold Astroga, with the supplies being brought up from Ponferrada (about forty miles away) to sustain the troops. Moore replied that he had determined upon a retreat into Galicia 'because his troops required a rest'.[10]

Indeed, the men did need to rest. Rifleman Harris saw just how exhausted the troops were:

> I came up with a cluster of poor devils who were still alive, but apparently, both men and women unable to proceed. They were sitting huddled together in the road, their heads drooping forward, and apparently patiently awaiting their end. Soon after passing these unfortunates, I overtook a party who were being urged forward under charge of an officer of the 42nd Highlanders. He was pushing them along pretty much as a drover would keep together a tired flock of sheep. They presented a curious example of a retreating force. Many of them had thrown away their weapons, and were linked together arm-in-arm, in order to support each other, like a party of drunkards. They were, I saw, composed of various regiments; many were bare-headed, and without shoes; and some with their heads tied up in old rags and fragments of handkerchiefs.[11]

Joseph Sinclair was, like the rest of the troops, under the impression that Moore was going to halt at Astorga:

> On the 30th, we reached Astorga. Which we were led to believe was to be our resting place, and the end of our fatigues … This was what we all wished, though none believed. We had been told so at Benavente; but our movements had not the smallest appearance of a retreat, in which we were to face about and make a stand; they were more like a shameful flight.[12]

One thing that especially upset Sinclair was that along with the items that were of no use to the retreating troops were things that would have been of immense value to the men, particularly shoes. He, and possibly a quarter of the army, was in desperate need of new boots, and large quantities of footwear were destroyed rather than them being distributed to the men.

'We now began to see more clearly the horrors of our situation,' wrote Rifleman Harris with the rear-guard, 'and the men to murmur at not being permitted to turn and stand at bay – cursing the French, and swearing they would rather die ten thousand deaths, with their rifles in their hands in opposition, than endure the present toil.'[13]

Charles Stewart saw the effects of Moore's decision to hurry on to Corunna:

> In Astorga, the blowing up of ammunition waggons, the destruction of intrenching tools, and the committal of field equipments to the flames for a whole division, gave signal for all the bad passions of those who witnessed it, the fact cannot be denied, that from that hour we no longer resembled a British army.[14]

Captain Gordon also expressed his dismay with the news that the army was not going to halt at Astorga, but when he saw the state of Romana's troops he saw that the British had been misled about the Spanish forces that Moore was supposed to co-operate with:

> The officers told us that the Spanish army, estimated at 120,000 men, was in cantonments in the town and adjacent villages, and that it was determined our combined forces should await the arrival of the French army, and give it battle in the plain. It is difficult to conjecture how such an absurd report could have originated or obtained credit; the town was, in fact, occupied by the Marquis de la Romana's corps, in consequence of which we found it difficult to get quarters. This Spanish force amounted to about 6,000 men in the most deplorable condition. They were all ill-clothed; many were without shoes, and even without arms; a pestilential fever raged amongst them; they had been without bread for several days, and were quite destitute of money. In short, their state could not be more justly described than in that French bulletin which, alluding to Romana's army, says: 'These miserable wretches fill every hospital.' Miserable indeed they were, and almost every house in Astorga contained some of their dead or dying.[15]

The Spanish could be of no effective use to Moore, despite Romana's admirable desire to fight the French. Moore's only concern, now that he had drawn the French from Madrid and disrupted

Napoleon's plans for the subjugation of Spain, was to save his army. There was no need to expose his troops to any further risk by fighting the French. Napoleon had a huge number of troops in Spain and Moore could not fight them all with the small force he commanded. Even if he did defeat Soult in front of Astorga, it could only be a temporary reverse as French reinforcements, which would inevitably be sent, would compel him to retire, if he had not already done so through a want of food. Whatever course of action Moore chose he would, ultimately, have to withdraw to the coast. So rather than give battle, the only certain consequence of which was that numbers of his men would be killed and wounded, Moore decided to retreat, even leaving behind 400 sick who would slow down the retreat. The following is how Moore explained this to his government:

> With respect to me, my Lord, and the British troops, it has come to that point which I have long foreseen. Abandoned from the beginning by everything Spanish, we were equal to nothing by ourselves. From a desire to do what I could, I made the movement against Soult. As a diversion, it has answered completely; but, as there is nothing to take advantage of it, I have risked the loss of the Army for no purpose. I have no option now but to fall down to the coast as fast as I am able. I found no provision here: the little which had been collected has been consumed by Sir David's corps in their passage; and there is not two days bread to carry the Army to Villafranca. I have been forced to push on the troops by divisions, without stopping.[16]

As might be expected, Napoleon saw things in a different light. 'I have been pursuing the English for some days,' he wrote in a letter to the Empress Josephine on the 31st, 'but they are fleeing in a terrified fashion. They have abandoned the debris of La Romana's army to avoid delaying their retreat by a single half day. More than a hundred baggage wagons have already been taken.' To his brother Joseph he wrote: 'The English are running away as fast as they can, and are abandoning their supplies and baggage ... They have abandoned the Spaniards in a shameful and cowardly manner.'[17]

Napoleon had driven his men on at a terrifying pace in his bid to entrap the British, as Baron de Marbot recorded in his memoirs:

> The Emperor was in such a hurry to overtake the enemy that he required his army to march this distance in one day, though it was the 31st of December and the days were very short. Seldom have I made such a fatiguing march. An icy rain wetted us to the skin; men and horses sank into the marshy ground. We only advanced with the utmost effort; and as all the bridges had been broken by the English, our men were five or six times compelled to strip, place their arms and clothes on their heads, and go naked through the icy water of the streams.
>
> It is painful to relate that I saw three veteran grenadiers of the guard, unable to march any further, and, unwilling to fall to the rear at the risk of being tortured and massacred by the peasants, blow out their brains with their own muskets.[18]

Yet it had all been in vain, for the British were always ahead of their pursuers. Napoleon's men had become so exhausted that he allowed them to recover, spending all of News Year's Day resting at Astorga. It was there that Marbot recorded an unusually touching gesture given by Napoleon:

> Just as the corps of Soult and Ney were marching past the Emperor outside Astorga, cries were heard from a great barn. The door was opened, and it was found to contain 1,000 to 1,200 English women and children, who, exhausted by the long march of the previous days through rain, mud, and streams, were unable to keep up with the army and had taken refuge in this place. For forty-eight hours they had lived on raw barley. Most of the women and children were good-looking, in spite of the muddy rags in which they were clad. They flocked round the Emperor, who was touched by their misery, and gave them lodging and food in the town; sending a flag of truce to let the English general know that when the weather permitted they would be sent back to him.[19]

The next day, as the troops were awaiting the orders to move off in pursuit of the British, a messenger, described by Marbot as an aide-de-camp from the Minister of War, arrived with despatches from Paris. Exactly what information the despatches contained has never been verified. It is usually stated that the Emperor was concerned with the possibility of Austria taking advantage of his absence from Paris (and that of a large portion of the Grande Armée from Germany) to launch a surprise attack on France, Oman offers another reason for Napoleon's abrupt departure from Spain – political intrigues in the French capital. It has also been said that the Emperor saw that the British were going to escape, and he did not want to be associated with any kind of failure.[20]

Regardless of his motives, Napoleon set off back to Paris, taking his Imperial Guard with him, handing over responsibility for chasing Moore to Soult. He left the marshal with four infantry divisions, those of generals Merle, Mermet, Bonnet and Heudelet, totalling around 25,000 men, and la Houssaye's and Franceschi's cavalry divisions which numbered approximately 6,000. In distant support were the 16,000 men of Ney's VI Corps.[21] It was more than enough to drive the British into the sea.

Regardless of the strength of the French force, Moore sought only to take his army safely back to England, as he told Castlereagh in what would prove to be his final despatch:

> There is no means of carriage: the people run away, the villages are deserted; and I have been obliged to destroy great part of the ammunition and military stores. For the same reason I am obliged to leave the sick. In short, my sole object is to save the Army. We must all make forced marches to the coast, from the scarcity of provisions, and to be before the Enemy; who, by roads upon our flanks, may otherwise intercept us; but, after a time, the same difficulty which affects us must affect him; therefore, the rear once passed Villafranca, I do not expect to be molested.

There would be no respite in the punishing drive to reach Corunna, and conditions were about to get far worse.

The army began its march from Astorga on 30 December. The Marquis de la Romana's men took the road to Foncebadon, which continued to the port of Vigo where the British fleet had been ordered to wait. Moore also sent Robert Craufurd's Light Brigade and Alten's brigade of the King's German Legion to Vigo, via the road through Ponferrada and Orense. At this stage of the retreat Moore had still not entirely made his mind up about which port he would fall back to, but why he divided his army in this manner and sent some of his best troops away has never been entirely satisfactorily explained. Certainly, Professor Oman was highly critical of this move, stating: 'They never saw a Frenchman, embarked unmolested [on the ships] at Vigo, and were absolutely useless to Moore during the rest of the campaign. It is impossible to understand how it came that they were sent away in this fashion, and nothing can be said in favour of the move.'[22]

However, the true purpose of this move by Moore was explained by Brigadier General Alten. Moore 'informed me,' Alten later wrote, 'that the object of the separate movement which was to be entrusted to me, was, first to secure the bridge over the Minho at Orense, which place, the enemy being actually nearer to it than the British army were, might be occupied by the French; and, secondly, after securing this point, to proceed to and occupy Vigo, where were assembled the whole fleet under Sir Samuel Hood, on which the safety of the army depended.' Alten marched as quickly as he could, sending a detachment of 300 volunteers from both brigades under the command of Major Stuart of the 95th by forced marches to seize the bridge at Orense. This was accomplished on 6 January. The main object having been achieved, Alten's next task was to secure Vigo. Alten again takes up the story: 'It was at Orense that I received a letter from Colonel Murray, the Quartermaster General, informing me, by command of Sir John Moore, of the general's alteration in his plans and intention to embark at Corunna. I was at the same time directed to transmit immediately Sir John Moore's orders to Sir Samuel Hood for the requisite number of vessels to go round to Corunna.'[23]

It is quite clear from this, that the two brigades under Alten and Craufurd were sent ahead to secure Moore's line of retreat to Vigo, should he decide to use that port to embark his army. So it was, that these 3,500 men, including some of the best of the army's regiments, left the road to Corunna and headed for Vigo.

Craufurd's brigade along with Henry Paget's cavalry had, up to this point, formed the rear-guard of the army. With the Light Brigade's departure, Major General Edward Paget's Reserve Division, consisting of the 20th, 28th, 52nd, 91st and the 1st Battalion of the 95th Rifles, along with Carthew's Company, Royal Artillery of six light 6-pounders, took on this responsibility. As the cavalry would be of limited value in the narrow mountain roads, only one regiment was left with the Reserve, the 15th Hussars, with the other four pushed up to the front.

With the main body of the column was a private of the 42nd:

> We entered the mountainous district that lay between us and Coruña. By this time the army was in a wretched condition, from the want of provisions, shoes, and blankets; insubordination began visibly to shew its capricious front in more brigades than ours. When we got amongst the mountainous roads, we found them covered in deep snow; and our march that day was very long and fatiguing.

The rear-guard left Astorga on 31 December, following the rest of the army heading up the road that wound through the pass on the summit of the Monte Toleno. Assistant Commissary Schaumann was also with the Reserve, having been given sole responsibility for supplying Paget's men's needs, 'with no money, no assistants, no food and no transport.' He had to walk through the dark and stormy night as the road was too slippery for him to risk riding. 'The road was incredibly bad,' he noted in his memoirs, 'and we sank knee-deep in mud and snow. On the mountain hung clouds of driven snow which from time to time blew in our faces.'[24] Such was how the bedraggled men of Sir John Moore's army welcomed in the first hours of 1809.

'What a New Year's Day,' complained Joseph Sinclair of the 71st Highlanders:

> Drenched with rain, famished with cold and hunger, ignorant when our misery was to cease. This was the most dreadful period of my life. How differently did we pass our Hogmanay, from the manner our friends were passing theirs, at home? Not a voice said, 'I wish you a happy new year;' each seemed to look upon his neighbour as an abridgment to his own comforts. His looks seemed to say, 'One or other of the articles you wear would be of great use to me; your shoes are better than those I possess; if you were dead, they would be mine!'[25]

As the private of the 42nd had seen, morale, and with it discipline, collapsed as soon as the men knew they were retreating instead of fighting. Had it been summer, and if the men had been properly equipped at Astorga before the stores were destroyed, then the retreat might have been tolerable. But the men had set off from Astorga in poor condition, and the weather they experienced was truly dreadful. 'Carts overturned and dead cattle had begun three days before to trace strongly the retreat of the British Army,' Captain Pierrepoint observed on 1 January. 'My horse who at first started and turned back at the sight of a dead carcass, was then brought to pass horses killed on the road scarcely noticing them.'[26]

Quite naturally, the men were angry and exhausted, and it was a brave officer indeed who attempted to enforce strict discipline in such circumstances, even if he were capable of anything more than looking to his own survival.

Moore also drove the men on as fast as he could push them along. Having decided upon retreat to save the army, he had no intention of allowing the enemy to catch him. All this proved too much for many men, who simply lacked the strength to continue.

Dispirited though many were, Sir John Hope, for one, was satisfied with the turn of events, writing on 31 December that, 'It was now perfectly evident that the greater portion of the enemy's force had been diverted from the projected enterprise against the Southern Provinces of Spain and aimed against us – the object therefore of our diversion was accomplished.'[27]

Perhaps being aware of what they had achieved, up to this point in the retreat there had been no more than 'murmuring' amongst the officers about the situation Moore had placed them in, Assistant Commissary Schaumann, commented. But the men 'who knew of no restraint', did not care what they said about their commander. Schaumann, on the other hand, saw things a little differently:

> Situated as we were, however, it was impossible, even with the best will in the world, to relieve our privations; for the cause of our sufferings lay in the fact that we were a large army all pursuing the same narrow road through the mountains, and could not avail ourselves of the resources which would have lain

to our left and our right had we been marching in three or four separate and parallel columns over roads covering a larger area of the country.[28]

What Schaumann also noted was that the troops who reached a village or town first repeatedly went on the rampage, resulting in vast amounts of food and other supplies being ruined and wasted. If officers had maintained discipline, in the way that both Paget brothers did with their respective commands, then there would have been far more food and drink saved that could have been shared throughout the army. The men complained of their privations, yet much of their suffering was self-inflicted. 'Every soldier took what he liked, everything was plundered, carried away, and trampled underfoot; the casks of wine were broken open, so that half their contents were spilt over the floor.'

Joseph de Naylies of the 19th Dragoons described the conditions the French encountered as they left Astorga in pursuit of the retreating British on 1 January:

> After having marched all day, we found ourselves on the summit of a high mountain … There we were assailed by a terrible storm: men and horses were blown over by the wind, while the eddying snow prevented us from seeing further than four paces. The road that we followed the next morning – the Corunna highway – was one of the best in Spain, but, as the snow had frozen as soon as it had fallen, it had been turned into a sheet of ice …we were in a deplorable condition … oppressed by cold, covered with snow and leading their horses … on foot, many of our riders were fainting from exhaustion and want.[29]

'The mountains were now becoming morewild-looking and steep, as we proceeded; whilst those few huts we occasionally passed seemed so utterly forlorn and wretched looking, it appeared quite a wonder how human beings could live in so desolate a home,' observed Rifleman Harris.'After the snow commenced, the hills became so slippery (being in many parts covered with ice), that several of our men frequently slipped and fell, and being unable to rise, gave themselves up to despair, and died. There was now no endeavour to assist one another after a fall; it was every one for himself, and God for us all!'[30]

A sergeant of the 43rd marched into Bembibre with Beresford's Brigade, and it was here where the strained discipline of the army, in some regiments more than others, all but fell apart, the town being a large local wine depot:

> On arriving at Bembibre, the immense wine-vaults established there exhibited such temptations, that hundreds of men, unable to exert themselves, or even stand, were left behind. That refreshment was needed, no one can doubt; but it is more difficult to be temperate than abstemious; the first healthful draught led to many an inordinate one … There was a heterogeneous mass of marauders, drunkards, muleteers, women, and children.[31]

It was Major Patterson of the 50th Regiment who first stumbled upon the large wine stocks in the town: 'At the hour of midnight, during the course of that dismal route, when struggling on against the pitiless pelting of the storm, which raged with its usual violence, and when the black clouds that gathered round our heads poured down in torrents, we entered Bembibre, a small and truly wretched place, buried amid the recesses of the wildest mountain scenery.'

Ahead of the troops the men of the Quartermaster's Department had gone forward to allocate billets for each battalion. When the troops arrived they found each property consisted of 'one small room below, with a ladder conducting to another of the same dimensions above, [and] were all deserted, the doors being locked and fastened as securely as almost to defy the power of entrance.' Nevertheless, Patterson was not going to be denied a place for his men, so, selecting one property he used force to gain entry. When finally he entered, he found it was a wine-store filled to its only entrance with casks of wine. Others soon made similar discoveries. 'By the approach of dawn next morning I went round the quarters to get the men under arms,' wrote Patterson, 'when I discovered that this wine-store, with many others, had been ransacked during the night; the wine-casks scattered about the streets, the wine spilled in all directions, a number of men lying drunk in the streets and in the houses, several totally unable to move.'[32]

The Reserve arrived at Bembibre on the morning of 1 January, just as Baird's division marched out of the village on the road to Cacabelos, leaving behind those still too drunk to move. After their march through the night, the men of the Reserve expected to be allowed to rest, but to theirs and Blakeney's disappointment, there was still work to be done:

> Bembibre exhibited all the appearance of a place lately stormed and pillaged. Every door and window was broken, every lock and fastening forced. Rivers of wine ran through the houses and into the streets, where lay fantastic groups of soldiers (many of them with their firelocks broken), women, children, runaway Spaniards and muleeteers, all apparently inanimate, except where here and there a leg or arm was seen to move, while the wine oozing from their lips and nostrils seemed the effect of gunshots … some lay senseless, others staggered … savage roars announcing present hilarity were mingled with groans issuing from fevered lips disgorging the wine of yesterday … We were employed the greatest part of the day (January 1st, 1809,) in turning or dragging the drunken stragglers out of the houses into the streets and sending as many forward as could be moved. Our occupation next morning was the same; yet little could be effected with men incapable of standing much less of marching forward.[33]

The arms and accoutrements of those unfit to move were placed on the baggage wagons but the 'unfortunate victims to brutal and disgraceful drunkenness,' were simply abandoned and, according to Patterson, 'became soon after an easy prey to the pursuing enemy'[34].

The Reserve did all it could to drive the stragglers out of Bembibre, but there were still hundreds left behind as Paget's men set off for Cacabelos, leaving a small piquet to warn of any approach by the enemy. Scarcely had the Reserve moved out when the leading brigade of General la Houssaye's dragoons appeared. The French cavalry broke through the piquet and rode into the town.

'In a moment the road was filled with the miserable stragglers, who came crowding after the troops, some with loud shrieks of distress, others with brutal exclamations,' wrote a sergeant of the 43rd:

> Many, overcome with fear, threw away their arms. Many more who preserved theirs, were so stupidly intoxicated that they were unable to fire; and kept reeling to and fro, insensible both to their danger and disgrace. The enemy's horsemen, perceiving this confusion, bore down at a gallop, broke through the disorderly mob, cutting to the right and left as they passed.[35]

Blakeney watched as the apparently lifeless stragglers who moments before, despite every effort by the men of the Reserve, could not be roused, suddenly found the use of their limbs, but the disorganised rabble stood no chance against the French cavalry:

> Frantic women held forth their babies, suing for mercy by the cries of defenceless innocence; but all to no purpose. The dragoons of the polite and civilised nation advanced, and cut right and left, regardless of intoxication, age or sex. Drunkards, women and children were indiscriminately hewn down.[36]

The Reserve moved on to Cacabelos, just beyond which the high road to Corunna was carried over the small Cua river on a single bridge. A British engineer had identified this spot as being the best place between Astorga and Lugo for fighting a defensive battle and had accordingly informed Moore. The Cua was swollen by the winter rain and snow, and the rising ground to the west of the river was ideal for defence. Though Moore had chosen not to make a stand here, Paget saw this as an opportunity to hold back the French and give the main bulk of the army chance to put distance between it and the pursuers.

After dismissing the men, Paget left one squadron of the 15th Hussars in Cacabelos with half of the 95th Rifles on the French side of the stream to watch the road from Bembibre. He then placed the Carthew's artillery on the western side of the Cua to command the bridge supported by the 28th Regiment. The rest of his division was hidden behind a line of vineyards and stone walls that ran parallel with the river.[37]

While these troops waited for the French to appear, the rest of the Reserve was ordered to form a punishment square. After witnessing the scenes in Bembibre, Edward Paget was determined to maintain discipline amongst the men under his command, knowing that once order had been lost it could never be recovered. Paget was determined to make an example of those that had been arrested by the provost. A hollow square was formed on the heights above Cacabelos with the troops facing inwards to witness the punishment. A drum-head court-martial sat at the rear of each regiment, and once the verdict had been announced, the punishment was carried out in the square where triangles had been formed, to which the culprits were tied to receive the number of lashes that had been ordered in full view of their comrades. Quite a large number of men had been arrested, it would seem as the punishment continued on all four sides of the square for 'several' hours.

During this time vedettes rode up to Paget to warn him that the French were approaching. But Paget remained unmoved and the punishments continued. Among the prisoners were two who had committed a more serious crime than just stealing – they had been caught actually robbing a civilian. For this the sentence was death. Paget ordered them to be hanged.

According to Rifleman Green, each prisoner had a rope around his neck fastened to the branch of a tree and he was sat upon two men's shoulders with his cap drawn over his face. He sat there waiting for the signal for the two men to let him drop.[38]Amongst those who witnessed this was John Dobbs of the 52nd:

> Everything was ready, and a square formed round the gallows, when a hussar rode in from the rear, reporting to General Paget that the enemy was close at hand. He coolly received the report, and proceeded to address the troops, stating the disgrace attached to the crime, but that he would pardon them if they would refrain from such excess; but that, if this promise was not made, they should die, if the enemy were firing into the square. There was a general exclamation of 'We will! We will!' He made a sign to the Provost Marshal, who immediately liberated the prisoners.[39]

The whole affair angered Paget, whose sympathy lay with the men who had been driven to such excesses by Moore's headlong rush to the coast. 'My God!' Grumbled Paget. 'Is it not lamentable to think that, instead of preparing the troops confided to my command to receive the enemies of their country, I am preparing to hang two robbers?'

The alarm raised by the hussar was because, at around 13.00 hours, the French cavalry had trotted up, in the form of General Auguste-François-Marie de Colbert-Chabanais' cavalry brigade of Ney's VI Corps, consisting of the 3rd Hussars and the 15th Chasseurs à Cheval.

Seeing just one squadron facing them, the French charged, driving the 15th Hussars before them, 'but at the entrance of the town we fronted them,' wrote Captain Gordon, 'and fought hand to hand, disputing every inch of ground. For some minutes we were so jammed together in a narrow street that it was impossible for either party to advance or retire. At this period of the conflict one of our men decapitated a French *chasseur* at a single blow; the head was not entirely separated, but remained attached by a muscle or part of the skin of the neck.'[40]

The single squadron of the 15th was forced to retreat to the bridge over the Cua, followed by the 95th which, somewhat unusually, appears to have been taken by surprise. Also taken unaware was Colborne, Moore's Military Secretary, who, along with other Staff officers, was in Cacabelos:

> We had to wheel round and ride as hard as we could, and expected them on us every moment. When I saw a Cavalry officer draw his sword, I thought it was high time to draw mine too … We were nearly as possible taken. We had no idea they were so near … At last we got to the bridge – covered with Rifles, all jammed up on it.'

Moore watched with anger from the heights above as the both the infantry and cavalry tried to cross the bridge at the same time, with the French on their backs. Neither the artillery nor the 28th Regiment, covering the bridge, could do much to help the retreating mass with the French so close behind. Some of the 95th were ridden down by Colbert's men, with some thirty or forty being taken prisoner. But the 95th would shortly have its revenge.

Seeing the near-panic his men had caused the British rear-guard, Colbert believed he had a chance to take the bridge with a bold charge, which Blakeney described in his usual detailed fashion:

> The French cavalry advanced at a quick trot down the hill. Our guns instantly wheeled out upon the road, and played upon their column until they became screened from their fire by the dip in the road as they approached the bridge. Here they were warmly received by the 52nd Regiment, now freed from our own dragoons, and the 95th; and upon this they [the French] made a most furious charge at full speed over the bridge and up the road towards our position. During this onset they were severely galled by the 95th, who by this time had lined the edges on either side of the road within a few yards of their flanks, and by the light company immediately in their front, whom it was evidently their intention to break through, as they rode close to our bayonets.[41]

Colbert had made a mistake in trying to take the bridge – and it would cost him his life. In what was possibly the most memorable action undertaken by a private soldier in the course of the Peninsular War, Rifleman Thomas Plunkett, considered the best shot in the 95th, spotted Colbert on his grey horse leading his men in the attack, conspicuous in his general's uniform. According to Edward Costello, Paget had ridden up to the 95th and offered his purse to any man who would shoot the French general. Plunkett took up the challenge: 'He ran about 100 yards nearer to the enemy, threw himself on his back on the road (which was covered in snow), placed his foot in the sling of his rifle, and taking deliberate aim, shot General Colbert. Colbert's trumpet-major, who rode up to him, shared the same fate from Tom's unerring rifle.' Paget, we are told made good on his promise and handed Plunkett his purse.[42]

Plunkett's shot has been the subject of much consideration. While all manner of ranges have been suggested for the shot, even as far as 600 yards, the most likely scenario is that Plunkett ('a smart, well-made fellow, about middle height and in the prime of manhood'[43]) ran forward to place himself at a distance where he could be fairly certain that he would hit his mark. Remarkable though the shot was, it was probably taken within the normal operational range of the Baker rifle at not much more than 200 yards.[44]

After the withdrawal of Colbert's brigade, another cavalry unit, that of General la Houssaye's Dragoon Division, moved to the front. Having witnessed the repulse of Colbert's two squadrons, some of the dragoons tried to ford the river, but found that the rocks in the river and vegetation along the bank precluded any possibility of mounting a charge. They dismounted and began skirmishing with the British infantry, but stood little chance against the 52nd and the 95th. Just before dusk Merle's Infantry Division arrived, the voltigeurs of which took over from la Houssaye's Dragoons. After about an hour of firing across the river, the French infantry formed into column and tried to charge across the bridge. The dense mass was an easy target for Carthew's well-posted six guns, and Merle's men were driven back in disorder. Paget's stand had given the main column a full day's start on its pursuers and it was evident that Merle would have to wait for the rest of Soult's force to come up before another attempt could be made at crossing the river. Nevertheless, Moore had learned of a position where he could deploy his entire force and give his men the battle they so passionately sought. Under cover of night, the Reserve slipped away.

Chapter 8

The Loss of the Military Chest

The road to Villafranca was, according to Charles Stewart, all but impassable, but it was the conditions rather than the terrain, that caused the army the most problems – as well as the lack of shoes and food. Villafranca itself was soon packed with troops who had trudged wearily into the town:

> You could hardly turn round in the place. Every corner of it was full of men. And many regiments had to bivouac. Most of the mules and draft-bullocks and pack-horses seemed only to have lasted out up to this point, and now fell down and died. Very soon we could neither drive nor ride through the streets … In the end Villafranca was literally plundered, and the drunkenness that prevailed among the troops led to the most shameful incidents. Down by the river the artillery destroyed all their stores, and lighting big fires burnt all their ammunition wagons which they broke up for the purpose. They also threw all their ammunition into the river. Several hundred horses which could go no further were led to the same spot and shot. Day and night we could hear the sound of pistol fire. Everything was destroyed. Discipline was at and end.[1]

The sad killing of the horses was, in many instances, the result of the repeated destruction of so much equipment at various stages of the retreat. This was remarked on by Blakeney. 'Upon my enquiring of the men how it was that horses in apparently tolerable condition were incapable of at least proceeding quietly along, the invariable answer which I received was, that from the roughness of the road, hardened by continued frost, they cast their shoes, and that they had not a nail to fasten on those picked up, nor a shoe to replace those lost; and they added that there was not a spare nail or shoe in any of the forage carts.'[2]

The men had also been burdened with their heavy packs until they reached Villafranca, where they were told to get rid of anything that might slow them down. According to Bombardier Miller, 'At this town we destroyed the remainder of wagons, stores, and ammunition, about 500 waggon loads, and even burned our knapsacks, so that we only had a few rounds of ammunition for each cannon left.'

The men were now 'light enough', continued Miller, but: 'our backs [were] almost bare, our bellies empty, and no shoes to our feet. Our greatest burden [though] was the Spanish lice; the few rags we had left were covered in them.'[3]

There were, of course, consequences of leaving behind their knapsacks, but as William Green and others of the Rifles knew all too well, there was one thing they dare not leave cast aside:

> We did not mind parting with our kits so we left them by the roadside. But then we had enough to carry: fifty round of ball cartridge, thirty loose balls in our waist belt and a flask and a horn of powder, and a rifle and sword, the two weighing fourteen pounds. These were plenty for us to carry with empty bellies and the enemy close at our heels, thirsting for our blood!

The men were issued two days' biscuit and three days' salt beef and pork at Villafranca, but what they needed most of all were shoes. Yet because Moore had ordered that nothing of value should fall into the hands of the enemy, most of the shoes were destroyed. 'There were a great many of the men who got shoes,' complained one private, 'but it was by forcing their way into the store, and breaking the casks in which the shoes were packed up. When I saw this, I endeavoured to get a pair; but the crowd was so great, I could not get near the entrance, and I could not tarry, for the bugle was sounding to fall in. The provost then came with his guard of horse, and cleared the store. In a short time, notwithstanding our wretchedness, and wants, and bleeding feet, all that was in the store was destroyed.'[4]

The Reserve marched through Villafranca during the night of 3–4 January without halting. Bringing up the rear was Alexander Gordon:

> The town presented the most dreadful scenes of riot and distress. Parties of drunken soldiers were committing all kinds of enormities; several houses were in flames; and a quantity of baggage and military stores, for which there was no means of conveyance, were burning in the plaza. The kennels were flowing with rum, a number of puncheons having been staved in the streets, and a promiscuous rabble were drinking and filling bottles and canteens from the stream. Every avenue was crowded with bât-horses, mules, and bullock-cars.[5]

Lord Paget was determined not to allow his cavalry to fall apart as the infantry had so clearly done and any instances of ill-discipline were immediately addressed. When, therefore, at Villafranca, three men of the 7th Hussars were seen wearing clothes they had stolen from one of the houses and trying to break open a box that clearly did not belong to them, they were arrested. Looting was punishable by death, but Lord Paget ordered just one man to be executed as an example to the rest of his command. 'These three poor fellows drew lots which should suffer death, and it fell to the lot of a man named Day, of Captain Treveake's troop, previously a very steady, good soldier,' recalled Colonel Vivian. 'He was shot in front of the brigade; and in justice to him, poor fellow, be it said that he met his fate with the most undaunted courage – I may say, with the most perfect sangfroid.'[6]

Day was placed in a kneeling position with his face turned towards a large tree. A detachment of twenty men of his regiment stood behind him with their carbines at the ready. In a strong voice, the regiment's adjutant cried 'Fire!' He died instantly. The rest of the brigade was made to walk past the corpse.[7]

The main body of the army had left the previous day to embark on what was to be the worst part of the retreat, but many remained in Villafranca on the evening of the 4th even though Paget's men warned as many as they could that the French were close behind. It was only when an officer of the Engineers galloped through the streets shouting that by 18.00 hours that evening the bridge over the river that runs to the north of the town was to be blown-up that the stragglers finally appreciated the danger they were in: 'Now the uproar began!' wrote Schaumann: 'Women, children, the sick, and baggage wagons all tried to get across at once.' Suddenly, gunfire rattled round the streets, as the leading French units arrived and were engaged by the rear-guard. 'One or two sapper officers ran hither and thither, urging everyone to proceed to the bridge, for the gate of the town was not going to he held after the bridge was blown. Now all who still happened to be in the town made haste to escape.' Schaumann was lifted up with the crush of the terrified mass and carried bodily across the bridge.[8]

Most got away, but Kerr Porter considered what the troops had experienced so far was but 'a faint sketch' of the 'horrors of death and desolation' that was to come over the next few days:

> We were now in the heart of a stupendous country cleft into abyss-like ravines, and over-laid with a deep and trackless snow … in many parts above the clouds, with no provisions to sustain nature, no shelter to shield us momentarily from the storm, no fuel to warm us, no safe spot whereupon to linger for an instant to rest; but all one waste of severest winter.[9]

Some indication of the conditions through which the men (and women) shuffled along can be gauged by the observation made by David Baird's biographer, who wrote that the snow on each side of the road on the upper ground and summit of the mountain was 'much higher than the points of the men's bayonets when carried fixed to their firelocks'.[10]

Joseph Sinclair of the 71st also wrote that, dreadful as the retreat had been so far, after leaving Villafranca, it became, 'The march of death':

> There was nothing to sustain our famished bodies, or shelter them from the rain or snow. We were either drenched with rain or crackling with ice. Fuel we could find none. The sick and wounded that we had been still enabled to drag with us in the wagons, were now left to perish in the snow. The road was one line of bloody foot-marks, from the sore feet of the men; and, on its sides, lay the dead and the dying.[11]

Adam Neale concurred, writing that, 'All that had hitherto been suffered by our troops was but a prelude to this time of horrors … Our men had now become quite mad with despair.'

Large numbers of British troops simply could not take the punishing pace. One of those was Sergeant Stephen Morley:

> We had neither an adequate supply of food or clothing, and our feet were dreadfully hurt from want of shoes; many were actually barefooted … The poor women were deeply to be pitied. One of them … with no covering but her tattered clothes … gave birth to a son … The road all the way was strewed with men unable to proceed … Discipline was forgotten, none commanded, none obeyed … Seeing smoke issue from a large building off the road, I crawled rather than walked to it. It was something like a barn, and full of our men who had made a fire. I found a spare corner, and, putting my pouch under my head, fell into a sound sleep … When I awoke, I was told the army had gone.[12]

Morley paid the price for his desertion from the ranks by being captured by the pursuing French.

Sergeant David Robertson of the 92nd Highlanders described how: 'our clothes were falling off our backs, and our shoes were worn to the welts. From the officer down to the private, we were overrun with vermin, bearing alike the extremities of hunger and cold, and forming altogether a combination of suffering sufficient to appal the stoutest heart, and break down the strongest constitution.[13] The Highlanders, nevertheless, were more fortunate in one respect than the rest of the troops. 'There was a great deal of dysentery,' remembered Dobbs of the 52nd, 'and there were prisoners taken by the enemy in consequence of men being obliged to fall out. In this the Highlanders had a great advantage over the Reserve, who wore trowsers [sic].'[14]

Thomas Graham wrote in his diary of that march: 'The whole is a scene of desolation; so many horses and carriages, and some dead bodies remaining on the road.'[15] The men became so exhausted that they fell asleep as they were marching and, as John Dobbs was carrying one of the 52nd's colours, the man in front often received a bang on his head as the flagstaff slipped from Dobbs's hands, whilst Dobbs frequently knocked his head against the butt of the musket of the man ahead of him.[16]

Charles Stewart, with the cavalry, saw the worst effects of the punishing march:

> The condition of the army was melancholy; the rain came down in torrents; men and horses foundered at every step; the former worn out through fatigue and want of nutriment – the latter sinking under their loads, and dying upon the march. Nor was it the baggage-animals alone that suffered – the shoes of the cavalry horses dropped off, and consequently, they soon became useless. It was a sad spectacle to behold these fine creatures goaded on till their strength utterly failed them, and then shot to death by their riders, to prevent them falling into the hands of the enemy. Then, again, the few ammunition wagons which had hitherto kept up, fell one by one to the rear; the ammunition was immediately destroyed, and the wagons abandoned. Thus were misfortunes accumulating upon us as we proceeded; and it appeared extremely improbable, should our present system of forced marches be persisted in, that one-half of the army would ever reach the coast.[17]

It was probably the horses that suffered the most, being pushed on until they could not take another step. This included those of the cavalry, which was of concern to Edward Hodge of the 7th:

> About midnight we reached the highest mountain in Galicia, which we found covered with snow, the road covered with baggage of all sorts. Artillery, men, women and children laying frozen and freezing to death without a possibility of rendering them assistance, and our horses, with those of the Artillery, so fatigued they were dropping every hundred yards, where we were obliged to cut their throats and leave them. It snowed the whole way over the mountain and so piercing a wind I never remember. A Sergeant of ours fell dead from his horse, overcome by cold and fatigue. When we reached Los Nogales the horses were obliged to be lined in the fields and the men [to] lie down with them, and the only astonishment is that one half survived.[18]

In light of what was about to occur to the military chest, it is interesting to note the observations of Sergeant Robertson:

> The army had now commenced to ascend the Gallican mountains. Here there had once been a good road, but it was so destroyed by the heavy rains, and cut up with the carriages that had gone over it, that we could not go a step without sinking to the knees in mud. The first who stuck on the road was the Paymaster-General of the army. He had brought his lady with him out to Spain, and had got for her convenience a four-wheeled carriage, which was drawn by two fine English horses … Here at last, the vehicle stuck fast, all the efforts made to extricate it proving abortive, and it had to be left where it was.[19]

This experience should have warned the Paymaster at an early stage what was likely to occur to the military chest for which he was responsible.

During the long descent to Nogales, where the road runs along the edge of the mountain with a deep precipice on one side and 'bold' projecting rocks on the other, a horse-drawn artillery wagon, on which a number of women and children had been allowed to travel, rolled down the steep slope. The women and children were saved when the wagon crashed into a clump of trees and shrubs. No one was killed – only the poor horses.[20]

Henry Percy was one of Moore's aides-de-camp. He wrote the following in his journal:

> Until the 5th nothing occurred except the most fatiguing marches and the sad sight of Soldiers and their Wives lying dead with fatigue and cold above the mountains above Nogales. Indeed, the march of the army might have been traced by the dead animals lying on the road from this latter place. We were constantly followed by the enemy who, being close upon our rear, and until we pointed a gun they followed us firing continually upon our Rear Guard.[21]

The destruction of everything in the path of the retreating army had one positive consequence, which was, according to Lieutenant

Albert J.M. de Rocca of the French 2nd Hussars, that the devastation caused by the British troops helped slow the French pursuit:

> The country the English left behind them in their retreat was totally wasted, and, every night, Marshal Soult's troops had to seek provisions at very great distances from the beaten road, which considerably retarded their march, and augmented their fatigues.[22]

The French suffered no less than the troops they were pursuing, as sous-lieutenant Joseph de Naylies of the French 19th Dragoons noted: 'After having marched all day, we found ourselves at the summit of a high mountain. There we were assailed by a terrible storm: men and horses were blown over by the wind, while the eddying snow prevented us from seeing further than four paces.'[23] According to de Naylies, the French cavalry was 'in a deplorable condition ... oppressed by cold, covered with snow and leading our horses on foot many of our riders were fainting from exhaustion and want'.[24]

Gordon of the 15th Hussars, an outspoken critic of Moore, saw no reason for the headlong rush to the coast:

> After quitting Villafranca, every step of the road offered points where a single company of grenadiers, with one or two field-pieces, might have kept an army in check for some hours, and would have given more serious interruption, of course, to a corps of cavalry, unsupported by infantry or artillery. The road for several leagues wound along the side of steep mountains, and at almost every turn a well-served battery would have caused a heavy loss to an advancing column.[25]

Gordon also observed that the French would have been seriously impeded if the mountain road would have been broken up. This could have been easily achieved by the Royal Engineers with a few barrels of gunpowder. Such was the severity of the mountainside along which the road ran, the French would not have been able to bypass any such obstacle and would have to wait until their own engineers could make the road passable again. But, of course, much of the equipment the Engineers might have used had been destroyed at Astorga.

Hussey Vivian, who was also highly critical of Moore's conduct throughout the campaign, wrote the following in his journal:

> The strength of the country – full of defiles, and consequently defensible by a small body against even a very superior force, with the circumstance of its containing only one road passable for artillery – rendered the retreat of our army at its leisure perfectly feasible; the more so as the road leading to Orense, which was the only one by which it was possible for an enemy to advance on our flanks, was defensible by a very small body of light troops … This circumstance, however, never appears to have entered the head of the Commander-in-Chief, and perhaps the greatest error committed was the manner in which he hurried his retreat from Astorga.[26]

The Reserve reached Nogales after a forced march of thirty-six miles, having gained twelve hours' start over their pursuers. But here a sergeant of the 43rd found that the road was choked with stragglers and baggage – and with Spanish peasants trying to escape. The Spaniards feared both sides equally and drove away their precious cattle and carried off their belongings into the mountains. What angered the sergeant was that while the peasants were all armed they made no attempt either to help the British or stop the French, even though large numbers of the men sent to help them fight the invaders were collapsing by the roadside:

> The soldiers, barefooted, harassed and weakened by their excesses at Bembibre and Villa Franca, were dropping to the rear by hundreds. Broken carts, dead animals, and the piteous appearance of women with children, struggling or falling in the snow, complete the picture of war and its desolating results.[27]

With the Reserve, and frequently being called upon to form the rear-guard, was the 20th Regiment whose Light Company was commanded by Nathaniel Steevens who explained that: 'We were often within shot of the enemy's first line of Dragoons, but we did not fire at each other, our objective being to reach Corunna as expeditiously as possible, and to avoid engaging, our enemy being so superior in point of numbers, for the strength of the French was about double ours.' When Steevens' battalion reached Nogales, 'there was a bridge to be blown up, and my company was nearly taken prisoners, through some mistake with respect to an order.' Steevens was told to station his men on the side of the bridge next to the French to provide cover for the engineers who were placing their charges to demolish the bridge. Unfortunately, whoever was responsible for sounding the bugle call that would signal the Light Company to withdraw, forgot this important instruction.

As the minutes ticked by, and there was no signal call from the other side of the river and as the enemy approached, one of Steevens' junior officers suggested they had better cross the bridge – and quickly. Steevens, who had become increasingly anxious, took that advice, 'and immediately made for the bridge the advance-guard of the French cavalry being but a short distance from us ... We retreated in double quick time, and it was fortunate that we did so, for, as soon as we crossed the bridge, our engineer blew it up.'[28]

The Reserve also encountered the vast number of stores of all kinds that had been abandoned by the main column. This included between thirty and forty waggons filled with arms, ammunition, shoes and clothing which had been sent out from Britain for La Romana's army. These had been sent forward by the Junta of Galicia 'with incredible carelessness' as the Junta was aware that the British army was retreating.[29] 'There was no means of carrying them back,' wrote Robert Southey, 'such things as could be made use of were distributed to the soldiers as they passed, and the rest were destroyed. Indeed, the baggage that was with the army could not be carried on: nearly an hundred waggons, laden with shoes and clothes, were abandoned on this ascent.'[30]

Schaumann also saw the horses and the bullocks collapsing in ever greater numbers under their burdens, never to rise again, and one particular sight he remembered well:

> I saw one bullock cart, belonging to the Paymaster-General's department, loaded with six barrels full of Spanish dollars, standing on the side of the road, with its back resting against a rock. The bullocks were lying on the ground under their yokes, utterly exhausted. A soldier with a bayonet fixed stood guard

over the treasure, and with a desperate air implored every officer that passed by to relieve him of his duty. But of course, no one dared to do so! If only those dollars had been bread! Now, however, nobody paid any heed; the most confirmed thief passed by unmoved.[31]

At least one man, however, was tempted by the money, and was spotted by Assistant Quarter Master General Pierrepoint:

> The loss of the military chest was only delayed 24 hours by the exertions of General Paget. Among carriages of every description I had passed along the road, my attention had scarcely been attracted by several small carts, each laden with three small barrels, & drawn by two bullocks, under the supposition that the contents were ammunition or salt meat. I neglected enquiring, until I met a soldier creeping along with one of them under his charge, 'so that beef or port? said I. 'No, Sir, dollars.'[32]

Charles Stewart witnessed the army becoming ever more unfit for action with the passing of every single hour, and its resources wasted at every mile:

> Whole waggon loads of clothing, arms, shoes, and other necessaries, which had just arrived from England for the purpose of refitting Romana's army, were met, and after the men had helped themselves to those articles of which they stood in need, the residue was destroyed … everything was done now as if our case was absolutely desperate – as if the utmost that could be expected was to escape with our persons, at the expense of the whole of our *materiél*. Guns were abandoned, as fast as the horses which dragged them were knocked up; and the very sick and wounded were left behind in the waggons, when our bullocks or mules could proceed no further.[33]

After a much-needed rest at Nogales, the Reserve was back on the road again at daybreak on 5 January, and almost immediately the French cavalry was upon them, having made up the ground since being left behind at Cacabelos.

Sergeant Peter Facey of the 28th Foot was with the rear-guard which was composed of the flank companies of the 28th, a company of the 95th Rifles, and a composite squadron of the 15th Hussars and the 3rd Light Dragoons (Hussars) King's German Legion:

> On the 5th of January, at 6 in the morning, we again marched, passing the worst of roads, every step half way up to the knee, and the French advance guard keeping sight of our rear guard consisting of cavalry and one rifleman behind each cavalry man. Accordingly, at every turn of the road, or height that would command the road, the riflemen dismounted and striving to annoy our rear guard, and every ridge that we came to was, as soon as the baggage troops passed, blown up, not waiting for stragglers that might be in the rear, of which there was a great many, all who always fell into the hands of the enemy. Marching over mountains covered with snow, sometimes without provisions or spirits, and marching night and day, the want of sleep proved in the extreme very fatiguing.[34]

A sergeant of the 5th Regiment, described the route of the army through the mountains:

> In this pass our flanks were protected by nature from assault. The road generally would not admit of more than a section abreast, say seven or eight men, defended on one side by impassable mountains, and on the other by inaccessible valleys: but amidst this security, celerity was imperative, from two causes, the proximity of the enemy, and our necessities. We had neither an adequate supply of food or clothing, and our feet were dreadfully hurt from want of shoes; many were actually barefooted, indeed we might be considered destitute of everything, but that with which a brave man parts with, only his life, courage.[35]

In Whinyates history of 'C' Troop, Royal Horse Artillery, the following is included in the entries for 4–6 January:

> This was a dreadful march over an immense snow mountain, with ruts cut into the snow-ice two feet deep and large holes, so that the horses could scarce move. The road blocked up with ordnance-carriages and others of every description; numbers of dead horses; men, women, and children frozen to death ... An immense quantity of dollars left on the road, and thrown over the

1: The bridge over the River Esla at the village of Castrogonzalo near Benevente, looking from the British side. A number of the British soldiers commented that they saw Napoleon on the heights above the river on the opposite bank. Would that be the high ground in the distance in this photo? A plague on the bridge has one sentence concerning the retreat: 'The bridge had problems of conservation by the frequent crossing of the Esla [and] the blowing up of some of its sections in 1808 by the English troops of General Moore. (David Rowlands)

2: It was somewhere in this part of the River Esla that General Lefèbvre-Desnoëttes was captured. (David Rowlands)

3: The chapel of Nuesta Señora de la Puente was where a number of the wounded from the combat at Sahagun were treated. (David Rowlands)

4: The bridge over the River Valderaduey outside Sahagun over which a few of Debelle's chasseurs escaped to warn Soult of the presence of the British army. (David Rowlands)

5: The old walls of Astorga. (David Rowlands)

6: The accounts of the troops in Bembibre referred to subterranean vaults of wine casks, and many of the older houses in Bembibre, such as this renovated one, still have doorways whose bottoms are below street level. (David Rowlands)

11 & 12: The bridge over the Rio Cruzul where the Reserve held back the pursuing French for an hour. (David Rowlands)

13: The road down to the bridge over the Cruzul. (David Rowlands)

14: A milestone on the Camino Real beyond Nogales. (David Rowlands)

15: Cadoalla, where numbers of people in the past have dug in search of buried treasure. (Angel Perez)

16: Del castillo de Doncos, where local legends claim Moore's treasure is hidden. (Angel Perez)

17: The road leading down to the hamlet of Toralla, where the so-called 'stone of treasure' was, certainly matches the descriptions given by many of Moore's soldiers. (Robert Mitchell)

18: The road to Constantin reaches its highest point at Alto de Campo de Arbore but, as can be seen, the terrain there does not fit the descriptions given in the eyewitness accounts. (Robert Mitchell)

19: The place on the Roman road which travels over the Pass of Piedrafita where it is said by locals the military chest was discarded

20: The Camino Real as it travels from Alto de Campo de Arbore through Retorta to Constantin

21 & 22: The place that fits most of the criteria for the point where the military chest was thrown down the ravine near Cereixal. The distant bottom of the ravine, with a road running along it, can only just be seen far to the left of the upper image. (David Rowlands)

23: Looking up from near Cadoalla towards where the military chest was most probably discarded. The track from where this view was taken is only half-way down this very deep ravine. The gradient of the road above can clearly be seen. (Robert Mitchell)

24: An old building on the Camino Real which was once part of the estate of Vicente Rivera. (Angel Perez)

25: When the National N-VI was built, it cut through the former estate. (Angel Perez)

26: So near, yet …

27: The bridge at Constantin, though to be perfectly accurate, the bridge is at Baralla. (David Rowlands)

28: The rebuilt bridge across the River Mandeo at Betanzos, the original having been destroyed by the Royal Engineers. (David Rowlands)

29: The old village of Elviña is virtually unchanged from the time of the Battle of Corunna and one can easily imagine Napier fighting through its narrow streets. (David Rowlands)

30: Commemorations to the Battle of Corunna by the old church at Elviña. (David Rowlands)

31: The tomb of Sir John Moore in the Jardin de San Carlos, Corunna. (David Rowlands)

32: Bust of Sir John Moore – this, though, is not in Spain, but on the esplanade at Sandgate near Shorncliff Camp in Kent where Moore established his reputation as a trainer of light infantry. (Author)

hill on this day's march … About 10,000 pounds' worth of dollars thrown over the hill this day.[36]

Likewise, Colonel Vivian made the following notes in his journal of 5 January:

> From Villa Franca to Lugo, seventeen leagues (over a most immense mountain, on which several hale men were soon dead from the intense cold and fatigue, and on which guns, ammunition, and money were stuck and were destroyed), the cavalry marched at a rate almost incredible. The 7th were twenty-six hours only completing it, out of which they were halted four; but this rate of marching had the effect of destroying the horses, which never recovered it.
>
> The infantry also began to be fatigued. Hundreds that would not come on either died or were shot on the road; and several hundreds, who for want of shoes had dropped behind, others who straggled to villages for the sake of plunder, and others who were fatigued and in bad health, fell into the hands of the enemy, all together amounting to a very considerable number … From Astorga this hurry appeared no longer necessary.[37]

The Reserve and the French dragoons continued to skirmish throughout the morning. As Peter Facey had noted and was confirmed by Bugler William Green of the 95th, the French had a light infantryman (which Green called a rifleman) mounted behind each dragoon:

> And when any good position, or bushes by the road side, gave them any advantage to give our men a few shots, those riflemen would dismount and get under cover of the bushes, so that we were obliged to do the same; their dragoons at the same time dismounting and laying their carbines on their saddles, with their horse standing in front of them for a sort of defence, would give us a few shots as well. In this way we were obliged to make a stand and drive them back. We used to laugh to see the riflemen run to the road, put their feet into the stirrups, and mount behind the dragoons and gallop back. We served many of these fellows off; and then we had to run to get up to the regiment. This was the sport for many days' and we could not avoid it.

The French continued to hound the Reserve until the British reached a bridge over a stream at the foot of a hill. Beyond the bridge, the road zig-zagged its way up the steep slope of the hill. The Reserve would be horribly exposed to the long carbines of the dragoons on the opposite bank of the stream as they climbed slowly up the meandering mountain path. How Paget solved this typified the brilliance he showed throughout the retreat, being one of the few senior officers to emerge from the Corunna campaign with an enhanced reputation.

He ordered the Reserve to move quickly across the bridge and start the climb up the winding road, but Carthew's six artillery pieces were unlimbered and prepared for action, the horses being taken to the rear. This gave the appearance of the Reserve making a stand, and it kept the French back out of artillery range. When the rear-guard, in the form of the 28th, was safely beyond musket range, it was halted. The job of the 28th was now to cover the guns.

The French were held back for about an hour, to allow the rest of the other divisions to gain a lead of four or five miles. The French, amassing in ever-increasing numbers, were attempting to outflank the position, so Paget calmly ordered the guns to be limbered up and the rear-guard made off unmolested.

The French light troops were soon over the bridge and, once again, on the tail of the rear-guard. At around midday, the rear-guard halted at a place where the mountain on its right was 'stupendous, covered with snow, and rose nearly perpendicularly from where we stood', and on the left was a very steep precipice, 'its steepness bearing proportion to the sudden rise of the mountain above.'[38]

This was an ideal defensive spot as the severity of the slopes on either side meant that the enemy could only attack frontally along the road. Paget decided to halt at this point and the 28th turned round to face its pursuers.

Shortly, the French arrived. They saw that it was impossible climb up the mountainside to turn the British position, so they sent some infantry and cavalry down into the valley below. The thick covering of snow made it difficult for the French to keep their footing on the uneven ground, and it afforded the 28th 'much amusement to see men and horses tumbling head over heels as they advanced through the valley'.

As the British troops happily watched the French slipping and slithering in the snow in a futile bid to outflank Paget's position, at around 14.00 hours,[39] an officer wearing a blue coat rode up from behind Blakeney as the Light Company faced the enemy. Upon asking the whereabouts of General Paget, the men directed the officer to Blakeney, who was stood not five yards away. When he asked Blakeney where Paget was, the general himself answered, asking the officer what he wanted. Blakeney was able to hear every word:

> 'Oh, beg pardon, sir,' said the blue-coated officer; 'I am paymaster general … The treasure of the army, sir, is close in the rear, and the bullocks being jaded are unable to proceed; I therefore want fresh animals to draw it forward.'
>
> 'Pray, sir,' said the general, 'do you take me for a bullock-driver or a muleteer, or, knowing who I am, have you the presence of mind coolly to tell me that through a total neglect or ignorance of your duty you are about to lose the treasure of the army committed to your charge, which, according to your account, must shortly fall into the hands of the enemy?'

As he spoke, Paget pointed to the French advance guard which was closing in upon the Reserve. 'Had you, sir, the slightest conception of your duty,' continued a very angry Paget,

> you would have known that you ought to be a day's march ahead of the whole army, instead of hanging back with your foundered bullocks and carts upon the rearmost company of the rearguard, and making your report too at the very moment when that company is absolutely engaged with the advancing enemy. What, sir! To come to me and impede my march with your carts, and ask me to look for bullocks when I should be free from all encumbrances and my mind occupied by no other care than that of disposing of my troops to the best advantage in resisting the approaching enemy! It is doubtful, sir, whether your conduct can be attributed to ignorance and neglect alone.

According to Blakeney, Paget continued to harangue the paymaster as the French began to fire on the 28th, 'to give the man of money an opportunity of witnessing how the rear-guard were generally occupied, and to show him the different use of silver and lead during a campaign.'

Paget told the paymaster general that he ought to be immediately hanged for his incompetence. But the general, as he had said, had more pressing matters to attend to, with the rear-guard coming under fire from the enemy, whose main column had now reached the front. It was time for the 28th to retire, and it soon came upon the two carts of the Paymaster, which were guarded by a subaltern's party from the 4th (King's Own) Regiment. The bullocks were so exhausted they were scarcely able to move the carts. It was evident that, with the French so close, either the money would have to be left to fall into the hands of the French or be disposed of. As a fortune in stores had been destroyed at Bembibre and Villafranca, Paget had little compunction in ordering the money to be thrown into the ravine below the road.

As the Light Company of the 28th passed to the rear, Paget ordered the regiment to draw up close to the carts. Paget then ordered Lieutenant Joseph Bennet of the 28th to dispose of the treasure, telling him to shoot the first man who attempted to grab any of the money. 'The casks were rolled over a precipice,' wrote one commentator, and being quickly shattered by the rocks, the good Spanish dollars were liberated, and descended in a glittering shower into the abyss. The French advanced guard, however, arrived just in time to gather up a few dollars which had fallen upon the road.'[40] 'As they rolled down the precipice,' Blakeney wrote,'their silvery notes were accompanied by a noble bass, for two guns were thundering forth their applause into Soult's dark brown column as they gallantly pressed forward.'

The incident was noted by Schaumann, who, we have seen, had earlier passed what was probably that very same bullock cart:

> Among the disasters that befell us while ascending this dreadful mountain, was the fact that we found ourselves compelled to rid our wagons of the load of Spanish dollars which constituted our war treasure. Most of the mules and bullocks that were drawing it had fallen down dead, and we had no fodder for those that still remained. The speed with which the French were pursuing

us, moreover, left us no time in which to take any measures to save this money … As, therefore, it was impossible to conceal the stuff, the barrels containing it were rolled over the side of the precipice, where they smashed to pieces, and hurled their bright silver contents tinging into the abyss. And there, when the snow melted, many a poor shepherd or peasant must have found his fortune.[41]

According to William Napier, there had been a chance to save the money earlier:

An officer of the guards had charge of the cars that drew this treasure, and in passing a village another officer observing that the bullocks were exhausted, took the pains to point out where fresh and strong animals were to be found, but the escorting officer, either ignorant of, or indifferent to his duty, took no notice of this recommendation, and continued his march with the exhausted cattle.

Charles Stewart believed the money could have been saved, and that throwing it away was 'unwise' and unnecessary. 'Had it been distributed among the soldiers,' he argued, 'there is little doubt that they would have contrived to carry it along; whereas, the knowledge that it lay among the cliffs, tempted many men to lag behind, who fell into the hands of the enemy or perished from cold.'[42] Though they must have known that they were taking an enormous risk by holding back in the hope of picking up some of the treasure, the men had just witnessed more money being thrown away than they would ever see in their lives. So, not only money was lost when the military chest was scattered across the mountainside but men also.

The distribution of the money to the soldiers had earlier been proposed by the man who wrote the first historyof the Peninsular War, Robert Southey:

Had the resolution of sacrificing them [the dollars] been determined upon in time, they might have been distributed among the men: in this manner, [a] great part might have been saved from the enemy, and they who had escaped would

151

have had some little compensation for the hardships they had undergone.[43]

The questions of why the coins were not distributed amongst the troops or that more effort was not made to save the money was considered by Captain Pierrepoint:

> Of all our losses, none so unaccountable, so unjustifiable in the eyes of the public as that of the dollars, why not halt to give time to the carts to get on? Why not distribute them among the troops? From the nature of the ground a halt might have been attended without much risk, a division among the troops must have caused great irregularities. I hope some high authority will ask the commissary or Pay Master General, why did you trust the military chest to country carts drawn by two oxen each, whilst daily experience must have taught you that such of those animals destined for the use of the troops could hardly keep up with the army?
>
> The road was then tapering along the flank of a steep ridge which did not allow us to face the enemy with advantage. The commander of the forces ordered the casks (19 in number each containing 5000) to be rolled down the precipice. Two hours after the shape of the hills enabled us, but too late, to face about we halted; an hour after we continued our march, they followed.[44]

In light of the manner in which the infantry behaved during the retreat, Pierrepoint might be correct in believing that the distribution of the money to the men would have caused great irregularities. It was one thing for the mounted cavalry to carry heavy coins, but the infantry, hundreds of whom could not put one foot in front of the other to save their own lives, were in no condition to carry any extra weight. The only consequence would have been that even more men would have fallen by the wayside.

An explanation as to why the money was not distributed among the men was given by Captain Steevens of the 20th Regiment:

> Previous to the money being thrown away, it was proposed, I heard, that the officers and men should carry a certain number of dollars, but whether so being so hard pressed by the enemy, we had not time to distribute the money, or whether the men were

unwilling to carry it, I cannot exactly say, but I believe the latter was the case, for everyone seemed so fatigued that they wanted no additional weight to carry. For my own part I should have been sorry to have carried even twenty or thirty dollars in my pocket, (such were my feelings at the time) wishing to keep myself as light as I could, and I am sure that many were of my opinion.[45]

The loss of the coins had at least one beneficial consequence for the retreating troops, however, as General la Houssaye's dragoons abandoned their pursuit to try and recover as much of the treasure as they could gather from the snowy slopes. This meant that the rear-guard was left unmolested for around two hours. The French cavalry only reappeared around evening. That night French troopers weighted down with silver dollars were selling 1,000 francs in silver for 100 francs in gold. Several young British girls who had been captured by the French that day were put up for auction with the horses captured with them. 'I was scandalized to see,' wrote Edouard de Fantin des Odoards, 'that the former were not always the preferred items.' One can only speculate on what the French soldiers did with the horses that so shocked Odoards![46]

The army stumbled on towards Lugo, where Moore had to decide whether to join the Light Brigade and the King's German Legion at Vigo or continue to Corunna, or possibly even Ferrol. On the morning of 6 January, he received a report from his chief engineer, Colonel Richard Fletcher, who had spent the previous few days galloping round all three harbours. Fletcher reported in favour of Corunna, where the surrounding hills would give Moore a strong position from which he would be able to cover the embarkation if the French were still in contact with the rear-guard.

Captain George Napier was handed the task of informing Baird, his division being at the rear of the main column, that the army was to stand and give battle at Lugo. Baird then sent an orderly dragoon to pass on this information to Hope and Fraser, who were far in advance. Charles Stewart explained what happened:

> It unhappily fell out that the dragoon got drunk, and the packet miscarried; but the misfortune was not discovered till the following morning, when fresh orders were instantly sent off.

That loss of time nothing could repair. General Hope with his division, was already a full day's march beyond Lugo; and though he wheeled about immediately on receipt of Sir David's communication, he did not arrive at Lugo till after the rear-guard had come in; and even then his troops were so fatigued, that their fitness for immediate service was problematical.[47]

Stewart wrote that many of the horses attached to Hope's division had been driven so hard that theydropped down dead in the streets of Lugo and others were so beaten up that they had to be killed. Some 400 stragglers had been left behind and a number of Baird's men who had reached Lugo also collapsed and died. However, Hope's dispirited troops received heartening news when they reached Lugo – the army was going to turn and fight its pursuers. At last Moore had found a position which he believed was strong enough for him to stand and give battle.

Chapter 9

At Bay

The Battle of Lugo

Moore had at last decided to turn and face the enemy, but his army was in no fit state to fight a battle: 'All order or subordination was now at an end,' wrote Archibald Alison, 'the soldiers, exhausted with fatigue, or depressed by suffering, sunk down by hundreds by the wayside and breathed their last; and the army, in frightful disorder, at length reached Lugo late on the evening of January 6.'[1]

The arrival of the army at Lugo was described by Lieutenant Andrew Leith Hay of the 29th Regiment:

> There might be seen the conductors of baggage toiling through the streets, their laden mules almost sinking under the weight of ill-arranged burdens swinging from side to side … These were succeeded by the dull, heavy sound of the passing artillery; then came the Spanish fugitives from the desolating line of the armies. Detachments with sick or lamed horses scrambled through the mud while, at intervals, the report of a horse pistol, knelled the termination of the sufferings of an animal, that a few days previously, full of life, and high in blood, had borne its rider, not against, but over the ranks of Gallic chivalry.[2]

Hussey Vivian recorded that: 'The British commander was well aware of the condition of his troops and issued a stern General Order from Lugo on the 6th':

> Generals and Commanding Officers of Corps must be as sensible as the Commander of the Forces, of the complete disorganization

of the army. The advanced-guard of the French is already close to us, and it is to be presumed that the main body is not far distant; an action may, therefore, be hourly expected. If the Generals and Commanding Officers of Regiments (feeling for the honour of their country and of the British arms) wish to give the army a fair chance of success, they will exert themselves to restore order and discipline in the regiments, brigades, and divisions which they command.

The Commander of the Forces is tired of giving Orders which are never attended to: he therefore appeals to the honour and feelings of the Army he commands; and if those are not sufficient to induce them to do their duty, he must despair of succeeding by any other means. He was forced to order one soldier to be shot at Villafranca, and he will order all others to be executed who are guilty of similar enormities: but he considers that there would be no occasion to proceed to such extremities if the Officers did their duty; as it is chiefly from their negligence, and from the want of proper regulations in the regiments, that crimes and irregularities are committed, in quarters and upon the march.[3]

Such criticism seemed unjust to some of the officers, who had already been angered by what they considered Moore's insulting tone in the address he gave at Benavente. Moore had driven the men on at a pace that many simply could not maintain. Had the troops been properly fed and clothed, much of the disorder in the ranks would not have occurred. But the men, thirsty, starving and threadbare had witnessed thousands of pounds' worth of stores of all descriptions needlessly destroyed. Little wonder, then, that so many had strayed from the columns. The rebuke by Moore certainly offended Alexander Gordon, who saw Moore's conduct, 'the primary cause of the evil'.

Nor did La Romana's troops behave any differently than those of John Moore faced with the same circumstances, as the parish priest of one of the villages through which the Spanish troops passed, testified:

The streets and houses were strewn with the dead and dying. What with the stench and filth of the former and the cries and groans of the latter, a more horrible spectacle had never been seen … All this accompanied by robbery, insult and outrage as men besieged by hunger or accustomed to a life of crime, assailed road and home alike … It was not possible to move an inch without exposing oneself to every sort of vexation.[4]

The degree to which discipline had broken down in the British ranks is seen in the episodes recorded in the diary the quartermaster of the 71st, Ensign William Gavin, in which the men were actually fighting each other:

> Marched to Lugo under torrents of rain. Our sufferings were indeed pitiable. Orders were given to send off the baggage and sick to Corunna and to halt the army. The men were to be completed to sixty rounds of ammunition each. The writer [Gavin] and Adjutant Anderson were ordered to proceed to a magazine about two miles from town, to get the complement of our regiment, on which occasion (our tempers were so soured by fatigue and hunger) that we drew our swords and actually commenced a regular combat, when some friends interfered and effected a reconciliation.
>
> In this town I got into the house of a priest with Lieut. John Graham. A soldier if the 18th Dragoons entered and demanded provisions, when Mr Graham, remonstrating with the violence of his conduct he deliberately drew out his pistol and discharged it at Mr Graham, but fortunately it missed him.[5]

The situation, though, was about to change, albeit temporarily. For at Lugo was a large depot containing four or five days' provisions for the entire army. At last the men were fed and clothed and the horrors of the retreat quickly forgotten. But the appearance of thousands of soldiers at Lugo caused chaos in the small walled town. 'Arrived at Lugo and were obliged to remain (both horses and men) in the streets, the town and environs being so extremely crowded with nearly the whole of the British army,' wrote an officer of the 15th Hussars. 'The sick and dismounted men [those who no longer had horses] ordered to proceed to Corunna under charge of an officer … Cornet Laroche went to Corunna sick. Sick indeed, why the whole army is sick and sorry too! and in addition extremely mutinous.'[6]

Nevertheless, at the prospect of battle the spirits of the troops rose immeasurably. In a flash the mutinous rabble had become an army – one that was ready to fight.

By standing to face the French, Moore gave the numerous stragglers chance to catch up with their regiments as well as giving the transports more time to sail round to Corunna, and the position at Lugo was a strong one where he could feel confident of holding his ground against a frontal attack. Moore placed his regiments along a low hill, all along the front of which there was a line of low stone walls, which marked the boundaries of fields and vineyards. On its right the British position touched the unfordable River Minho, on the left it rested on rocky and inaccessible hills. Below it there was a gentle down-slope of a mile, up which the enemy would have to march in order to attack, being under the eyes of the defenders throughout.[7] The position was certainly well-suited for defence, as the stone walls and cultivated fields would break up the French formations and limit their momentum.

The number of troops available to Moore to man this position has been estimated at around 19,000, some 500 or 600 sick or wounded who were too ill to be moved having been left at Astorga and a further 2,000 or so had been lost on the march over the mountains. The halt at Lugo, though, gave a few hundred stragglers time to catch up, and they were able to re-join the army. Moore disposed his force to face the enemy with Hope's division on the right, next to the Guards, who had their right on the River Minho, which was impassable from the heavy rains. Fraser's division was in the centre, and Sir David Baird on the left.

Soult, with la Houssaye's dragoons and Franceschi's mixed light cavalry division, and Merle's infantry behind, reached Lugo on the 6th, close behind the Reserve. The two armies settled down for the night in clear view of each other. It rained heavily at intervals during the night, but not sufficiently to extinguish the numerous fires that blazed along the front of the two armies, and marked in flame the hostile lines.

It continued to drizzle as day broke on the morning of the 7th. Soult began to test the strength of the British positions, no doubt expecting that Lugo was held only by the rear-guard. Moore knew that the French had no choice but to try and drive the British from their position in front of Lugo, and he issued another General Order, the tone of which was in marked contrast to his order of the previous day, and reflected the mood of the army as a whole:

> The Army must see that the moment is now come when, after the hardships and fatiguing marches they have undergone, they will have the opportunity of bringing the Enemy to action. The Commander of the Forces has the most perfect confidence in their valour, and that it is only necessary to bring them to close contact with the Enemy in order to defeat them; and a defeat, if it be complete, as he trusts it will be, will, in a great measure, end their labours.
>
> The General has no other caution to give them, than not to throw away their fire at the Enemy's skirmishers, merely because they fire at them; but to reserve it till they can give it with effect.[8]

The sergeant of the 43rd saw the effect the prospect of battle had amongst the troops: 'Scarcely was the order issued, when the line of battle, hitherto so peeled and spread abroad, was filled with vigorous men, full of confidence and courage.'[9] The effect was 'magical', wrote John Fortescue. 'Stragglers and absent men presented themselves from all sides, and the ranks, lately so thin, became suddenly and mysteriously full; and, in spite of all adverse circumstances, Moore found himself in command of nineteen thousand vigorous and confident men.'[10]

Joseph Sinclair also remarked on how the chance to fight the enemy had revitalised the troops:

> From the first moment of the attack, and as long as the French were before us, discipline was restored, and the officers were as punctually obeyed as if we had been on parade at home. We felt not our sufferings; so anxious were we to end them by a victory, which we were certain of obtaining.[11]

Expecting only to be faced with Paget's Reserve, Soult ordered up a battery (the maximum of which would have been eight field pieces) to blast a hole in the British line through which he would send his cavalry. The response must had surprised the Duke of Dalmatia. For the French salvo was answered by fifteen guns. Evidently there was more than just a rear-guard facing Soult's force, and the French battery was withdrawn while the marshal sought to learn more about the dispositions of the enemy.

Soult's next move was to feint with his left, sending a column against the British right, but this was easily repulsed by the Brigade of Guards. But then a more serious attack was delivered against Moore's left. Merle's Division with five artillery pieces fell on the outposts of Leith's brigade of Hope's Division, on the lower slopes. The outpost line fell back in some confusion upon its parent body as the French advanced, gaining confidence.

Seeing the danger, Moore galloped over to the threatened point, encouraging the men to hold firm. A soldier of the Highland Light Infantry was one of those engaged:

> Twelve men out of each of the other companies, and the whole of ours, were sent out to stem their way. I was among the party that was placed as a reserve: in this situation the enemy began peppering us with cannon-balls, upon which we had recourse to our old system of sitting down. Happening to be under a tree, it was struck several times, and the man who sat next to me got his musket broke to splinters in his hand, without receiving the slightest injury.[12]

The matter was finally decided when Leith, at the head of the 59th Regiment, counter-attacked, and did so with such ferocity that at least 300 of Merle's men were killed or captured.

It was clear that most, if not all of Moore's army was present and Soult knew that he would have to wait for the rest of his force to come up before he could risk engaging the British again. So there was no further action that day, and both sides settled down in their positions to await the morrow, with Soult hoping that Moore would remain where he was for a few more days. He sent a message to Ney to hurry his 6th Corps to Villafranca and to despatch one division round by the Val des Orresto Orense on the road to Vigo, and from there to take the minor road to Lugo from where he could fall on Moore's right flank. As we know, this would have been in vain as the brigades under Alten and Craufurd had been sent in that direction, so Moore's flank was reasonably secure.

On the morning of the 8th, both armies were under arms again. Some reinforcements had reached Soult, who now had 20,000 men with fifty guns at his disposal. Moore hoped that Soult would attack, as did his troops, who were eager to get to grips with the men who had been pursuing them for so long. 'We firmly expected to attack this morning,' Thomas Graham confided to his diary, 'and waited with much impatience for an opportunity to beat the enemy – the confident expectation of every man in the Army, which was of the highest.'[13]

Soult, though, wanted Moore to remain exactly where he was until the 6th Corps could outflank the British position. All day the British troops waited for the French attack, but Soult was happy to bide his time. Nor could Moore risk taking the initiative and launch an attack upon Soult. The British commander knew that Soult could only get stronger with the passing of every hour as more reinforcements came up, and an attack would be foolhardy. This also meant that the longer the British remained at Lugo, the more danger it was in, as eventually the enemy would reach overwhelming strength. Moore had to move on.

William Napier of the 43rd agreed with Moore's decision: 'The British army was not provided to fight above one battle; there were no draught animals, no means of transporting reserve ammunition, no magazines, no hospital, no second line, no provisions; a defeat would have been ruin, a victory useless.'[14]

Though Moore did not get the battle he had hoped for at Lugo, the men had recovered not only their composure but also, to a great degree, their physical strength. The twenty-four hours without action plus the provisions they had found at Lugo, had helped the soldiers considerably. But Moore was only too conscious how quickly they broke ranks, and broke down, when they had to retreat. He, therefore, issued another Order of the Day before the army left Lugo:

> It is evident that the Enemy will not fight this Army, notwithstanding the superiority of his numbers; but will endeavour to harass and tease it upon its march. The Commander of the Forces requests that it may be carefully explained to the Soldiers, that their safety depends solely upon their keeping their

divisions, and marching with their regiments; that those who stop in villages, or straggle on the march, will inevitably be cut off by the French cavalry; who have hitherto shewn little mercy even to the feeble and infirm, who have fallen into their hands. The army has still eleven leagues to march, the soldiers must make an exertion to accomplish them; the rear-guard cannot stop, and those who fall behind must take their fate.[15]

Joseph Sinclair of the 71st voiced his opinion of Moore's order which, no doubt was felt by many: 'Before our reserve left Logo, general orders were issued, warning and exhorting us to keep order, and to march together; but, alas! How could men observe order amidst such sufferings! Or men, whose feet were naked and sore, keep up with men who, being more fortunate, had better shoes and stronger constitutions? The officers, in many points, suffered as much as the men. I have seen officers of the guards, and others, worth thousands, with pieces of old blankets wrapt [sic] round their feet and legs.'[16]

At 21.30 hours, night having set in, the army slipped quietly away from the positions it had held for two days and set out on the final leg of the retreat to the coast, leaving fires burning along the picket lines to deceive the enemy on the heights opposite. On duty on the picket line was a sergeant of the 5th Regiment:

> We, in our turn received orders to follow, after putting all the fuel we could find upon the fires. When we reached the road, we found it nearly impassable from an immense quantity of snow and rain which had alternately fallen, and was at this juncture again hardened by the frost; and in the morning, our route might have been traced by the blood on the snow.[17]

Captain Thomas Downman's troop of the RHA remained with the rear-guard and was amongst the last to leave Lugo, whilst Lieutenant Colonel George Cookson led the rest of the artillery as the army marched out of the town on the road to Corunna:

> It was so intensely dark and the ground so heavy that I was apprehensive at one time that I should never have gotten in the Main Road with my Brigades. The guns frequently stuck fast in

going over the plow'd ground from which the heavy rain was completely saturated – however by great exertions tho' very late we reached [the] Corunna gate out of Lugo; here the confusion of men, horses, carriages etc. forcing their way out of the town was far beyond description. Not far from the gate a number of Spanish field pieces were collected together and their carriages etc. [put] on fire to prevent them being useful to the enemy.[18]

As well as artillery pieces, the depot at Lugo also included a large quantity of ammunition, more than could be used, or carried, by Moore's army. It could not be left to the enemy, as Captain Adam Wall of the Royal Artillery described in his *History of Operations*:

Colonel Harding, Commanding the Artillery, arrived with Sir John Moore at Lugo, when a number of troops were employed with the Artillery in destroying ammunition, provisions and stores, which had been brought from Corunna, and for want of a mode of conveyance could not be removed; the quantity of musquet [sic] ammunition was immense, together with a number of Artillery carriages; the conflagration through the whole day appeared as if the whole of the city was on fire.[19]

The burning carriages were noted by Neale when he glanced back to view Lugo as the main column set off on the final stages of the march to Corunna:

As I quitted Lugo, I took a last look at its mouldering walls, which frowned over the glowing embers of our artillery-waggons. The inhabitants had all fled with whatever little property they possessed, and the empty streets and desolate houses sent back a thousand echoes to the clatter of our horses' hoofs.[20]

A similar scene was recorded by Schaumann:

It was dark; the bulk of the inhabitants had fled, and the ring of our horses' hoofs was gruesomely echoed by the deserted streets and open houses. When we got outside, I cast one more look upon the decayed and blackened walls of the town, which loomed darkly above the glowing embers of the fires that had been made with broken-up ammunition wagons.[21]

Behind them, the troops had to leave behind several thousand loaves of bread prepared by the commissaries, having no means to carry them, the streets of Lugo being choked with dead horses.[22]

Precautions had been taken to mark the correct track that the troops should follow as they left Lugo in the dark by the placing of bundles of straw at certain distances, and officers were appointed to guide the columns. But, as the men marched out of Lugo they walked into a dreadful storm, and the bundles of straw were blown or washed away. 'It was, indeed a miserable night,' complained a soldier of the 71st, 'thrust out into the storm, and the rain lashing on me in torrents, I threw myself down in the mud, on the lee side of a stone dyke, as the best shelter I could find. Certainly there was no respect of persons here; the elements are remarkably impartial in such cases as these, and on looking round the field I saw Colonel Pack squatting close by my side.'[23] While some tried to shelter from the storm, others stumbled around in the dark, scarcely able to see where they were treading. 'The night was extremely dark,' recalled Captain Gordon. 'Our route to the town [of Betanzos] lay over broken ground and through intricate lanes; the country was also much intersected by dry stone walls, enclosing the fields and vineyards, which made it difficult to keep the squadrons together, as no man could see his own horse's head, much less his file leader.'[24]

In such circumstances, and with bundles of hay markers destroyed, the divisions became hopelessly lost almost as soon as they had left Lugo. The Reserve, which managed to keep on track, discovered that some of the other divisions, which had wandered around the countryside, had fallen behind the rear-guard. This meant that Paget's men had to slow down to allow the troops behind them to catch up. As muddled-up battalions marched up behind the Reserve, the men had to stop, turn and be ready to fight in case it was the enemy that was approaching.

Commissary Schaumann wrote that, as the storm of sleet and hail struck his face, it stung like molten lead and he could hardly keep on his saddle:

> The army, which had spent this appalling night, almost without rations, in a cold bivouac, were marching slowly

in the direction of Quitterez, in a straggling throng, weary, discouraged, hungry, wet to the skin and covered with mud. All the inhabitants had flown; all the villages were deserted and were therefore immediately plundered. Many of the soldiers lay down completely exhausted in the ditches, never perhaps to rise again. Few women were still to be seen, the majority lay behind somewhere between Villafranca and Lugo. In one of the villages through which we went I saw one of them sink up to her waist in a bog, whereupon, the mud and slime preventing her from rising, she fell, and the whole column marched over her.[25]

Another officer wrote that: 'the rain, sleet and snow came down alternately, while the piercing wind, blowing in gusts through every crevice in the rocks, or through the defiles, in loud and successive squalls, made the earth tremble before our very feet.'[26]

Worse still, was what Blakeney called 'one of our greatest plagues' that began at the dirty miserable village called Guitiriz (Schaumann's Quitterez).[27] The leading divisions reached this place at around 01.00 hours on the morning of the 9th. The village offered the troops, or at least the officers, a chance to escape from the storm. The men, ravenous hungry, soaked and chilled to the bone, were left to their own devices outside in the teeming rain to await the arrival of the other divisions. Predictably, the men went in search of food and drink. They plundered the houses and the remaining commissariat wagons. Casks of wine were found as well as a cart-load of salt fish and rum. According to Schaumann, the combination of raw fish and rum resulted in the death of many men, while several others went mad.

This included, according to Rifleman Green, a man of the 1st Battalion of the 95th (Thomas Baxter), who was so full of red wine that he could no longer walk. The colonel of the regiment was so angered by this man's behaviour he ordered the buttons to be cut off his jacket so that he would not disgrace his regiment when he was taken by the enemy. He was never heard of again.'[28]

Wherever the exhausted infantry came across a large bundle of straw the men would roll themselves up in it and immediately fall asleep. Hussey Vivian's 7th Hussars found that the only way to wake such sleepers was to 'prick' them with their swords.

When the cavalry had eventually driven the men out of Lugo, it took up its usual station at the rear of the column again. According to Hussey Vivian, the road presented an even more distressing sight:

> Fine fellows, willing and anxious to get on, their feet bleeding for want of shoes, and totally incapable of keeping up; others, whose spirit was better than their strength, actually striving till the last to join their battalions, and several of this description perished in the attempt.
>
> I myself saw five dead on the roadside, and two women, whilst every now and then you met with a poor unfortunate woman, perhaps with a child in her arms, without shoes or stockings, knee deep in mud, crying most piteously for that assistance which, alas! we could not afford her. One poor wretch of this description actually died with two children at her breast, one of whom was also dead.[29]

The troops, who for two days had eagerly expected a set-piece battle, once again found themselves fighting a dismal and unrewarding rear-guard action. 'This change of scene produced a considerable alteration in our affairs,' bemoaned one officer. 'Instead of being the assailants, or ourselves assailed, in the open field – where with fair play there is always something encouraging to hope for – we were forced to defend ourselves against superior numbers in a country of truly Alpine wildness; pent up, formed in files or sections, within the limits of a narrow, rugged and hilly road, in many parts almost impassable by huge projecting rocks, between whose craggy fissures the mountain torrents rushed with fearful violence – at every step we took the winding route became more desolate.'[30]

On 8 January Vivian, whose 7th Hussars were the last to leave Lugo, wrote:

> Although I left the advanced posts, which were four miles in advance of the town, full four hours after the retreat of our army, I found the houses on the outskirts of the town full of stragglers. Many of these I succeeded in driving out by force or persuasion. Others were so ill and harassed that nothing could move them.

From this instant the road presented one constant string of stragglers, many of whom no efforts of ours could drive before us; although the certain consequence of their dropping behind was their becoming prisoners, as the enemy would certainly follow early in the morning.

Every house was full (I may say, out of some we drove upwards of a hundred) of these stragglers, and such was the state of carelessness and the total want of spirit occasioned by fatigue, &c., that on being told that the enemy would certainly shoot them, many replied, 'They may shoot us, sir, as you may shoot us, but we cannot stir'; and although there were many instances in which our men actually proceeded to severe measures to force the people on, hundreds remained immovable; of these several were almost in a dying state, and two or three were found actually dead.[31]

One of those who fell behind through exhaustion brought on by 'alarming' diarrhoea, left an account of his capture by the French cavalry:

The road all the way, was strewed with men unable to proceed. Here and there, we saw some calmly at rest. Morning arrived, and it was said we were only four leagues from Corunna … Seeing smoke issue from a large building off the road, I crawled, rather than walked to it. It was something like a barn, and full of our men who had made a fire … I found a spare corner, and putting my pouch under my head, fell into a sound sleep, leaving the army and the enemy to take care of themselves.[32]

When this sergeant of the 5th woke up he found that the army had indeed taken care of itself and had long gone. Though at first he was too stiff to move, the sleep had revived the NCO, nevertheless, he had slept throughout the day and it was dark by the time he felt able to march on to catch up with the army. He decided to wait until daylight. It was the wrong decision: 'Next morning at daybreak, shots whistled through our tenement, some of the men jumped up, ran out, discharged their pieces, and then were shot dead on the spot. To surrender was the prevailing opinion.' Before giving themselves up, the men looked out through a hole in the barn and saw just eight or ten French dragoons. The men in the barn numbered seven fit enough to handle their muskets. At such odds, the men chose to fight, and walked out of the barn to form up, ready to defend themselves:

> The French observing the poverty of our numbers, galloped up to us. I had brought my piece down to a level, and the instant the re-bound announced its discharge, a sabre was plunged into my left arm, while the man who made the thrust, sprang up from his saddle and fell a corpse … [However] our cartridges being expended, the dragoons invited us to surrender, pointing at the same time to their army, which was advancing … I therefore of course complied.[33]

According to Blakeney, more men fell away from the ranks during this 'disastrous' march from Lugo to Betanzos than during the whole previous part of the campaign. The road to Betanzos, which had seemed in very good condition to Baird's men who had marched from Corunna just a few weeks before had, according to Gordon, completely broken up by the frequent changes in the weather and the continual passage of the heavy carriages of the army. The men, who were in a state of near collapse, took sixteen hours to march just fifteen miles, often being forced to wade through mud more than a foot deep. According to Ensign Gavin, only 150 men of Brigadier General Catlin Craufurd's brigade were still with the colours when they marched into Betanzos, and they were 'barefoot, covered with old blankets, and many without arms'. At the start of the retreat, Craufurd's brigade numbered around 2,500.[34]

'The miseries to which the troops were exposed increased at every step,' wrote Captain Gordon:

> Many of the officers were destitute of shoes or stockings, with their clothes in rags; it may therefore be imagined that the privates were in a most deplorable condition. Straggling had increased to such a degree that, if the retreat had continued three days longer, the army must have been totally annihilated. The men were so much exhausted by incessant fatigue and want of food, added to the effects of violent dysentery which raged amongst them, that many who lay down to rest themselves at a little distance

from the roadside had not sufficient strength to rejoin the line of march, and fell into the hands of the enemy. Soldiers of different corps were mixed promiscuously together, and the Colours of one regiment – the Fiftieth, I think – entered Betanzos without a single man to form them.[35]

'It was melancholy to see the brave soldiers, who feared no mortal foe, thus beaten by the elements, and crouching from their fury,' wrote another, 'they lined the ditches which border the road, creeping along under the dwarf banks and enclosures, to screen themselves from the cutting sharpness of the tempest; – the calls and exhortations of their officers unheeded and unattended to, not from any feeling of disrespect or insubordination, but literally and purely from animal exhaustion.'[36]

The anonymous soldier of the 71st was suffering such excruciating pain from his cut and bruised bare feet, that he threw himself down on the ground, 'with a fierce indifference to my fate; death had no longer any terrors for me.' While lying in this condition, he saw one of the generals (who he incorrectly identifies as Major General Ferguson) with a number of other field officers and aides-de-camp, riding around entreating those that, like the soldier of the 71st, had given up the struggle and had collapsed onto the ground, to make one final effort as they were now close to Corunna. 'The general came up to two men who lay close by me, and persuaded them to rise, and crawl on; coming next to me, he attempted to encourage me with hopes of a speedy arrival at the ships, and so on; but I told him in firm, but respectful terms that "I felt myself unable to even move".'[37]

However, the soldier of the 71st Regiment and other stragglers were given a second chance to re-join their regiments, as the whole army halted at Betanzos on the 10th. 'On arrival at this town,' continued Gavin, the men 'threw themselves down in the streets … [and] though literally starving, their want of sleep and fatigue were such that it was impossible to rouse them to receive their rations'.

So many men had dropped by the wayside on the march from Lugo that when the French cavalry caught up with the stragglers on the morning of the 10th, they found themselves faced by a considerable body of men. The stragglers formed up in reasonable order and presented such a solid front that the enemy horsemen were held off. General Paget, with the Reserve, saw that the stragglers were quite capable of looking after themselves and did not bother sending them any assistance. 'He declared in presence of the men,' Blakeney recounted, 'who from a natural impulse wished to move down against the cavalry, that his reason for this was that he would not sacrifice the life of one good soldier who had stuck to his colours to save the whole horde of these drunken marauders who by their disgraceful conduct placed themselves at the mercy of their enemies.'[38] This, of course, was unjust to the men who had been driven on through the harshest terrain in the very middle of winter without adequate food, drink, clothes or shoes. But Paget was making a point, and he needed the Reserve to hold together for just a few more days.

To reinforce his message, once the French cavalry had withdrawn, Paget sent a strong piquet to 'prick' the stragglers forward, and drive them onto Betanzos. By Blakeney's estimation, there were around 1,500 of these men who were sent under escort to be dealt with by their respective corps.

The men with Alten and Robert Craufurd marching for Vigo, though not pursued by the enemy, were still suffering, being pushed hard by Alten, 'through a most difficult and mountainous country, during inclement weather', in his bid to secure the bridge over the Minho at Orense and then reach the port. 'Forced marches under such peculiar circumstances,' wrote Alten, 'necessarily involve the necessity of leaving behind the sick and stragglers, which, during the latter part of the march amounted to a considerable number … The procuring [of] provisions during this march was attended with much difficulty. The country was poor and thinly inhabited.'[39]

Lieutenant John Brumwell was with the 1st Battalion, 43rd Regiment on its march to Vigo: 'After we left the road for Corunna we had no provisions for four days [not so much as] a morsel of bread, but you [cannot] form any adequate idea [of the miseries during the] retreat. We were obliged to break open the [Spaniards'] doors to procure [food, and we had to] march wet to the skin and miserable in every respect. The mountains in the provinces of Galicia, where we had to march over, were dreadful. [We marched] for 16 to 17 days over these mountains without a halt. The [soldiers were] falling out of the ranks sick by dozens together. Many of our men were walking without their shoes [or stockings], for there were hardly anything to be got in Spain … The Spaniards would turn out upon the sick soldiers that were left on the road with firelocks and … rob them of everything they had.'[40]

But for the troops under Moore, from the hills around Betanzos the end of their ordeal was, quite literally, in sight – the sea. Commissary Schaumann wrote that his heart leapt for joy when, standing on a height just beyond the River Mandeo he saw a strip of blue sea on the horizon and the masts of a few ships: 'Thank God! We are now safe!' he declared.

At what must have been exactly the same spot, the 15th Hussars also got their first glimpse of the sea:

> New vigour appeared to be suddenly infused into our ranks, and a lengthened shout of exultation burst from the troops when, upon reaching the summit of a hill about a league from Corunna, we descried that element upon which the British flag reigns unrivalled, and distinguished its colours on the vessels in the bay.[41]

All the troops were rejuvenated at the sight of the sea, even the weary infantry. 'When I saw the vessels in the harbour,' recalled a private of the 42nd, 'I was so rejoiced, that in a few hours I was a new man again.'

But the masts the men could see in Corunna harbour were not the masts of the fleet of transports. It would be many more days before the ships would arrive, and by then the French would be upon them. Before they could sail for home, the exhausted, hungry, bedraggled survivors had one more battle to fight.

Chapter 10

A Melancholy Aspect of Affairs

Before dawn on the 11th, the army was assembled for its final march into Corunna. The men, naturally, were elated, despite the evident fact that the transports had yet to arrive, and the ships they could see in the harbour were insufficient to carry off the army. These, it was soon learnt, were only store ships and hospital ships. Despite this, Joseph Sinclair of the 71st was particularly happy that day: 'How shall I describe my sensations at the first sight of the ocean! I felt all my former despondency drop from my mind. My galled feet trod lighter on the icy road. Every face near me seemed to brighten up … The sea and home appeared one and the same.'[1]

The troops marched down from Betanzos and across the Mandeo. Once across this river, there was nothing to prevent the army reaching the coast, providing the bridge was destroyed behind them. They tramped towards the port through fields of rye, orange orchards and gardens of flowers. The snow and sleet of the mountains was already a memory, but one that would not be forgotten. 'They were a mere rabble,' remarked one officer who watched the troops pass by, 'marching in groups of twenty or thirty each. Looking quite broken-hearted and worn out, many without shoes or stockings, the colours of several regiments detached and moving with an officer or two and some of the sergeants only.'[2]

Moore went off ahead of the army to examine the positions his troops would take up at Corunna, leaving Paget in command. He established his headquarters at 13 Canton Grande, in a street in an unwalled part of the town that was within easy reach of the harbour.

The rear-guard was also largely left alone by the French until the British troops reached the Mandeo. An engineer was detailed to demolish the bridge to ensure that Soult could not follow them into Corunna before the troops embarked for England. The 28th Regiment was detailed to protect the engineer and his party as they prepared the bridge for demolition. 'The desired explosion now took place by which it was confidently expected that for a short time at least we should be separated from our teasing pursuers,' Blakeney confidently asserted.

> Our expectations were, however, blasted by the explosion itself; for as soon as the rubbish had fallen down and the smoke cleared away, to our great surprise and annoyance we perceived that one half of one arch only had been destroyed, the other half and one of the battlements remaining firm.[3]

A dismayed, but not entirely unsurprised Paget, asked the engineer to account for 'another abortion'. The engineer believed that there had been a break in the powder train and that he would be able to ignite the remaining barrels if he was given another twenty minutes. Accepting the engineer's word, and with Franceschi's cavalry now bearing down on the bridge, Paget ordered the 28th across the river to take up a position to hold off the enemy whilst the engineer completed the job.

Unfortunately, the 28th took a wrong turn as they moved down towards the bridge and by the time they realised their mistake, and crossed the bridge, the French cavalry was amongst them. The dragoons gave a loud cheer and charged. 'I had not time to turn round, for at that moment a French officer, darting in front rode full tilt at me,' continued Blakeney:

> I cut at him, but my sword approached no nearer perhaps than his horse's nose; in fact my little light infantry sabre was a useless weapon opposed to an immense mounted dragoon, covered, horse and all, with a large green cloak, which in itself formed a sufficient shield. After the failure of my attack I held my sword horizontally over my head, awaiting the dragoon's blow, for it was far more dangerous to turn round than to stand firm. At this critical moment a man of the company, named

Oats, cried out, 'Mr. Blakeney, we've spun him!' and at the same instant the dragoon fell dead at my feet. I flew with a bound to the rear … The cavalry were now up to our bayonets, covering the whole pontine isthmus.[4]

The 28th had held its ground, and the opposing forces faced each other across the remnants of the bridge. French infantry had now arrived and occupied a building at the end of the bridge, from where they were able to command the length of the bridge. This meant that there was no chance of the engineer being able to re-ignite the barrels of powder. The great hope of being able to delay the French at the river while the army embarked peacefully at Corunna had been lost. The best that could be hoped for was that the rear-guard could hold the French back long enough for the rest of the army to cross the bridge over the River Mero at El Burgo. At this point, the tidal river was just four miles from Corunna and was the army's last hope of holding back Soult.

The rear-guard, therefore, held firm. Every attempt by the French to cross the damaged bridge met, as Blakeney described it, 'a wall of steel'. Eventually, Paget considered that the main body had been given enough time to get well ahead, and he withdrew from the bridge. Ten minutes after Paget's men had pulled back, the French warily followed, maintaining, according to Blakeney, 'their courteous distance'. There was, though, a little skirmishing between the respective cavalry forces and the French managed to capture David Baird's travelling coach and baggage.[5]

Blissfully unaware of the danger that once again threatened its rear, the main body marched on towards the port. Believing that he was now safe, the anonymous private of the Black Watch pondered on the extraordinary march that the men had lived through:

When we came in sight of the sea we fancied all was well. When I saw the vessels in the harbour, I was so rejoiced, that in a few hours I was a new man. What is man made of that he can endure all this? How comes he to adapt himself to such mysterious fortune? These and many other reflections crowded on my mind at the sight of the salt sea … we advanced by the thought that if we could but reach it, our salvation was sure.

175

Paget's reserve caught up with the main body of the army before Corunna and, for the first time in the campaign, with the exception of the men under Alten and Craufurd heading for Vigo, the whole force marched together. Under the watchful eye of its commander, and with the prospect of an end to their sufferings, the rumblings of discontent were muted and discipline was fully re-asserted. According to Blakeney, 'every commanding officer headed his regiment, and every captain and subaltern flanked his regularly formed section; not a man was allowed to leave the ranks until a regular halt took place for that purpose.'

As Moore watched his men trudge into Corunna, one body of men in particular caught the British commander's eye at a distance for its fine military bearing. 'Those must be the Guards,' he said, according to Sir John Fortescue:

> and presently the two battalions of the First Guards, each of them still eight hundred strong, strode by in column of sections, with drums beating, the drum-major twirling his staff at their head and the men keeping step, as if in their own barrack-yard. As the remaining battalions went past him Moore addressed every commanding officer, and instructed such as needed the lesson – and these were far too numerous – in their duties when on the march. He can hardly have failed, as we may conjecture, to point out that the senior regiment of the British infantry had set an example to the whole army, and that it was only vicious systems and neglectful officers that had prevented every battalion from behaving as the Guards.[6]

Nevertheless, that was all in the past and the army crossed the River Mero and marched through the villages of Piedralonga and Eiris and down to the port. 'The state of the army when it arrived at Corunna was indeed truly deplorable,' Major Edwin Griffith of the 15th Hussars remembered, 'a sickness had spread throughout it, and the men and horses were worn down with fatigue, and perfectly bare foot. Notwithstanding all this they were in excellent spirits.'[7]

Further south, the men heading for Vigo were also in good temper, having reached the hills above the port to see the transports in the harbour. 'The view of the town, the shipping, and the sea, broke all at once upon us,' wrote William Surtees on 12 January:

> It was a most delightful prospect, and it was highly amusing to observe the joy which seemed to animate the woe-worn countenances of our ragged and dirty soldiers. Fellows without a shoe or a stocking, and who before were shuffling along with sore and lacerated feet like so many lame ducks, now made an attempt to dance for joy; laughter and mirth, and the joke now succeeded to the gloomy silence with which they had in general prosecuted their wearisome journey for several days past, as the friendly element before them promised shortly to put a period to long and toilsome wanderings.[8]

Rifleman Harris described the condition of the men as they arrived at Vigo: 'Our beards were long and ragged; almost all were without shoes and stockings; many had their clothes and accoutrements in fragments, with their heads swathed in old rags, and our weapons were covered with rust; whilst not a few had now, from toil and fatigue, become quite blind.'[9]

Despite the terrible hardships the men had endured, the army – Britain's only disposable field force – had been saved, as James Carrick Moore was quick to point out in his brother's defence:

> The British Army thus arrived at Corunna entire and unbroken; and, in a military point of view, the operation was successful and splendid. Nearly 70,000 Frenchmen, led by Buonaparte, with a great superiority of cavalry, had endeavoured in vain to surround or to rout 26,000 British. Two hundred and fifty miles of country had been traversed; mountains, defiles, and rivers, had been crossed, in daily contact with their Enemy. Though often engaged, even their rear-guard was never beaten, nor thrown into confusion; but was victorious in every encounter. Much baggage undoubtedly was lost, and some three-pounders were abandoned; but nothing was taken by force.[10]

The reserve reached El Burgo that evening. Here 'extraordinary' measures had been taken to ensure the destruction of the bridge over the Mero. Having failed at the Mandeo, the Engineers were determined that this time they would succeed.

Once again it was the Light Company of the 28th, along with a company of the 95th, which had the job of holding the bridge until it was demolished. Though some of the men complained that they had been posted too close to the bridge, they were sneered at by the Engineers. Thus, wrote Blakeney, 'high-bred scientific theory scorned the vulgarity of common sense'. So the infantrymen waited pensively for the powder to ignite. 'The explosion at length took place, and completely destroyed two arches', continued Blakeney:

> large blocks of masonry whizzed awfully over our heads and caused what the whole of Soult's cavalry could not effect during the retreat. The light company of the 28th and Captain Cameron's company of the 95th broke their ranks and ran like turkeys, and regardless of their bodies crammed their heads into any hole which promised security. The upshot masonic masses continuing their parabolic courses passed far to our rear, and, becoming independent of the impetus by which they had been disturbed, descended and were deeply buried in the earth.[11]

One man of the 28th was killed, being almost cut in two by a flying piece of stone, and four others so severely wounded that they had to be carried down to Corunna. There was another fatality on the river that day. Further upstream at Cambria was another bridge over the Mero and it was thought that this should also be destroyed. Unfortunately, the supervising officer stayed too close to the mine and was blown up, to add to the Royal Engineers dismal catalogue. Nevertheless, both bridges were demolished and infantry pickets were placed on the eastern banks of the river opposite the broken bridges to prevent attempts by the French to repair them.[12]

Soult's cavalry reached the Mero later in the evening, watched by the rear-guard, which had taken up positions in houses in El Burgo with advance posts in the rubble of the bridges and along the banks of the river. The rest of the reserve was posted between El Burgo and Santiago.

The first of the French infantry arrived at the Mero on the morning of the 12th, opening fire on the British troops across the river. With large stocks of ammunition at Corunna, the 28th and 95th were able to return fire without reservation and it was evident that the rear-guard could hold El Burgo almost indefinitely. 'The advanced posts of the contending armies were only the breadth of two arches of a bridge asunder,' explained Blakeney. 'keeping up an incessant fire, so long as we could discover objects to fire at.'[13] So relaxed were the officers of the 28th, that evening they prepared a 'sumptuous' meal from the provisions sent up from Corunna. 'The men made fires and cooked our meat,' recalled Rifleman Green, 'took off our belts, sponged out our rifles, got a fresh supply of ammunition, took off our jackets, and found plenty of vermin on our bodies, which in some cases had found their way into flesh, as well as appearing outside. As knapsacks, and razors, and kit, were all thrown away, some of the older men had beards like Jews; not having been shaved since the commencement of the retreat.'[14]

All their troubles, it was confidently believed, were at an end. Unfortunately, Franceschi's cavalry found a bridge that had not been destroyed downstream at Cela. This oversight would cost the British army dear, and Moore his life.

As the transport convoy was still somewhere out in the Atlantic, there was no way of knowing when the ships would arrive, so the troops settled peacefully in and around Corunna, grateful for the rest after the terrible ordeals of the retreat. The evidence of the suffering that had been endured was most graphically portrayed by the effect the punishing pace over rough roads and lack of food had upon the horses. Robert Kerr Porter described the pitiful scenes in Corunna:

> Our cavalry and artillery horses on entering this city were found in such a state of debility and irremediable lameness from the want of shoes, that many fell dead in the streets, and more were obliged to be shot in mercy to their sufferings.
>
> The streets, the grand square, and piazzas are now being filled with their putrefying bodies. Horrible is the sight, and more horrible is the sound, for not a minute of the day is permitted to elapse without our hearing the report of some pistol or musket depriving these once noble creatures of life. The heavy rains have swollen and burst many of the carcasses; and the infected air hovers so rancorously about our heads, that it is almost

impossible to pass in any direction without feeling violent convulsions of stomach, and prognosticating all the calamitious effects of imbibed putrefaction.[15]

Preparations for the withdrawal of the army in anticipation of the arrival of the transports continued, most notably with the destruction or removal of a large number of barrels of gunpowder that had been sent to Corunna from England some months earlier, to prevent them falling into the hands of the enemy. Some 4,000 of these barrels ('unappropriated and unregarded by a nation infested with three hundred thousand enemies' complained William Napier) had been stored in a magazine on a hill three miles outside Corunna, with a further 1,500 barrels in another storehouse close to the first. These were both destroyed on 13 January, 'the inferior one blew up with a terrible noise, which shook the houses in the town; but when the [powder] train reached the great store,' wrote Napier, 'there ensued a crash like the bursting of a volcano':

> The earth trembled for miles, the rocks were torn from their bases, and the agitated waters rolled the vessels as in a storm; a vast column of smoke and dust, shooting out fiery sparks from its sides, arose perpendicularly and slowly to a great height, and then a shower of stones, and fragments of all kinds, bursting out of it with a roaring sound, killing many persons who remained too near the spot.[16]

What actually happened was related by the man responsible for dealing with the magazines, Lieutenant Colonel Cookson:

> I was put in orders to move 300 barrels of powder in Corunna. I placed the officers and men at a distance of 10 yards asunder to hand the barrels on to about 200 yards off to the wagons as it was very dangerous to have them nearer owing to the quantity of powder scattered about the magazines. I had removed about 200 barrels when I heard a murmuring among the men saying after such a distressing half-starved long march to be made porters of was too bad. This was followed up by swearing, they were completely knocked up and throwing the barrels down, some of

them burst and made the situation still more dangerous … After this unpleasant duty was settled an order was brought to me to prepare for blowing up the magazine.

After preparing the magazines, and making them safe from accidental explosion, Cookson went to find Moore, to tell him everything was ready. He found Moore with Hope and reported that the magazine was all set for destruction. 'Well then, Colonel,' said Moore, 'let them be blown up immediately, only take care that the neighbourhood and the troops are made acquainted with it so that there may no lives be lost.'

Cookson decided to ignite the smaller magazine first. So, when he laid the two fuzes, he cut half an inch off the one that ran to the smaller magazine. Cookson estimated that it would take twenty minutes for the magazines to explode after the fuses had been lit. When all was ready, the NCOs under Cookson's command lit the fuzes and the party retired. 'When we were about a quarter of a mile off,' continued Cookson:

I mounted my horse and rode to a position to have a full view of the explosion and looking at my watch I found the *portfires* had been lighted 23 minutes. The surrounding officers said that something must have happened to the train of powder. They had scarcely finished the sentence when the smaller magazine blew up followed by the larger immediately.

The sight of 12,000 barrels of powder, the quantity stated by the Spaniards, was terrifickly [*sic*] grand. The explosion from the well which was filled with barrels of powder had a very curious effect; some barrels absolutely blew up in the air. The running fire upon the ground was curious. The inhabitants of Corunna ran out of their houses exceedingly alarmed fancying the French were bombarding the town.[17]

According to Anthony Hamilton:

Corunna shook, as if convulsed by an earthquake. Huge masses of rock were cast from their pedestals. The calm waters of the bay became furiously agitated. A vast column of smoke and dust arose perpendicularly and slowly to a great height, and then bursting with a roaring sound, a shower of stones and fragments of all kinds reverted to the earth, killing several persons who had incautiously remained too near the scene of peril.[18]

It was not only the Spaniards who thought Corunna was under attack. Commissary Schauman, who was talking to three hussar quartermasters in his temporary office in the town, believed the French had begun to shell Corunna:

> Suddenly two such fierce flashes of lightening and claps of thunder burst over the town that my windows flew into our faces in a thousand pieces, the doors sprang open, the slates rolled from the roof, while I, who had just been rocking myself in my chair and talking, was flung backwards by the gust of hot air that poured in at the window. Even the quartermasters, who believed a bomb had fallen in the room and burst, ducked under the table ... Pulling ourselves together, we stared at each other in dumb amazement, when the streets suddenly filled with piteous cries. The whole population, particularly the women ... dashed out of their houses with despair written on their faces, and shouting like maniacs tore the hair from their heads.[19]

In fact, the French, having crossed the Mero far upstream, had attacked, but not with their artillery. Being on the outskirts of the town, the magazines were close to the outlying French pickets, and the British artillerymen were fired upon as they made a rapid retreat to Corunna. The enemy was getting closer.

The gunpowder was not the only item destroyed by the British troops. Moore had no intention of leaving anything behind that could be of use to the French, or that could not easily be taken on board the transports when they arrived – the most important thing was to save the men. Consequently, artillery wagons were thrown over the cliffs into the sea, and the horses of the artillery and the cavalry that were considered to be in such a poor condition that it was not worth trying to save them, were slaughtered. Many of the men that had suffered the trauma and trials of the retreat with unflinching resilience, broke down when they were compelled to kill these creatures. Amongst those who was moved by this dreadful sight was Captain Gordon, who saw how 'the hearts of the soldiers were more affected with feelings of pity and grief than by all the calamities and misery they had witnessed during the retreat':

> On this occasion the town exhibited the appearance of a vast slaughter-house. Wounded horses, mad with pain, were to be seen running through the streets, and the ground was covered with mangled carcasses of these noble animals; for, in consequence of their uncertain aim with the pistol, the men were latterly directed to cut the throats of the horses instead of attempting to shoot them.[20]

The sight shocked even a tough Scot of the 71st Highland Light Infantry:

> The beach was covered with dead horses, and resounded with the reports of the pistols that were carrying this havoc amongst them. The animals, as if warned by the dead bodies of their fellows, appeared frantic, neighed and screamed in the most frightful manner. Many broke loose and galloped alongst [sic] the beach with their manes erect and their mouths wide open.[21]

Only around 250 cavalry horses were considered fit enough to be saved, and some 700 artillery draught animals. The remainder, more than 2,000 in number, were killed and thrown into the sea.[22]

Barbaric and unnecessary such action may seem, the historian of the King's German Legion explained the reasoning behind the slaughter of the crippled animals: 'The embarkation of these in the face of an enemy would have been attended with difficulty and delay, and, therefore, in order to prevent them falling into the hands of the French, where their sufferings would have been protracted, they were ordered to be shot.'[23]

Aware that the French had found a means of crossing the Mero, Moore knew that he might have to fight Soult with the sea at his back, and that the chance of a peaceful embarkation had been lost. On the evening of the 13th, the Reserve was ordered to evacuate El Burgo with immediate effect. Paget, though, did not want to alert the French to the Reserve's departure, so the men were told that 'no regular formation whatever was to take place, neither regiments, companies, nor sections; every man was to move out independently.' The last to move out was the Light Company of the

28th: 'In obedience to this order the reserve commenced moving out of the town, directing their steps towards Corunna in the manner indicated,' wrote Blakeney:

> The light company perceiving the village evacuated by all except themselves, prepared to follow the example by moving out of the hothouse which they had occupied for two days, when all of a sudden we were not a little startled by a tremendous crash; a cannon-shot, followed by another and another, passed through the roof, shattering tiles, beams and every article that opposed.[24]

As the French had spotted the withdrawal of the Reserve, there was no longer any need for stealth and the 28th left El Burgo as rapidly as possible. The French had placed a battery of guns on the summit of a hill that overlooked the village. Paget had spotted this and realised that if his men formed up in the usual manner they would have made excellent targets for the French gunners. Thanks to Paget's instructions, the Reserve evacuated El Burgo without loss.

That day, the 13th, with the transports still at sea and in the expectation that he would most likely have to fight a major battle, Moore penned what would prove to be his last letter to Castlereagh, which was delivered by Charles Stewart, who could explain the campaign in detail:

> Your Lordship knows that had I followed my own opinion as a military man, I should have retired with the army from Salamanca. The Spanish armies were then beaten; there was no Spanish force to which we could unite; and I was satisfied that no efforts would be made to aid us, or favour the cause in which they were engaged. I was sensible, however, that the apathy and indifference of the Spaniards would never have been believed; that, had the British been withdrawn, the loss of the cause would have been imputed to their retreat; and it was necessary to risk this army to convince the people of England, as well as the rest of Europe, that the Spaniards had neither the power, nor the inclination, to make any efforts for themselves. It was for this reason that I marched to Sahagun. As a diversion it succeeded: I brought the whole disposable force of the French against this

army, and it has been allowed to follow it, without a single movement being made to favour its retreat.

The Marquis de la Romana was of no other use to me but to embarrass me by filling the roads by which I marched, with his cannon, his baggage, and his fugitives …

My position in front of this place is a very bad one; and this place, if I am forced to retire into it, is commanded within musket shot; and the harbour will be so commanded by cannon on the coast that no ship will be able to lay in it. In short, my Lord, General Stewart will inform you how critical our situation is.

If I succeed in embarking the Army, I shall send it to England – it is quite unfit for further service until it has been refitted, which can best be done there.

It was the following day, the 14th, that the bridge at El Burgo was rendered practicable for artillery, and Soult sent two infantry divisions with their accompanying guns, those of Merle and Mermet, and one of cavalry, over the river. Moore now knew for certain that there would be no easy embarkation, even though that evening the ships from Vigo hove in sight and soon after the transports – more than 100 of them – and the escorting twelve warships entered the harbour. Their arrival brought Robert Kerr Parker great joy, 'we saw in them an asylum from all our fatigues; and every exertion was made for instant embarkation.'

There was, indeed, no time to lose in case the wind should change. As it was likely that the French would try to take advantage of the disorganised state of his army as it broke formation to embark, Moore had to plan his withdrawal carefully. The nature of the defensive stand the British would have to adopt would present little opportunity for cavalry action, particularly as the ground between Moore's main position on the Monte Mero and Corunna was, according to Captain Basil Hall, 'a complete network of walls, hedges, and rows of olive-trees and aloes, of such intricacy that I should imagine it nearly impossible to have formed fifty men abreast anywhere'.[25] Paget's mounted regiments, therefore, and their remaining horses, were embarked, along with the sick, during the course of the night. If the British had to embark in a hurry the artillery, with its heavy guns, horse teams and caissons, would be a considerable encumbrance. It would help a speedy embarkation if the artillery could also be taken on board the transports during the night, but Moore could not leave his infantry without some form of artillery support. He decided to keep nine pieces with the infantry and embark the remainder. All this was accomplished by morning. Of the nine guns, three were given to Paget and the other six were distributed in pairs along the British positions.

The French had moved from El Burgo to occupy the Heights of Palavea and Peñasquedo, which rose to 600 feet and dominated the approaches to Corunna. Moore had considered occupying these hills, but they were far too extensive for his depleted band of 15,000 men. This was referred to by Schaumann, who had a view of the harbour from the window of the house of a Don Bernardo Mascoso where he was quartered:

> Corunna lies on the narrowest part of an irregular peninsula, and is protected by a chain of bastions. At one end stands the Citadel, which forms a sort of horn or arm encircling the harbour. At the other, which is the San Diego Point, there is a fort, in the middle of which on a rock there stands to castle of St. Antonio. To the south of the town there is a double chain of hills, along the lowest and flattest of which our army will take post.[26]

The positions actually adopted by the British army were described by Charles Stewart:

> There is a range of hills, or rather of swelling knolls which form an amphitheatre round the village of Evina, at the distance of perhaps a mile, or rather more, from the town of Coruna. Upon these Sir John Moore resolved to draw up his army; for, though there was a much more formidable range a mile or two further in advance, his numbers were inadequate for its occupation. He accordingly, stationed General Hope's division upon the left, posting it along a ridge which commanded the Betanzos road, and which sloped away, with a rearward inclination towards Elvina. At this place, Sir David Baird's Division took up the line, covering the hills which still bend in, and extend to a valley which divides this range from another on the opposite side of the Vigo road. Across that valley, the rifle corps threw itself in extended

order; and it was supported by Frazer's division, which covered the road to Vigo, and protected a principal approach to Corunna. The reserve, under General Paget, took post at a village, about half a mile in the rear of General Hope.[27]

Sir Charles Oman, writing 100 years later, described the British position as an excellent one. It was about two miles beyond the walls of Corunna and stretched for approximately 2,500 yards. It had one glaring defect identified by the late professor and fully understood by Moore. This was that the western end of the heights upon which the army was posted could be turned along low open ground that extended as far as the gates of Corunna.[28] There was also the possibility that Baird and Hope, to the south-east, could be separated from the rest of Moore's force around half a mile to the north-west.

There were mixed views amongst Moore's officers about the advisability of fighting a battle with their backs to the sea, being worried that in the event of a reverse the British would be trapped. Captain Boothby, on the other hand, believed that the position occupied by Moore's regiments was ideal:

> The hill itself, [Monte Mero] was very well against assault, because the side was very much intersected by steep banks and fences which, defended by our troops, could not be carried … The fortification of Corunna was infinitely better than any entrenchment thrown up occasionally. It was much improved and strengthened by us, and though its being fatally commanded, without bomb proof, and many other faults and disadvantages, natural and incurred, would prevent its pretending to withstand a regular siege, yet as a barrier against assault for a certain time it was as good as could be; 1,500 men might stand behind it and defy 20,000. Nothing, therefore, could be better to cover the tail of an embarkation.[29]

According to Moore's brother James, however, some of the experienced senior officers were:

> So impressed with the melancholy aspect of affairs, as to consider the state of the Army almost desperate. They thought

it their duty to represent to the Commander of the Forces the little probability there was of being able to resist the attacks of an Enemy cannonading and pouring upon them from the hills, while they were waiting for shipping. And even should the transports arrive, to embark in the face of a superior Enemy could not be accomplished without an enormous loss. From these considerations they counselled Sir John Moore to send to the Duke of Dalmatia, and propose to enter into terms with him, to permit the British army to embark unmolested.[30]

Andrew Leith Hay explained why some officers were worried about becoming involved in a full-scale battle:

the accoutrements of the soldiers lost or damaged during the retreat; the arms, in many cases, out of repair, and nearly rendered unserviceable, from the constant snow and rain which had fallen, when no time could be granted for putting them in a better state; the minds of officers and men harassed and dispirited by the disastrous aspect of affairs, or feeling the effects of excessive fatigue, encountered in the depth of winter, under circumstances of peculiar hardship, rendered the prospect of an action not so desirable as usual with British troops.[31]

Soult, though, was in no state to attack. The divisions of Heudelet and Delaborde were still struggling over the mountains, and the Duke of Dalmatia had fewer men under his immediate command than his British counterpart. Soult, no doubt champing on the bit, had no choice but to wait for the rest of his force to join him. Throughout the 15th, the opposing armies stared at each other across the valley between the two ranges of hills. As the hours ticked by, Moore began to believe that Soult would not attack.

The Duke of Dalmatia, however, was reinforced by Delaborde's division during the course of the day, and there was some skirmishing with Hope's outposts as the French took up their positions along the Heights of Peñasquedo. The opposing forces were now roughly equal in numbers, but with most of Moore's artillery having been embarked, Soult had a greater number of guns (figures vary between twenty and forty), and he saw the opportunity that the commanding Peñasquedo heights offered

him to make good use some of those guns, as a commissary called
Pierre Le Noble explained:

> Having occupied [the Heights of Peñasquedo], Marshal Soult
> immediately realised that it was an excellent position from which
> to open fire. A cannon placed there could enfilade the English line,
> he saw that this could do great damage. Orders were therefore
> quickly given to the commander of the artillery … to establish
> a grand battery there. We did not command any road that led to
> the position, and, given … the nature of the terrain, the obstacles
> that had to be overcome to get the artillery up there can easily
> be imagined. However, our gunners again proved that there was
> nothing they could not do, and by the morning of the sixteenth
> we had eight cannon and two howitzers in battery.[32]

On those rocky heights the rest of Soult's men were still moving
into position for the assault upon the British line as darkness fell on
the 15th. According to the men of the 95th, the French bands played
and excited shouts could be heard across the divide throughout
the night, signalling the certainty of a general action on the morrow
and with it, the enemy believed, the destruction or capture of the
British army.[33]

Chapter 11

'I Hope the People of England will be Satisfied!'

Moore went to bed late on 15 January and was woken at some time between 02.00 and 03.00 hours by his military secretary, with Major John Colborne reporting to Moore at the house he had taken on the Canton Grande. As there was still no indication that the French were willing to attack, Moore told Colborne that: 'if there is no bungling, I don't see why we should not all be off safely tomorrow.'[1]

Moore then arranged for the following General Order to be issued to the troops:

> Head Quarters, Corunna, 16th January, 1809.
>   The Commander of the Forces directs that Commanding Officers of Regiments will, as soon as possible after they embark, make themselves acquainted with the names of the ships in which the men of their regiments are embarked, both sick and convalescent: and that they will make out the most correct states of their respective corps: that they will state the number of sick present, also those left at different places: and mention at the back of the return where the men returned on command are employed.

The Reserve would be the first to embark at midday, having been told that 'in consequence of general good conduct during the retreat, and having covered the army at Corunna for two whole days', the men would be allowed to make themselves comfortable before the rest of the army joined them onboard.

The morning passed without incident and, from the Penasquedo Heights Captain Louis Florimond Fantin des Odoards of the French 31st Light Infantry, looked across the valley on a deceptively tranquil scene:

> As a light fog dispersed, an eminently picturesque view appeared to us. On the opposing heights were English troops, and beyond one could see the city of Corunna, its port and bay crowded with countless ships. A clear sky, brilliant sunshine and all the warmth of early spring completed the panorama. Nothing broke the complete silence that reigned in valley between the two armies.[2]

With no sign of any threatening movements from the French, about noon Moore decided to start embarking the rest of his force. He sent for his adjutant-general, Colonel Anderson, to finalise arrangements for the embarkation of the infantry. He told Anderson that if Soult had not attacked by 16.00 hours he,

> intended, if the French did not move, to begin embarking the Reserve at that hour. And that he would go out himself, as soon as it was dark, to send in the troops by brigades in the order he wished them to embark. He continued transacting business until a little after one o'clock, when his horse was brought. He then took leave of Colonel Anderson, saying, 'Remember, I depend upon your paying particular attention to everything that concerns the embarkation; and let there be as little confusion as possible.'[3]

Moore set off in 'good spirit' to discuss the arrangements for the withdrawal of the divisions from the Monte Mero. He had not gone far when he received a message from Hope, 'that the Enemy's lines are getting under arms,' which was confirmed by a deserter who had made his way into the British camp.

Suddenly, Soult's cannon opened fire, and a Royal Navy officer who had been walking along the British line, Captain Basil Hall, watched the response of Moore's men:

> The whole of the British troops, from one end of the position to the other, started on their feet, snatched up their arms, and

formed in line with as much regularity and apparent coolness as if they had been exercising on parade in Hyde Park. I really could scarcely believe my eyes when I beheld these men spring from the ground, full of life and vigour, though but one minute before they had been stretched out listlessly in the sun ... now, however, there could be heard a loud hum, and occasionally a jolly shout, and many a peal of laughter, along the distance of nearly a mile. In the midst of these sounds the peculiar sharp 'click-click-click' of fixing bayonets fell distinctly on the ear, very ominously.[4]

Major James Viney had been placed in command of the few artillery pieces left with the infantry after the remainder of the guns had been embarked. These consisted of eight light 6-pounders and four Spanish 8-pounders. These were formed into two brigades under captains Truscott and Wilmot. Six of the 6-pounders were with Paget's Reserve, with the others in forward positions. With these advanced guns was Bombardier Miller:

On 16 January, 1809, I was ordered out with the guns attached to the 'Forlorn Hope' Picquets to keep the enemy's advanced picquet at bay ... we were in a very poor state to wish for a battle, but, however bad our condition, fight we must, or be driven into the sea, for the enemy, perceiving our shipping [had] come and [was] ready for us to embark, they sent out strong parties to oppose our 'Forlorn Hope' picquet. We began to fire on them thinking they were only going to relieve their night picquet, but finding they advanced past their picquet and [were] beginning to fire, we began to think it a signal for a general action (or a 'killing day' as we soldiers term it).[5]

According to Miller, Moore and Baird were standing near the gun the Bombardier was commanding. The two generals went up to Miller and looked over the wheel of the gun with a spy-glass at the enemy. Moore apparently said: 'don't fire any more, Artillerymen, for I don't think it will come to a general engagement today'. Moore, though, was soon to see he had misread the situation, for the French bombardment signalled the start of the Battle of Corunna.

'That formidable battery opened the fight with a slaughtering fire,' wrote Captain William Napier, 'sending its bullets crashing through the English ranks from right to centre.' The anonymous Private of the 42nd, had not thought of having to fight until that moment, even though he was aware that his battalion was within cannon shot of the enemy. He reflected that there was a 'kind of fear' which had pushed the idea of a battle from his mind.

As the grand battery hammered relentlessly upon the British line on the Monte Mero, the French began to move. Merle's 1st Division and Delarborde's 3rd Division sent skirmishers out to engage Moore's left and centre, whilst Mermet's 2nd Division, with la Houssaye's dragons, moved towards the British on the right of the Monte Mero.

It was Mermet's 31st Light Infantry that led the attack against the Baird's light infantry outposts in Elviña. Marching with the 31st was Captain Odoards:

> To reach the enemy position, we had to go into a deep gully and climb its other side. At the same time, a powerful battery thundered from the heights we had left towards those of the English; they responded with a hot fire, and it was under a canopy of cannonballs criss-crossing over our heads we reached the enemy position.[6]

The advance of Mermet's battalions was watched from above by Major Charles Napier of the 50th Regiment:

> I stood in front of my left wing, on a knoll, from whence the greatest part of the field could be seen, and my picquets were fifty yards below, disputing the ground with the French skirmishers: but a heavy French column, which had descended the mountain at a run, was coming on behind with great rapidity, and shouting 'En avant, tue, tue, en avanttue!' their cannon at the same time, plunging from above, ploughed the ground and tore our ranks.

As it was now clear the French attack signalled the start of a major engagement the British troops looked for their commander. Major Napier shared his men's anxiety:

> Our line was under arms, silent, motionless, yet all were anxious for the appearance of Sir John Moore. There was a feeling that under him we could not be beaten … Where is the general? was now

heard along that part of the line where I was, for only of what my eyes saw, and my ears heard, do I speak. This agitation augmented as the cries of men stricken by cannon-shot arose. Suddenly I heard the gallop of horses, and turning saw Moore. He came at speed, and pulled up so sharp and close he seemed to have alighted from the air; man and horse looking at the approaching foe with an intenseness that seemed to concentrate all feeling in their eyes ... He glanced to the right and left, and then fixed his eyes intently on the enemy's advancing column, at the same time grasping the reins with both his hands, and pressing the horse firmly with his knees: his body thus seemed to deal with the animal while his mind was intent on the enemy, and his aspect was one of searching intenseness beyond the power of words to describe: for a while he looked, and then galloped to the left, without uttering a word.[7]

After eating lunch, Paget's Reserve had set off for the port when the roar of the opening shots of the battle reverberated around the valley. 'Our minds were occupied by thoughts of home; but we had not proceeded above a hundred yards when we heard the firing of the guns,' recalled Blakeney:

The division halted to a man, as if by word of command; each looked with anxious enquiry. But we were not kept long in suspense. An aide-de-camp came galloping at full speed to arrest our progress, telling us that an extraordinary movement was taking place throughout the enemy's line ... We instantly countermarched, and passed through the village of Los Ayres, where but twenty minutes before we had bidden adieu to Spain, and considered ourselves on the way to England.[8]

The French advanced with their usual élan into Elviña. Bullets hummed and hissed among the stone walls, ricocheting among the rocks, thudding into the wood and the turf. One by one the houses fell into the hands of the French as the British light infantry fell back.

Waiting on the Monte Mero was Bentinck's brigade, of the 4th, 42nd and 50th Foot. The anonymous sergeant of the 42nd watched the enemy infantry approaching:

In two very large compact columns down on our brigade ... Our artillery fired a few shots and then retreated for want of ammunition. Our flankers were sent out to assist the pickets. The French soon formed their line and advanced, driving the pickets and flankers before them, while their artillery kept up a close cannonade on our line with grape and round shot. A few of the Forty-Second were killed, and some were wounded … We had not moved an inch in advance or retreat.

The few British accounts that we have of the battle all mention Moore's presence with their respective regiments. Read together, one is left with the impression that that the British commander was constantly galloping up and down the line to encourage his men. This was, it seems, because Moore was thrilled at finally having the battle he had so long wished for. This is certainly the opinion of Thomas Graham:

> During the whole of the anxious time of the retreat from Sahagun to Corunna I was always near the General, except when sent by him with special orders; this gave me the opportunity of seeing how deeply he felt the disappointment of not being attacked by the enemy at Lugo. But for having observed that, I could scarcely have believed it possible for a man so worn down with fatigue and anxiety to have been so transformed as he was on the 16th January, 1809. It was a transition from fixed gloom, bordering almost on despair, to a state of exultation at the prospect of being attacked before the embarkation could take place.[9]

With regard to the 42nd said, he apparently said, 'There is no use in making a long speech, but, Forty-Second, I hope you will do as you have done before.' With that he put spurs to his horse and flew off to another part of the line. The 42nd, encouraged or not by Moore's endorsement, still had to face the enemy. According to the sergeant of the 42nd, the ground was hardly conducive to the manoeuvres of formed battalions, being rocky and full of ditches:

> The French did not advance very rapidly, on account of the badness of the ground. Our colonel gave orders for us to lie on the ground, at the back of the height our position was on; and whenever the French were within a few yards of us, and then give them the bayonet. They came up the hill cheering as if there was none to oppose them, we being out of their sight.

To the left of the 42nd was Napier's 50th Foot:

> I walked to the right of my regiment, where the French fire from
> the village of Elvina was now very sharp, and our picquets were
> being driven in by the attacking column; but I soon returned to
> the left, for the enemy's guns were striking heavily there, and
> his musquetry also swept down many men. Meeting [Major
> Charles Banks] Stanhope, I ordered him to the rear of the right
> wing, because the ground was lower, it was his place, he was
> tall, the shot flew high, and I thought he would be safer. Moore
> now returned, and I asked him to let me throw our grenadiers,
> who were losing men fast, into the enclosures in front. 'No,' he
> said, 'they will fire on our own picquets in the village.' 'Sir our
> picquets, and those of the 4th Regiment, also, were driven from
> thence when you went to the left.'[10]

When he heard this Moore agreed with Napier, riding away along
the Monte Mero. Napier therefore turned to Captain Clunes of
the 50th, who had just galloped up from Corunna, and told him
to take the grenadiers and 'start the ball'. The six foot five inches
tall Clunes – a 'Goliath' as bulky as he was tall – immediately
responded and led the Grenadier Company down the slope
towards the advancing enemy.

There was no doubt that the main French attack was being directed
at the right of the British position on the Monte Mero, but already
Paget's Reserve was marching to intercept Mermet's columns.
Moore had also ordered up Fraser's Division from Corunna and he
was confident that Mermet would soon find himself in trouble.

Until Paget and Fraser could make their presence felt, Bentinck's
men had to hold Mermet's attack. Moore, therefore, galloped up
to the 42nd and told Lieutenant Colonel James Sterling to drive
the French back down the hill. The Highlanders, as we have read,
had been lying down to shelter from the French cannon but then,
upon Sterling's command they leapt to their feet:

> When they [the French] came to the top of the hill, all the word
> of command that was given was 'Forty-Second: charge!' In one
> moment, every man was up with a cheer, and the sound of his
> musket, and every shot did execution. They were so close upon

us we gave them the bayonet the instant we fired … and many of us skewered pairs, front and rear rank. To the right about they went, and we after them … When we had driven them in upon their other columns, we ourselves retreated.[11]

Around this time Moore rode up again to assess the French attack and was talking to Napier when a roundshot struck the ground between Moore's horse's feet and Napier's. Moore's horse shied away, but the general quickly brought it back under control, asking at the same time if Napier was hurt. Napier said that he was fine, but then more shots whistled through the air. 'A second shot had torn off the leg of a 42nd man, who screamed horribly, and rolled about so as to excite agitation and alarm with others,' remembered Napier. 'The general said, "This is nothing my lads, keep your ranks, take that man away: my good fellow don't make such a noise, we must bear these things better."'[12] With that Moore flew off again.

The remaining companies of the 50th Regiment were still in line on the Monte Mero, with a frustrated Napier watching the fighting unfolding below:

> I walked up and down before the regiment, and made the men shoulder and order arms twice to occupy their attention, for they were falling fast and seemed uneasy at standing under fire. The colours also were lowered, because they were a mark for the enemy's great guns: this was by the advice of old John Montgomery, a brave soldier who had risen from the ranks. Soon the 42nd advanced in line, but no orders came for me. Good God! Montgomery, I said, are we not to advance?

Montgomery told Napier that he thought the battalion should follow the Highlanders, but Napier had not received any orders to move and as the other battalion in the brigade, the 4th, had not moved he was reluctant to leave his allotted position. He also knew that if he did advance and start to fire on the enemy he would have great difficulty disengaging and any retrograde movement, apart from causing disorder in the ranks, would have a negative effect on morale. Far better, Napier considered, to do nothing than place his battalion in a compromising position.

The reason why the 4th had not moved was because Moore could see la Houssaye's four regiments of dragoons picking their way through the broken ground to the right of the Monte Mero. It was, therefore, essential that the 4th held its ground to protect Baird's flank. Indeed, Moore ordered Lieutenant Colonel James Wynch to throw back the 4th's right wing to form an angle to present a front facing the advancing French cavalry. The 4th manoeuvred with such precision that Moore called out to Wynch, 'That is exactly how it should be done.' Baird himself, unfortunately, was an early casualty, a cannon ball shattering his left arm, and so Moore left the 4th to issue instructions to the rest of the brigade.

The 50th still remained without any orders from Bentinck or Moore. Again Montgomery urged an increasingly anxious Napier to attack, saying that he would never be wrong to follow the famous 42nd! It was enough for Napier and he decided to move down the hill alongside the Highlanders but, as he wanted to keep his men in hand, he ordered them slope their muskets. The 50th moved off, with some of the men begging the major to let them open fire. 'Not yet,' answered Napier:

> At that moment the 42nd checked a short distance from a wall and commenced firing, and though a loud cry arose of Forward! forward! no man, as I afterwards heard, passed the wall. This check seemed to prove that my advance was right, and we passed the 42nd. Then I said to my men, Do you see your enemies plain enough to hit them? Many voices shouted, By Jasus we do! Then blaze away! and such a rolling fire broke out as I have hardly ever heard since.[13]

As the 42nd had halted, the 50th found itself on its own but Napier was committed and all he could do was continue with his counter-attack with as much determination as possible:

> After passing the 42nd we came to the wall, which was breast high and my line checked, but several officers, Stanhope one, leaped over, calling on the men to follow. At first about a hundred did at a low part, no more, and therefore, leaping back, I took a halberd and holding it horizontally pushed many over the low part; and again getting over myself I ran along, followed by my orderly

199

sergeant, Keene, with his pike. As we passed, four or five soldiers levelled their muskets together from the other side, but Keene threw up their muskets with a force and quickness which saved me from being blown to atoms.

Napier had come so close, quite literally, to being killed that his face was burned by the exploding French muskets. But the 50th could not stop now and eventually all the men were over the wall, though, according to Napier, it was only through the example of the officers and a few brave men:

> Now the line was formed beyond the wall … the check at the wall had excited me and made me swear horribly. We then got to marshy ground close to a village, where the fire from the houses was terrible, the howitzers from the hills pelting us also. Still I led the men on, followed closely by Ensigns Moore and Stewart with the colours until both fell, and the colours were caught up by Sergeant Magee and another sergeant. My sword-belt was shot off, scabbard and all, but not being hit I pushed rapidly into the street, exactly at the spot where, soon after, I was taken prisoner. Many Frenchmen lay there, apparently dead, and the soldiers cried out bayonet them, they are pretending. The idea was to me terrible, and made me call out No! no! leave those cowards, there are plenty who bear arms to kill, come on!

With small groups of the 42nd now following, the 50th charged on, but no longer in any semblance of order. This was exactly the situation Napier had sought to avoid, and the further he advanced the more perilous his position became:

> At this place stood the church, and towards the enemy a rocky mound, behind which, and on it, were the grenadiers [of the 50th] yet no officer met my sight, except Captain Harrison, Lieutenant Patterson, and Lieutenant Turner, and my efforts were vain to form a strong body; the men would not leave the rocks, from which they kept up a heavy fire.
>
> No time was to be lost, we could not see what passed on our flanks, we had been broken in carrying the village of Elvina, and as a lane went up straight towards the enemy, I ran forward calling out to follow: about thirty privates and the above-named officers did so, but the fire was then terrible, many shells burst

among us, and the crack of these things deafened me, making my ears ring. Half way up the lane I fell, without knowing why, but was much hurt, though at the moment unconscious of it.[14]

Seeing Napier fall, one of the 50th called out that the major was dead. But Napier got back on his feet and called out 'Not yet, come on':

We reached the end of this murderous lane, but a dozen of those who entered it with me fell ere we got through it. However, some shelter was found beyond the lane; for Brooks of the 4th had occupied the spot with his picquet the day before, and had made a breastwork of loose stones, which was known to me, having been there, and nearly killed the evening before, when visiting the picquet as officer of the day. The heap remained, and about a dozen of us lodged ourselves behind this breast work, and then it appeared to me that by a rush forward we could carry the battery above; and it was evident we must go on or go back, we could not last long where we were.[15]

The breastwork was only a 'slender' construction, offering but slight protection and three or four men were killed at Napier's side. Two were killed by the fire from the men in Elviña behind them. One of those was hit in the back of his head, crying out, 'Oh God! Major, our own men are killing us!'

Napier tells us that at that moment he recalled that his father had saved a man's life during fighting in the American Revolution by pulling a musket ball out of the soldier's head. Napier decided he would try to do the same, and began to probe into the hole in the man's skull. But he could not find the bullet and it made him feel sick pocking inside someone's head. Fearing that he would do more harm than good if he pushed his finger deeper, he left the man alone, and to die, on the ground, still crying that he had been shot by his own men.

Napier, and the few men that had advanced with him, remained detached from the rest of the battalion which, despite the urgings of Major Stanhope, refused to move forward. Mad with frustration, Napier leapt up:

I got on the wall, waving my sword and my hat at the same time, and calling out to the men behind among the rocks; but the fire was so loud none heard me, though the lane was scarcely a hundred yards long … My own companions called out to jump down or I should be killed: I thought so too, but was so mad as to care little what happened to me.

Having driven Mermet out of Elviña Napier then decided to search along the line to see if he could gather enough men from the 42nd to join him in charging the battery on the Peñasquedo Heights. Armed with just his sabre and without his spectacles (he was very short-sighted) he moved off alone. After almost blundering into the French positions, Napier walked back only to find his men had gone:

> I felt very miserable then, thinking the 50th had behaved ill; that my not getting the battery had been a cause of the battle being lost, and that Moore would attribute all to me. The English smoke had gone back, and my only comfort was that the French smoke had not gone forward. The battle seemed nearly over, I thought myself the last man alive belonging to our side who had got so far in front, and felt certain of death, and that my general would think I had hidden myself, and would not believe me to have done my best.

Disappointed and dejected, Napier turned back towards Elviña and the Monte Mero. On the way, he encountered a badly wounded man of the 50th. Napier bent down to help the soldier and was struck by a French musket ball, which broke a bone in his leg just above the ankle. Now only able to limp along, Napier had to leave the soldier who was still imploring the major to help him.

As Napier made his way back through Elviña, he met three privates of the 50th and one of the 42nd, who said that they were cut off and indeed Napier saw that parties of Frenchmen were running up the lanes on both sides. Seeing no escape, Napier chose what appeared to be the smallest of the enemy parties, he led the four privates in a wild bid to cut their way through the advancing French infantry:

> The Frenchmen had halted, but now run on to us, and just as my spring and shout was made the wounded leg failed and I felt a stab in the back: it gave me no pain, but felt cold and threw me

on my face. Turning to rise I saw the man who had stabbed me making a second thrust; whereupon letting go my sabre I caught his bayonet by the socket, turned the thrust, and raising myself by the exertion grasped his firelock with both hands, thus in mortal struggle regaining my feet. His companions had now come up and I heard the dying cries of the four men with me, who were all bayoneted instantly.

Napier's little group had been attacked from behind by enemy troops who had burst out of the house at the back of the four British soldiers. The four privates were killed but Napier fought on with the musket he had wrenched out of the hands of his attacker:

> At that moment a tall dark man came up, seized the end of the musket with his left hand, whirled his brass-hilted sabre round and struck me a powerful blow on the head, which was bare, for my cocked hat had fallen off.

The man raised his sword and struck at Napier again. The major ducked down trying to avoid the next blow, but it landed again on top of his head:

> Fire sparkled from my eyes, I fell on my knees, blinded, yet without quite losing my senses and holding still on to the musket. Recovering in a moment, I regained my legs, and saw a florid handsome young French drummer holding the arm of the dark Italian, who was in the act of repeating his blow.

That young drummer saved Napier's life. Napier was taken prisoner, though the French infantrymen tore his breeches as they robbed him of his watch and his purse.

Though Napier had thought his battalion had given way under pressure from Mermet's division, in fact Bentinck had ordered the 50th and the 42nd to withdraw. Napier's charge into Elviña had certainly blunted the French advance, but had left a large gap in the British line. Reports had also been received of la Houssaye's dragoons continuing to progress round the flank of the Monte Mero and Paget's Reserve, though marching hard towards the scene, had not yet arrived. Moore therefore needed to re-establish a solid line on the Monte Mero, calling back the remnants of 50th and 42nd and ordering forward Major General Henry Warde's two Guards battalions. Once order had been restored, Moore could mount another counter-attack with these fresh troops.

The situation at this point in the action was described by Thomas Graham:

> The Guards were ordered up to take up the ground where the 42nd and 50th had stood; the 4th, thrown back from the first, was protected by a deep hollow way and a garden wall, and kept up a heavy fire on the column which remained crowded in the village, where the enemy must have lost a great number of men. About this time the sun was setting, and the smoke hung entirely to our right.
>
> A report prevailed that the enemy had pushed a column round that way, and as nothing was heard from General Paget, the General [Moore] wished to make a diversion by an attack on their centre at the bottom of the hill, where, at the White House and Oak Wood, they were in considerable force.
>
> The left battalion of the Guards was advanced for this purpose, but owing to an improper formation, got into some confusion which obliged them to fall back and form behind a wall; at the same time the left company of the 42nd conceiving they were to be relieved by the Guards, retired up a narrow lane.[16]

Seeing the 42nd withdrawing, but possibly not realising why the battalion was retiring, Moore rode up to the Highlands and called out: 'My brave 42nd, if you've fired your ammunition, you still have your bayonets. Recollect Egypt! Think on Scotland! Come on my gallant country-men.'[17]

The 42nd immediately faced to the front again, and Moore, ceremoniously, took his hat off to them. It was shortly after this, as Moore watched the Guards moving up to take position with Bentinck's brigade, that a round shot crashed into Moore's left shoulder, almost ripping it from his body.

Thomas Graham recorded the moment in his diary:

> The enemy, whose artillery all day had been directed with much precision and rapidity against groups of mounted officers, continued firing at this spot, when at last a fatal ball took the General under the left arm, shattering the ribs and almost severing

the arm from his body; he fell at my horse's feet; but such was the invariable firmness of his mind, such the consciousness of his rectitude, that he bore this pain without an altered feature. I scarcely thought him wounded till I saw the state of his arm.[18]

Captain Henry Hardinge was also by Moore's side:

> The violence of the stroke threw him off his horse onto his back. Not a muscle of his face altered, nor did a sigh betray the least sensation of pain. I dismounted and, taking his hand, he pressed mine forcibly, casting his eyes anxiously towards the Forty-Second Regiment, which was hotly engaged, and his countenance expressed satisfaction when I informed him that the regiment was advancing. Assisted by a soldier of the Forty-Second, he was removed a few yards behind the shelter of a wall … The blood flowed fast [and] the attempt to stop it with my sash was useless from the size of the wound.
>
> He assented to being removed in a blanket. In raising him for this purpose, his sword … touched his wound and became entangled between his legs. I perceived the inconvenience and was in the act of unbuckling it when he said in his usual tone and manner, 'It is well as it is; I had rather that it should go out of the field with me.'[19]

Moore was carried off by six men of the 42nd, Hardinge's sash helping to support him. As he was being transported to the rear he frequently asked the Highlanders to stop and turn him round so that he could see the battlefield. What he saw was the French withdrawing across the whole front. The divisions of Merle and Delaborde had sent only their light troops against the centre and left of the Monte Mero but had made no impression upon the brigades of Hill, Leith and Manningham, and over to the right the Reserve had finally arrived from the west.

Paget's men immediately made their presence felt, with Blakeney's 28th Foot eager to exact revenge on those that had pursued them across the mountains:

> The enemy's column [that had] passed by Baird's right, flushed with the idea of having turned the right of the British army (since the 4th Regiment had retired their right wing), moved sternly

forward, certain, as they thought, to come in rear of our troops. But as they advanced, they met the reserve coming on with an aspect as stern and determined as their own; they now discovered the true right of the British army. The advanced troops of Soult's army during the march now formed his left; we recognised each other … A thousand passions boiled in every breast … We painfully recollected the wanton carnage committed on … defenceless stragglers … and the many the cold nights we [had] passed in the mountains of Galicia … The haughty and taunting insults, too, of our gasconading pursuers were fresh in our memory …

Thus urged forward by mutual hate, wrought up to the highest pitch by twelve days' previous fighting, and knowing the approaching conflict to be our last farewell, we joined in the fight.[20]

Moving along the right bank of the Menelos river, Paget's five battalions reached the edge of the Monte Mero whilst la Houssaye's cavalrymen were still winding their way around the walled enclosures and small buildings between San Cristobal and Elviña. Paget took his men up the slope to extend the British flank and so that they could face the French head on.

In open order, the 95th and the 52nd moved directly against the dragoons supported by the 28th and the 91st. The low walls, which gave excellent cover to the riflemen, rendered the French cavalry impotent. Sat high on their mounts and unable to charge or move at speed, the dragoons made perfect targets. Seeing his men being picked off with deliberate ease by the 95th, la Houssaye ordered them to dismount and fight on foot. Dragoons were, in theory, mounted infantry, and Napoleon's dragoons did often fight as light infantry, being trained and armed accordingly. Trained or not, the dragoons were no match for the British light infantry, among whom was John Dobbs of the 52nd:

The 52nd [was] ordered to relieve the rifle corps (their ammunition being expended and most of their swords out of order) which we did in extended order, sending the colours to the rear. Sir Sidney Beckwith met us, calling out, 'Come here with your bayonets, come here with your bayonets.' Reynett's company, in which I was one of the first engaged, and the first man hit was close by me; he fell apparently dead by the ball, it having entered the forehead and passed out at the back of the head, so that I said nothing could be done for him; but what was my surprise afterwards to find he was not killed, the ball having passed round the head under the skin.[21]

The dragoons were driven back as the Reserve steadily advanced, Paget's men even clashing with some of Mermet's infantry as they pushed on towards the lower slopes of the Peñasquedo Heights within striking distance of the grand battery.

It was evident that the French had been beaten and Moore had the satisfaction of knowing that he had won a famous victory. He knew also that he was dying due to the vast extent of his injuries, which John Colborne described as horrible: 'the ball had carried away his left breast, broken two ribs, shattered the shoulder, and the arm was scarcely attached to it, the whole of his left side lacerated.'[22]

He was taken to the headquarters room in Corunn accompanied by his old friend Paul Anderson. To each person that crept into the room he asked about the battle, being repeatedly reassured that victory was his. 'You know, Anderson', Moore said, 'I have always wished to die this way, I hope the people of England will be satisfied! I hope my country will do me justice!'[23] Though his country would indeed do him justice, many of the people of England were far from satisfied with Moore's conduct, as will shortly be seen

Chapter 12

Consequences

Night stole in as the fighting died down. The British had won what might be only a brief respite and the hours of darkness presented them with the chance to embark on the waiting ships that they could not squander.

Following the death of Moore and the injury to Baird's arm, Hope, 'a handsome man, with a bold military air', assumed command and was seen by Schaumann organising the embarkation, 'charging through the streets like mad, fresh from the battlefield, issuing orders left and right'. As senior officer, it was Hope who had the task of compiling the official report of the battle:

> The Troops quitted their Position about Ten at Night, with a Degree of Order that did them credit. The whole of the Artillery that remained unembarked, having been withdrawn, the Troops followed in the Order prescribed, and marched to their respective Points of Embarkation in the Town and Neighbourhood of Corunna. The Piquets remained at their Posts until Five on the Morning of the 17th, when they were also withdrawn with similar Orders, and without the Enemy having discovered the Movement.[1]

Robert Blakeney agreed with Hope that the withdrawal had been conducted efficiently:

> As darkness approached, our picquets as usual lit large fires; and the British army retired to Corunna, and embarked that night without the slightest confusion, so completely had everything been previously arranged. On the morning of the 17th, the picquets being withdrawn, the wounded were collected and with

the exception of very few put on board, covered by a brigade still left on shore for that purpose.[2]

Such descriptions conceal the true state of affairs in Corunna Bay. For with the night had come mist and while all the wounded and much of the rest of the army were safely on board by daylight of 17 January, the sailors rowing from ship to shore had often gone astray, as John Dobbs recalled:

> We found the boats waiting for us and immediately pushed off, but lost one another in the darkness, and some of us not knowing where to find our ships got on board the first we came to, sending back the boats for others who were waiting for them.[3]

Adam Neal was watching from onboard one of the ships in the harbour:

> About eight o'clock on the morning of the 17th, we were astonished, by observing that the enemy had got possession of the heights above St. Lucia, from which he opened a spirited fire from three pieces of cannon, upon the ships in the inner harbour. Nothing was now to be seen but the most dreadful confusion. The transports slipped their cables, and put to sea instantly; many running foul of each other, and carrying away yards, bowsprits, and rigging. Four or five ships, in attempting to run between the island of St. Antonio and the citadel, ran aground on the rocks, and bilged. A seventy-four gun ship immediately stood in towards the French batteries, and opened her guns upon them.[4]

Hussey Vivian also saw the transports come under fire, believing that: 'no fleet of transports ever got under weigh so quickly! In less than half an hour the bay was clear!'[5] The trouble was that hundreds of troops were still on shore – and now stranded.

The only ships that remained at Corunna were the Royal Navy vessels, and they began to take the remaining troops on board. But the men crowding together by the harbour steps offered the French gunners an easy target and they came under fire from the heights. One of the naval officers called out to the soldiers to make their way round to the lighthouse where they would find better protection, and the sloops would wait for them there.

The men had to march back through Corunna to reach the other side of the harbour. Here they found the water breaking 'furiously' on the rocks. Commissary Schaumann was one of those men:

> The sloops from the men-o'-war could not come up close, but were kept at a safe distance from the rocky boulders by means of their oars, while we had to go to the edge of the rocks which were being washed by the surf, and then, with the water splashing over our heads, take hold of one of the oars. Then we were grasped by the mighty fists of the sailors, who were leaning overboard, and seized and dragged in like sheep.[6]

This meant that it was not possible for the soldiers to take any baggage with them, and everything had to be abandoned or cast into the sea. The sloops raced out to sea, the soldiers being 'flung' onto the first ship that the sailors could reach.

Gunner Miller watched this from one of the transports:

> As we drifted down the harbour we saw hundreds of our soldiers, which had been doing duty in the garrison, sitting on rocks by the water's side at the back of the town, waving their hats and calling for the boats to take them off and as many women and children among them. They saw us pass without seeming to take any notice of them and expecting every minute to be made prisoners, not knowing there were two companies of artillery left on the batteries, which could keep the enemy out of the garrison for that night and indeed not knowing that boats would be sent for them in the night.

The situation was explained in an official report from the chief agent for transports, Captain James Bowen:

> The tide being out when it [the embarkation] commenced, the troops were obliged to wade into the Boats up to their necks in water, the night was excessively dark, the transports were obliged to lie at a considerable distance, a gale of wind coming on as the tide flowed and the surf greatly endangering the safety of the

boats. To all this may be added the utmost efforts of a persevering enemy whose fire more tremendous from its noise than from its effects. The latter part of the evacuation proceeded though he [the enemy] had not the satisfaction of sinking a boat or destroying a single man.[7]

The rear-guard was not embarked until the evening of the 17th, with Colonel Harding writing to the Deputy Adjutant General that:

> Captain Truscott's Company came in at night with the army, and occupied the Citadel with the Spanish Brigade. Capt Wilmott's [Wilmot's] retired at the same time, but could not embark the guns, owing to the Boats being occupied in embarking the remainder of the troops, during the night. Major General Beresford, with 3 Regiments of the Line and 3 Companies of artillery under Major Beevor, formed the rear guard, to embark on the night of the 17th instant. At the time I embarked on the 17th, boats were sent to embark Wilmott's [Wilmot's] guns at a cove in the rear of the town; but the wind blew so strong, and the swell was so high that I fear they could not embark before the evening; when it became more moderate.[8]

Beresford's brigade was the last to embark from behind Corunna's Citadel in the early hours of the 18th, leaving the small Spanish garrison to hold off the French. The Spaniards kept Soult's men at bay until the last of the British warships were far out at sea, and then 'rather tamely' surrendered.[9]

A total of 227 transports plus Hood's squadron, evacuated more than 26,000 men from Vigo and Corunna.[10] Though it had cost him his life, Sir John Moore had saved the army entrusted to his care.

After battling through tempestuous seas, in which two transports were lost off the Cornish coast, the ships reached ports along the south coast where the inhabitants were shocked at the site of the ragged, emaciated troops who were 'literally covered and almost eaten up with vermin, most … suffering from ague and dysentery, every man a living still active skeleton.'[11] 'We were strange figures,' wrote Captain Seton of the 92nd Regiment, 'all dirty, and the most of us almost naked … When we landed at Portsmouth I had neither shoes nor stockings but had to walk along the streets barefooted; the condition we were in with regard to clothing and cleanliness beggars description. When we came to our billets about six miles from Portsmouth, the inhabitants would not allow us to sleep in their beds, nor sit by the fireside, on account of the vermin that infested us.'[12]

The state of the troops, and the loss of so much equipment, horses and money for no apparent gain, led to much criticism of Moore's conduct. His daring bid to fall on Soult's II Corps had ended with a somewhat ignominious evacuation and, in the view of many at the time, Moore had shown himself to be fearful and indecisive. This was certainly the opinion of one of his young officers who was clearly close to the British commander:

> Sir John Moore proved lamentably deficient in those qualities of decision and firmness which he had so often displayed on former occasions, and which alone would have enabled him to extricate the army by some brilliant achievement, from the perilous situation in which it had been placed by his own ill-advised measures and the disasters of our Spanish allies. At this juncture, however, he appeared to labour under a depression of spirits so different from his usual serene and cheerful disposition as to give a mournful expression to his countenance, indicative of the greatest anxiety of mind; and it seemed either that his judgment was completely clouded or that he was under the influence of a spell which forced him to commit the most glaring errors.[13]

Alexander Gordon also believed that Moore's death at the moment of victory merely 'cast a veil of glory over the errors of his judgement.' Gordon went on to write:

> So fine and well appointed army as that under the command of Sir John Moore was probably never sent into the field either by this or any other nation; but in the space of four weeks – from the day on which the several corps were united – this force, which both for its appearance and behaviour had been the admiration of all who saw it, after a race of 260 miles, without having been

engaged and almost without having seen an enemy, embarked with the loss of the greater part of its baggage and stores, nearly a fourth of its numbers, and the remainder enfeebled by famine and disease. Yet this army, at the point of embarkation, in a disadvantageous position, and almost without artillery, defeated the very enemy from whom it had so disgracefully retreated. Such a complete disorganization of a well-disciplined army in so short a space of time, such a lamentable change in the character of the soldiers, can only be ascribed to the ill-judged precipitancy of the retreat, and the undecided measures of the commander, by which he forfeited the confidence of his troops.[14]

Another officer of the 15th, Edwin Griffith, expressed similar views to those of Gordon, agreeing that Moore had lost the confidence of the troops he commanded by his rush to the coast:

The province of Galicia is perhaps the strongest by nature, and is the easiest to be defended of any country on the face of the earth. Surrounded by mountains whose sides are almost inaccessible and height immense it would be hardly possible even for infantry to enter it except by passes; and in these passes there are positions where … a handful of men might arrest the progress of millions; there were also bridges thrown over chasms at the bottom of which run large and rapid rivers; had these been destroyed as soon as we had passed, it must have stopped the pursuit of the French cavalry for a certain time, and the artillery for many days. Unhappily these advantages were neglected, and trusting more to celerity of movement, than to the usual stratagems of war, Sir John subjected his army to the humiliating accusation of being actually driven into the sea by the French.[15]

Even Commissary Schaumann, not a man given to speculation, made the following comments, reflecting on what he had heard expressed by many in the army:

Many people blame General Moore very severely for having made his army retreat so fast across mountain and passes, which might have been so splendidly defended, and for having in this way allowed everything to go to ruin. Others say that he was obliged to do it, if he did not want to be cut off, enveloped, or starved to death. The wild mountains had neither corn nor bread. True, but there were flocks of sheep and goats among them, and there were also our horses, mules and draft-bullocks. With these we might at least have been able to hold out until the sick, the wounded, the ammunition and the war treasure had been sent to the coast in safety.[16]

Lieutenant Andrew Leith Hay agreed that there was no military need for the precipitous retreat, but he blamed it on the lack of knowledge of the country under which the British had to operate:

> It becomes a subject of regret that so little was known of the real state of the country, and of the possibility of the communications being cut off, as to occasion a rapidity of retreat unnecessary, and attended with the worst consequences: from the moment the British divisions had passed through Astorga there was nothing to endanger their safety: they retired upon their supplies, had the ports of Vigo, Coruña, and Ferrol, open to them; nor was there any practicable route by which a body of French troops, with artillery, could have penetrated through the mountains and fallen on the supplies, or obstructed the march of the British army. The Marquis de la Romana's force would have prevented any attempts on the right flank of Sir John Moore's army; and had there been a corps of the enemy in a situation to have operated on the left, it must have encountered all the difficulties attending a march through the mountains of Asturias and Galicia in the depth of winter, a movement it could not have executed without expending more time than would have been sufficient for the British to retire upon Coruña.[17]

John Colborne, who as Moore's military secretary was better informed than most of the difficulties his commander was faced with, explained why it had not been possible for Moore to make a determined stand in Galicia:

> The mountains of Galicia are formidable to an enemy, but had we attempted to defend the passes and Galicia in the winter by placing a regular army in position without cover or supplies

in a country exhausted by the continual passage of troops, it must have been exposed to such fatigue and privations as would have occasioned its destruction.

Near Astorga the ground is not sufficiently favourable to induce an inferior army to wait the attack of an accumulating force or risk an action. At Foncebadon, one of the points of defence of this mountainous district, an enemy might be opposed with advantage; but no important object was to be gained by halting there and defending that pass. The Galicias may be penetrated by roads from Zamora, Benevente and Braganza to Puebla de Sanabria, and thence by the Val de Jares and the valley of the Sil to Lugo. Magazines and cover for the troops would have been required had Sir John Moore halted, and the enemy, being able to choose his time of attack, would have compelled him to abandon the mountains, when his combinations might have rendered a retreat impracticable.[18]

Also in Moore's defence, his brother James pointed out that, 'neither Napoleon nor the Duke of Dalmatia won a piece of artillery, a standard, or a single military trophy, from the British Army'. It is also the case that Moore received little help in his operations from the Spaniards, a point made by many, including Kerr Porter:

Although many of them have shewed [sic] themselves to us from the mountain tops in arms; and well aware as they are of the use they might be in covering our retreat; yet no exertion has been attempted on their part to arrest the progress of the French even for a moment: such an effort could easily have been made from their knowledge of these native bulwarks ... I must confess, that on seeing these men with musquets [sic] &c., prowling about in large bodies amongst the heights, we took it for granted that they turned out to support us ... These valiant Galicians, these redoubted patriots, were only leaving their homes that they might not assist us.[19]

Moore himself was angered at the attitude of the Spaniards, making the following observation in his last letter to Castlereagh:

The people of the Gallicias, though armed, made no attempt to stop the passage of the French through their mountains. They abandoned their dwellings at our approach, drove away their carts, oxen, and every thing that could be of the smallest aid to the army. The consequence has been, that our sick have been left behind; and when our horses and mules failed, which on such marches, and through such a country, was the case to a great extent, baggage, ammunition, stores, and even money, were necessarily destroyed or abandoned.

Of course it is that money, which Schaumann and Moore both refer to, that is our primary concern in this book. Their comments reflect the peculiar circumstances surrounding the discarding of the military chest. The very act of, quite literally, throwing money away, is such an alien concept that it had a profound effect upon those who witnessed it and those who knew of it.

Nevertheless, the lack of support from the Spaniards, as we have seen, was a frequent complaint of Moore's troops, who could not understand why the Spaniards offered no help to the men who were trying to save their country from invasion, as Adam Neal made clear in his personal account:

Our soldiers were frequently incensed at finding that the offer of a dollar would not induce a peasant to part with a morsel of rusty bacon, a few garlic sausages, or a bit of bread, which often, in fact, were not intrinsically worth one-third of the sum.

On arriving of an evening at their villages, after a most fatiguing march – wet to the skin, yet expiring with thirst, these unfeeling mortals often refused, when requested by our men, to run to the adjoining fountain for a pitcher of water, or to procure a few heath-roots to make a fire.[20]

Similarly, young William Warre, who later rose to the rank of lieutenant general, placed all the blame for the difficulties the British troops experienced at the feet of the Spaniards: 'Never have a nation been more infamously deceived than the English about this country … We have not seen, since we have been in the country, a symptom of organisation or, till lately, a Recruit.'[21]

Captain George Napier, one of Moore's aides, expressed the same views: 'We have made a most *rapid retreat*; & the General most richly deserves the thanks of his Country, for saving this army, by his own Superior talents, for he received not the slightest assistance from the Spaniards, on the contrary, they seemed to wish for the success of the French; damn their souls.'[22]

As always, there are two sides to the story, and Thomas Graham had to admit that, 'The soldiers very disorderly, the officers negligent, the whole Army, with few exceptions, such as the reserve, disorganised in the most disgraceful manner.' Moore himself was shocked at the lack of discipline exercised by the officers under his command: 'I couldn't have believed it possible,' he wrote, 'had I not witnessed it, that a British army could in so short a time have been so completely disorganised. Its conduct has been infamous beyond belief.'[23] Colonel Lord John Proby found even stronger words to express his disgust with the actions of the troops:

> Englishmen are not capable of bearing all at once the fatigues which this army has undergone … Our line of march presents such a scene of desolation as I believe was ever occasioned by an army before, & our conduct in this respect has left an impression upon the country that is most unfavourable to us, & will not easily be effaced.[24]

This was echoed by the Marquess de la Romana, who was stinging in his condemnation of the British:

> The English have seized … the mules and oxen that drew our army's artillery, munitions and baggage train … They have stolen all the mules of the inhabitants of Benevente and the pueblos of the Tierra de Campos, and have left a multitude of carts abandoned by the wayside, some of them broken down and others smashed up on purpose. They have without necessity killed and eaten the oxen that pulled these carts and have not paid their value. They have killed three magistrates and various other inhabitants. After allowing anyone who wanted to drink their fill without paying a penny, they have poured away all the wine in the cellars. They have not paid for the carts and animals that they have used to move their women and their immense baggage trains … In a word the French themselves could not have found agents better calculated to whip up hatred of the British than the army commanded by General Sir John Moore.[25]

In all of this, it must not be forgotten that for more than 200 years England and Spain had been the most bitter of enemies. Gibraltar had been seized from Spain in 1704, and only three years before the English troops landed in Mondego Bay the Spanish fleet had been destroyed at Trafalgar. It was perhaps unrealistic to expect the Spaniards to suddenly embrace the soldiers of the nation that had caused them so much past and recent harm. It might also be recalled that it was from Corunna that the Spanish Armada had sailed in the bid to invade England in 1588. The two nations had rarely been on the best of terms for a long time.

Not a few laid blame for the entire episode on the British Government, with a debate on the decision to send an expeditionary force to Spain taking place in the House of Commons on 24 February 1809. In the opening speech, MP George Ponsonby pointed out that there had been no discussion beforehand in Parliament about sending an army to help the Spaniards, and the administration had taken upon itself the decision to become embroiled in the war in the Peninsula. According to Ponsonby, it was therefore incumbent upon ministers: 'to examine, with precision and accuracy, all the means in their reach to employ, and how far those means were adequate to the ends in view. Before they attempted to involve the country in the contest alluded to, before they ventured so to engage its wealth and its power, they should have taken care to make this examination, and, above all, to ascertain the real state of Spain … What was the spirit of the people, what the internal condition of the country, what the state of its parts, what its resources, both military and naval, what, in a word, the means upon which we could calculate for success in pursuit of the common object?'[26]

Ponsonby argued that when Moore learned of the fall of Madrid, he should have begun his retreat then, in which case it could have been undertaken in a far more leisurely fashion without being hounded by the enemy and, consequently, without the enormous losses to men, equipment, stores and money.

George Canning, the Secretary of State for Foreign Affairs, also opposed the government line, and attacked Moore, declaring that the late general 'retreated before a rumour'. He was against the government showing its support for Moore whom, he said, was wholly answerable for the mess he got himself into.[27]

Hussey Vivian, in his memoir, also questioned Moore's decision to continue with the campaign when it had become increasingly clear that the British were effectively on their own: 'what were the circumstances which occasioned so rapid a retreat so very immediately to follow the premeditated advance of the whole army to attack the French at Carrion and Saldana. And what made it necessary to make such haste through the Galicias – a country so strong by nature?' He answered this by pointing out that the information concerning the movements of the French was, in hindsight, incorrect but at the time it was understood at Moore's headquarters that the forces directed towards the British were in over whelming numbers and being led by Napoleon in person. 'The probability is,' Hussey Vivian wrote, 'that had Sir J. Moore received correct information of the force and movements of the enemy, he never would have altered his first determination of retiring from Salamanca.'[28] Had Moore been more forthcoming with his explanation of the situation instead of keeping his officers in the dark, such criticism of his conduct might have been avoided.

While the likes of Vivian heaped condemnation upon Moore, it must be remembered that the collapse in discipline during the retreat was only experienced in some units. The divisions led by the Paget brothers recorded very few cases of insubordination, and any such instances were dealt with both summarily and harshly. Consequently, the two generals maintained excellent discipline throughout the retreat. Had such measures been adopted by other officers, the story of the retreat might have been entirely different. It might, indeed, have been an orderly withdrawal in the face of overwhelming numbers in which the British Army would have emerged with great credit. While Moore was severely castigated, it was his subordinates – who escaped censure – who were the real villains of the piece. This can be seen in the words of a very revealing letter sent to the divisional commanders, signed by the Adjutant General, Clinton, on 3 January at Villafranca concerning the disorderly conduct of the troops under their command:

> Every village is pillaged with stragglers from all three corps, and their men have committed every species of disorder … on such

marches as this army has performed it was to be expected that the strength of many should fail ... but a very small part of the numbers which have left their battalions are of that description – the greater part have been in charge of the baggage. In direct disobedience of most pointed orders, in some instances non-commissioned officers have been left by order of officers in charge of a description of luggage which is not allowed.[29]

This puts an entirely different complexion on the issue of the disorder experienced throughout the retreat. The men with the baggage trains of the divisions were plundering the villages and then loading their ill-gotten gains onto the baggage wagons. Instead of using the wagons to carry the items necessary for the troops, they were being used to transport plunder – and wearing out the precious bullocks in the process. This was confirmed by Colonel Digby Hamilton: 'The habit of men quitting their ranks, upon the plea of fatigue, especially those detached with the Baggage of the Army, became at last an organised system, and it is a well-known fact that compacts were often made by them mutually to participate in the plunder which was acquired on alternate days.'[30]

Moore, therefore, demanded that the divisional commanders put in measures to inspect the baggage of every battalion and to dispose of all items that should not have found their way onto the wagons. They were likewise ordered to make frequent inspections of the soldiers' packs and, similarly, to remove any non-permitted articles. It is to be wondered how many men fell exhausted by the wayside in desperate efforts to carry some precious item they had stolen.

This was highlighted by Moore as he rode past the regiments on his way to Corunna, when he spotted that eight or nine stragglers had taken possession of a house where they found wine. The men were seized, and Moore halted the army, demanding to see the captains of the companies to which the prisoners belonged. He asked them how long the men had been absent from their regiments. When one of the officers tried to justify allowing the men to leave the ranks because they could not keep up with the rest, Moore cut him short, saying that when he gave out orders he considered 'that he addressed them to Military men'. According to the orders that had been issued, any men not able to march with the column was to be placed 'under the charge of an officer or a non-commissioned officer', and not allowed to wander off on their own. 'had I found plunder in the possession of this man,' he said to the captain, 'he must have been condemned to death; and you would have been the cause of his guilt.'[31]

There was clearly a dereliction of duty on the part of many officers. Baird's Military Secretary and aide, Lieutenant Colonel T.S. Sorrel, however, tried to justify the failure of the officers to maintain discipline among the ranks of their regiments:

> Any want of attention on the part of the officers, or of order and obedience in the men, ought, principally to be ascribed to the fatigues and privations they underwent, which made it physically impossible that they should properly fulfil all their duties as soldiers. Oppressed by want of sleep, and exhausted by constant marching, they moved on, silent and sullen, regardless of, and indifferent to, every object which surrounded them.

It has been said that the reason why the Reserve and the cavalry maintained order in the ranks was because they were in almost constant action with the enemy. This is entirely disproved by the statistics. Firstly, as D.W. Davies has calculated, in the 270 miles of the retreat, the opposing troops were engaged for only forty of those miles. Secondly, as can be seen in Appendix II of this present book, the regiments which, on the whole, lost the least amount of men were those that marched to Vigo. These men never saw the French after they left the main body, yet because of such strict disciplinarians as Robert Craufurd, they retired upon Vigo in good order. There is also an interesting take on all of this from a surgeon, who had been appointed to the Spanish service but joined Moore's army at Astorga, Henry Milburne. In his view, 'This retreat, from the distance marched, and the numerous difficulties by which it was attended, will long-remain a proud and honourable proof of the energy, perseverance, and valour of the British soldier.'[32]

It may also be the case, as John Colborne wrote, that the sufferings of the troops were exaggerated, and probably more so with each telling: 'What unheard-of difficulties, hardship and labours!' He exclaimed. 'Living on turnips! No sleep! All this frightful mama, but do not believe a quarter of what you hear.'[33]

Equally, those who condemned Moore for the speed of his retreat have overlooked the fact that they were pursued by the French at an equivalent pace. In fact, from Madrid, Napoleon moved a far greater number of men 200 miles in ten days – an average of twenty miles per day – whereas Moore moved his smaller force 270 miles in seventeen days, which is an average of less than sixteen miles a day. Yet the conviction that the British troops had been driven on beyond their capabilities was believed by those who pursued: 'The English troops had suffered, in their retreat …' wrote Albert de Rocca, 'when the soldiers are exasperated beyond endurance by fatigue; and, without having ever fought a pitched battle, they had lost more than 10,000 men, their treasure, a great deal of baggage, and almost all their horses.' The difference between the British and French experience may, in no small part, be due to the destruction of so many items by the former. Had the retreating troops been fed and supplied with shoes from the stores at Villafranca and Astorga, it is likely that many more would have survived. The French had no need to destroy anything that they carried with them or anything that that found abandoned by the British and were, as a consequence, better off. The destruction of so much valuable material had a far more detrimental effect upon Moore's army than any advantages Soult could have gained from its capture.

There is also another explanation for the different experiences of the British and the French in the race to Corunna, as the Duke of Wellington later made clear: 'The inhabitants of Spain and Portugal will not part with their provisions, even for money. There are no great markets for corn in any part of the Peninsula, excepting the seaports, and some of the very large and populous cities, and the inhabitants subsist generally upon stores formed in their own houses, or buried under ground; and if they are deprived of any considerable portion of their supply for the year, they must either starve, or must go to seek for a fresh supply at a great distance, as no neighbour has any to sell.' It is entirely understandable, therefore, that the Spaniards were unwilling to offer any of their precious stocks of food to the English. The French, on the other hand, were in enemy territory and simply took what they wanted. Wellington continued: They 'force from the inhabitants, under pain of death, all that they have in their houses for the consumption of the year, without payment, and are indifferent respecting the consequences to the unfortunate people.'[34] This, of course, led to the rise of the guerrillas who were to play such an important part in the Peninsular War.

Historians, looking only to the complaints of the British soldiers, have unjustly criticised the Spaniards. Their country had been invaded, its royal family removed, and its government dismantled. Little wonder that there was a breakdown in communications and of any properly co-ordinated opposition to the French. In the poorer regions of Spain, the Spaniards could barely support themselves let alone thousands of British troops. The responsibility of supplying Moore's army was principally the responsibility of HM Government which, after a slow start because of the suddenness of the outbreak of war in Spain, began to send considerable quantities of stores. It was the destruction of these stores, in the magazines Baird had formed on the road to Corunna, that was the reason for the terrible state the army found itself in, plus the lack of discipline that saw so much food, clothing and shoes wasted. It might be remembered that the Spanish troops, particularly those of the Marquis de La Romana which were encountered at Astorga, were in an even worse state than those of Moore's army, indicating quite clearly that large bodies of men could not hope to be provided for by the impoverished local populations. As we have seen, Wellington understood this well, and it was a factor which governed his operations throughout his campaigns in Iberia.

All that having been said, Moore's advance from Salamanca proved to have far-reaching consequences, that were spelt out by Sir Charles Oman:

> His main conception when he marched from Salamanca – that of gaining time for the rallying of the Spanish armies, by directing a sudden raid upon the Emperor's communications in Castile – was as sound as it was enterprising ... He was never for a moment in any serious danger of being surrounded ... [and] His plan of making a diversion was a complete success: he drew the Emperor,

with the 70,000 men who would otherwise have marched on Lisbon, up into the north-west of the Peninsula, quite out of the main centre of operations.[35]

Oman also saw that Moore had caused Napoleon 'to lose the psychological moment for striking at Seville' and had given the patriots three months to rally their forces.[36] That was certainly what Moore himself believed, as he told Romana on 27 December:

> The movement I made to Sahagun has answered every purpose I had a right to expect. A little more good fortune would have enabled me to cut up Soult's corps, but the attention of the enemy has at last been attracted from other objects. His march on Badajoz has been stopped, and the forces in the south will have time to be formed and to come forward. I shall continue my movement upon Astorga. It is there or behind it we should fight a battle, if at all. If the enemy follows so far, he will leave himself the more open to the efforts of the south. My opinion is that a battle is the game of Bonaparte, not ours. We should, if followed, take defensive positions in the mountains, where his cavalry can be of no use to him, and there either engage him in an unequal contest with us, oblige him to employ a considerable corps to watch us, or to retire upon Madrid, in which last case we should again come forth into the plain. In this manner we give time for the arrival of reinforcements from England. It gives time to your army to be formed and equipped, and that of the south to come forth.[37]

The respected historian Jac Weller, writing in the 1960s, concurs, believing that the advance from Salamanca changed the very course of the war in Iberia:

> Moore's advance on Napoleon's communications saved the southern half of Spain from French domination for several months. Had Moore not done so, British prestige in Spain would have suffered irreparably. Moore lost between 5,000 and 6,000 men, but left a legend of courage, efficiency and human virtue that still endures. It is possible that if Napoleon had overrun the entire country during the winter of 1808–9, the Spanish will to resist might have collapsed. Without this, the guerrilla armies, which aided Wellington greatly, would not have existed.[38]

Predictably, the British Government wished to paint the expedition as being a great success, and on 25 January, Castlereagh told MPs that:

> The next circumstance he should advert to was, the diversion effected by sir John Moore's retreat in favour of the Spaniards, and never was there in the military history of any country a more complete diversion; for he had completely succeeded in drawing to the northern extremities of the peninsula the efforts of the French forces from the track of the Spanish armies.[39]

Inevitably, not everyone saw the campaign that way, seeing no need for the precipitous retreat and evacuation, including a Spanish commentator:

> Suppose that the military maps which Moore had did not clearly explain the mountain geography so that he could find routes for the impressive army he commanded to fall back along. When he reached Villafranca, a slight inspection of the environs of the Pass of Piedrafita would have provided him immediately with precise information about the most suitable places to lay a good trap. Then, even with a small number of men, he could take the whole French army, which was always in pursuit with a long column of soldiers, by surprise, ruining any strategy. Bercian mountain geography provided a most imposing system fortified with bastions, which would not be found further ahead. There would have been no necessity at all to arrive at La Coruña exhausted.[40]

General Jomini believed that the British did not need to rush to the coast, nor did they need to evacuate Corunna:

> The road from Astorga to Corunna traverses a long defile of 30 leagues, bounded by high mountains on either side. A slender rear-guard would have defended that chaussee, and it was impracticable to manoeuvre on either side of it. That rendered it impossible for Soult to get at the enemy; and Ney, mountains entangled behind him in the defiles, could do nothing. This was the more unfortunate, as the English army, having prepared nothing on that line, stood in want of everything, and was in a

frightful state of disorder in consequence of the forced marches it took, for no conceivable reason. He (Sir J. Moore) cut the traces of their horses, and abandoned 3000 or 4000 stragglers or dying men when their line of operations was never menaced.

It is impossible to conceive why the English did not defend Corunna. It is not, indeed, a Gibraltar; but against an enemy who had nothing but field-pieces it surely could have been maintained for some time, the more especially as they could at any time throw in succour by sea. I could never understand their haste on that occasion, which the nation, it is true, have well wiped off in subsequent times, but which was inferior to no other of the same description.[41]

This was echoed by Hussey Vivian:

As to whether the British should have defended Corunna, or at all events not have deserted Spain by sailing direct for England. If the British could not have maintained their ground behind the strong battlements of Ferrol, or the weaker fortifications of Corunna, that might have afforded a good reason for bringing the troops round to Lisbon or Cadiz; but it was none for setting sail to England with the whole expedition, abandoning the contest in the Peninsula a shopeless, when the South was still unsubdued, and leaving10,000 English still in Portugal to their fate.[42]

It is true that at Corunna were supplies of every description, including gunpowder and ammunition. There was no immediate need for the army to be evacuated. It had defeated the enemy and could clearly hold its ground with Soult only able to add one more division to his force in front of Corunna. The British troops could be supplied by sea far easier than Soult could have dragged food across the already ravaged Galician mountains. If the British had tried to hold Corunna, there is little doubt that they would have been able to retain it. The French in Spain had far more pressing problems subduing the central provinces to divert the large forces necessary to evict the British from Corunna.

Some indication of the strength of the defences of Corunna can be gleaned from a letter sent by Lieutenant Colonel Robe on 20 January 1809, to the Deputy Adjutant-General, Royal Artillery

The 14th and I5th, the remainder of the Artillery [men] that could be spared from the embarkation of the Brigades were employed in destroying the guns and mortars on the sea front and island within the bay; upwards of fifty heavy guns were dismounted, spiked, and shot wrapped round with canvas rammed down to the bottom of the cylinders; the carriages were also destroyed and thrown over the precipice, and with the assistance of one hundred Royal Marines on the evening of the 15th twenty heavy mortars were also dismounted and thrown over.[43]

It may also be recalled that Baird suggested holding Galicia as a defensive base, and while Moore did consider it, by the time he had received Baird's letter, he had already determined on taking more positive action in attacking Soult. But, if Galicia was indeed defensible, as evidently Moore believed it was in early December, why then did he not try and hold the province when he heard that Napoleon was marching towards him? The answer to that was provided by Colonel Sorrel:

The question of a defence of Galicia was very different at the time when the letter alluded to was written, from what it became when we were retiring rapidly through the country, with an enemy pressing upon our rear. When the suggestion was offered, our strength was unimpaired, our equipment perfect, and the great body of the French was occupied with Madrid. Between the 8th of December, when the letter was despatched from Villa Franca, and the 29th, when we retreated through Astorga, much might have been done to improve our situation: besides, the enemy, in the hope of intercepting our retreat, were drawn on us, in consequence of our advance, earlier than would otherwise have been the case. In the breathing time which probably would have been allowed us, Lugo and other points might have been fortified, positions taken up and strengthened, depots established, and, by a judicious disposition of our force, the danger of being turned by the road through Orense, and by those from the north of Portugal and the Asturias might have been sufficiently guarded against.[44]

Such a clear observation must surely end further speculation regarding any alternative stratagems Moore might have adopted. For

Moore's decision to attack Soult not only saved the small British force in Lisbon but also saved the south of Spain, and in particular Andalusia which was at that time the country's wealthiest province. The Junta of Seville assumed overall authority of the various provincial juntas under the title of Supreme Central and Governing Junta and, when the French eventually invaded Andalusia in 1810, the Supreme Junta was able to find sanctuary in the fortress-port of Cadiz. With its garrison supplemented by a strong British contingent, Cadiz proved impregnable, and eventually became the home of the National Cortes. A Bonaparte might sit on the throne in Madrid, but the Spaniards recognised only their own government in Cadiz. The Spaniards, therefore, never considered themselves conquered and continued to resist the invaders.

This was certainly the opinion of most historians. The late David Chandler wrote of Moore's achievements in his unparalleled work, *The Campaigns of Napoleon*:

> He had overcome daunting difficulties for three long months. He had bearded Napoleon and entirely disrupted his plans for completing the conquest of Spain and Portugal, and he had brought his men through the horrors of a winter retreat over the mountains and made it possible for them to be safely evacuated. This meant that he had preserved the greater part of England's only field army … his work was vindicated a few months later when a new expeditionary force commanded by the able Sir Arthur Wellesley appeared off the Portuguese coast and prepared to renew the conflict. The running sore thus created by Moore and subsequently kept festering by the 'Iron Duke' was destined to impose a ceaseless drain on the resources of talent and lifeblood of the French Empire.[45]

Today, such views are almost universally accepted. Yet Napoleon did not rouse himself and move off from Madrid until 21 December. He abandoned his involvement in that pursuit on 31 December, just ten days later. While the ostensible reason for detaching himself from the pursuit of the British was to pre-empt Austrian mobilisation, the understanding now is that the Emperor had learnt that treasonous plots were afoot in Paris during his absence beyond the Pyrenees and only his presence in Paris would quell such disaffection.

If Moore had returned to Lisbon as soon as he was aware that the Spanish armies were incapable of offering any determined resistance, and Baird's corps had been shipped directly to the Portuguese capital instead of Corunna, Moore would have had, combined with the 10,000 left with Craddock, 40,000 men to defend Portugal.

We know, from the later campaigns in the Peninsular War that before an advance into Portugal would be practical, the border fortresses of Ciudad Rodrigo and Almeida, or Badajoz and Elvas, would have to be captured to secure the invaders' lines of communication. All of these were held by Spanish, Portuguese or British garrisons, which could have been further strengthened from Moore's army. When Marshal Masséna invaded Portugal in 1810/11, it took him more than two months just to capture Ciudad Rodrigo. And even when an all-Spanish garrison meekly surrendered Badajoz to Soult in 1811 it was only after repeated attempts over the course of almost three months. If Moore had made a determined defence of the Portuguese border, Napoleon and his Imperial Guard would have been long gone before any advance could have been made upon Lisbon, and the south of Spain would have remained unconquered. Moore, however, unlike the brilliant man who returned to Portugal to take over the British troops in the Peninsula, Sir Arthur Wellesley, did not believe he could hold Portugal.

'The frontier of Portugal is not defensible against a superior force,' he told Castlereagh on 25 November.'It is an open frontier, all equally rugged, but all equally to be penetrated. If the French succeed in Spain, it will be vain to attempt to resist them in Portugal. The Portuguese are without a military force and … no dependence is to be placed on any aid they can give. The British must in that event, I conceive, immediately take steps to evacuate the country. Lisbon is the only port, and therefore the only place from whence the army, with its stores, can embark. Elvas and Almeida are the only fortresses on the frontier. The first is, I am told, a respectable work. Almeida is defective; and could not hold out beyond ten days against a regular attack.'[46] How wrong he proved to be.

It may also be recalled that Moore had said that the concentration point of the army should have been in the south of Spain, rather than the north. The advantages of this would have been threefold.

Firstly, when Moore left Portugal heading for Seville, he would have been moving away from, rather than towards, the enemy. This would have put distance, and therefore time, between him and Napoleon – time that would have enabled him to join Baird, who could have been easily transported round to Cadiz.

Secondly, the roads from Lisbon to Seville and Cadiz were better than those actually taken by the army in its march to Salamanca. Moore, therefore, would not have needed to separate his artillery from his infantry.

Thirdly, Andalusia, as we have noted, was Spain's wealthiest region, which would have made finding transport and food for the army much easier than was experienced in Galicia.

All of this meant that if Moore had been hard-pressed by the French, he would have been able to retreat upon Cadiz with comparative ease. There would have been no disastrous retreat or humiliating escape, and the most important port in Spain would have been held by a powerful British force, just as it later was.

But Moore and Castlereagh were misled, as Colonel Sorrel makes clear:

> The plan of the campaign was framed in England by the British government, with the advice of the marquis de la Romana. It was intended that the British troops should advance towards the Ebro in support of the native armies, then represented to be in great force, and in the most efficient order. Indeed, such was the delusion which prevailed at the time in this respect, that the only fear expressed in Spain was, that the French might escape across the Pyrenees; and the plans most frequently discussed were those for an invasion of France.[47]

Of course, as we have seen, it was Moore's move against Napoleon's communications which disrupted the Emperor's plans for the subjugation of Seville and Andalusia. This, it is said, was Moore's great achievement. Had Moore marched directly to Seville, Napoleon could have advanced southwards from Madrid as soon as he became aware of the British presence. But we know that

Napoleon left Spain because of pressing matters elsewhere, so we can be reasonably certain that he would have left the conquest of Andalusia to his subordinates. The remnants of the Spanish armies could have rallied in the south alongside the British and, with the guerrillas operating freely in northern Spain, and many areas in the north unsubdued, it is likely that the French generals would have sought to consolidate central and northern Spain before attempting to do battle with a strong Anglo-Spanish force. The south of Spain might well have remained a Spanish stronghold whichever direction Moore had marched in.

Equally, when Joseph Bonaparte decided to invade Andalusia in 1810, he was able to conquer the region in just three weeks (7 January to 1 February 1810), so the fact that the south of Spain was free for twelve months was an irrelevance in military terms. And even though all of Andalusia, except for Cadiz, was in French hands, the war did not end. This was purely because of the continued existence and defiance of the Spanish government, in its various forms, at Cadiz. That resistance by the Spaniards at Cadiz was only possible because of the presence of a large British force, both military and naval, which helped render the fortress-port impregnable. By distracting Napoleon, Moore bought time for Cadiz's defences to be strengthened and a British garrison to be installed. However, if Moore would have marched to Seville, and then retreated upon Cadiz, that place, with Moore's 25,000 men to defend its walls, would have defied any attempt to storm it. Just as it subsequently did from early 1810 until the end of the war.

Fortescue offers the French view of the campaign, in which it is said that Moore's great gamble had no lasting effect: 'This perilous diversion, rendered no real service to Spain,'claimed Commandant Dominique Balagny:

> Because her hosts were already destroyed and Madrid was already conquered. No Spanish force existed except the fragments of vanquished armies under Galluzzo at Almaraz, and under Infantado at Cuenca. These were not relieved by the departure of the French army from Madrid; on the contrary they were still watched by Lefebvre and Victor, and presently met with their fate

at Almaraz and Ucles. The capital meanwhile was so strongly held that insurrection was impossible. The operations of the British army had consequently no influence on the southern provinces, nor on the armies which were being reformed there. Moore, therefore, by drawing immediately upon himself all the weight of a powerful army, risked the safety of his force without possibility of compensatory advantage.[48]

The French cavalry officer Lieutenant Albert de Rocca also offered an alternative strategy to Moore's attempt to strike a blow at Soult:

> From Salamanca, General Moore might have thrown himself behind the bridge of Almarez, over the Tagus, into an almost impregnable situation, where he could have reorganised the Spanish armies. It was there that he was most dreaded by the French. At all events, on leaving Salamanca, General Moore should have retired upon Lisbon than on Corunna, to shorten his own road, while he increased the difficulties of Marshals Lefevre and Soult, by widening [lengthening] the communications they had to maintain, and thus forcing them to weaken themselves, by leaving behind them a greater number of detachments. The English general would thus have furnished the troops of General Romana and the peasants of Galicia and Portugal with numerous opportunities of carrying on a petty war against the French detachments. This last operation has been performed since with the greatest success by General Sir Arthur Wellesley.[49]

The reality is that, through no fault of his own, Moore found himself alone in the midst of the enemy. His army might well have been better employed in the south of Spain, but that was not in his instructions. If he had retreated to Lisbon, the Spanish cause might well have been irretrievably lost. But his bold move against Napoleon's communications disrupted Napoleon's plans for the conquest of the south, which meant that half of the country remained free. It was that which kept the Spaniards fighting.

This, was the opinion of the man who came to understand the war in the Iberian Peninsula better than anyone else, Sir Arthur

Wellesley, Duke of Wellington. When talking many years later to FitzRoy Somerset, his military secretary, about Sir John Moore, the great man said: 'D'you know, FitzRoy, we'd not have won, I think, without him.'[50] Who can argue with that?

Nevertheless. an enormous quantity of stores, equipment, and horses had been lost on the retreat to Corunna – and, of course, the army's military chest.

Chapter 13

The Hunt

The first question that has to be answered in any search is, where do we need to look? So before I sent my little team clambering around the mountains of Galicia, I had to pinpoint as accurately as possible the spot where the barrels of coins were tipped down the ravine.

Robert Blakeney's account of the disposal of the military chest is the most detailed, and we should, therefore, read more of the relevant part of it. The following is his story of 5 January; the Reserve having set off 'about daybreak'. Just as the sky began to lighten the French cavalry, which had pushed on to Nogales through the night, engaged the rear-guard with their 'long' carbines:

> A few miles' distance from Nogales, as we approached a beautiful bridge, the skirmish became much more lively. This bridge, the name of which I do not recollect, presented a most romantic appearance. It was situated close to the foot of a hill. The stream immediately after passing through the bridge suddenly winding round the base of the high ground on the opposite bank, was entirely screened from our view as we approached the bridge, thus giving its numerous arches the appearance of so many entrances to subterranean caverns beneath the mountains, into which the current rushed. On the opposite bank and not far from the bridge, the road assumed a zigzag course … General Paget marched us quickly across, and having surmounted the zigzag road, halted us just beyond range of musket-shot from the opposite bank.

Such a specific description of this road and bridge should enable us to locate this point a 'few' miles from Nogales, or to the Galicians, As Nogais.

After holding this position for an hour, the Reserve moved off, the enemy's light troops crossed the bridge and the skirmishing resumed, which Blakeney wrote, 'was incessant during several miles' march'. As we have read previously, the 28th hurried on until 'about noon', Blakeney's Light Company halted at a place 'where we could only be attacked in front'. This, again, he records in detail:

> The mountain on our left, as we turned round to face the enemy, was stupendous, covered with snow, and rose nearly perpendicularly from where we stood. On our right the precipice was very deep, its steepness bearing proportion to the sudden rise of the mountain above.

It was here that the Paymaster-General, or his assistant, asked for help with the military chest. With the French pressing hard on the rear-guard, Blakeney's men were forced to continue their withdrawal:

> We now retired and soon came up to the treasure, contained in two carts lugged by foundered bullocks, moving so slowly as to render motion scarcely visible even in the wheels. The light company were now ordered to the rear in double quick time, to a village called, I think, Gallegos, about two miles distant, there to refresh and halt until called for … As the light company passed to the rear the regiment were drawn up close to the carts, and preparation prepared for the fall of the dollars.[1]

Charles Cadell was also with the 28th Regiment and he recorded the incident as follows:

> On the morning of the 5th, the Reserve left Nogales. We were detained at a bridge a little way on the road, covering the engineers, who were endeavouring to destroy it, but they did not succeed … About noon we came up with two cars laden with dollars; but the bullocks that drew them being completely exhausted, it was impossible to save the treasure. Under these circumstances, Sir John Moore decided that the whole should be thrown down the mountain, most judiciously considering, that if the casks were broken, the men would make a dash for the money, that would have caused much confusion, and might have cost the

lives of many. The rear-guard, therefore, was halted; Lieutenant Bennet, of the light company, 28th Regiment, was placed over the money, with strict orders from Sir John Moore to shoot the first person who attempted to touch it. It was then rolled over the precipice; the casks were soon broken by the rugged rocks, and the dollars falling out, rolled over the height – a sparking cascade of silver.[2]

Cadell also stated that it was only the coins which had spilled onto the road were picked up by the French, but that may have just been the French cavalry who were in touch with the British rear-guard. Others following may have had more time to wander down the mountainside. There are obvious flaws with this account, but it does confirm the timing of the incident, at around midday, and that it was after the bridge mentioned by Blakeney. He also states that the Reserve then marched onto 'Constantine', as does Blakeney, who wrote: 'After the money had been disposed of … We were instantly under arms; and the fight proceeded, and was well maintained on either side during several miles without the slightest intermission, until we came to a low hill within little more than musket-shot of the village of Constantino.'

Sir Thomas Graham recorded the following in his diary of 5 January:

> Marched about half-past eight, enemy advanced and skirmished with the rear guard. Obliged to throw away many casks of dollars and destroy much ammunition for want of carriage.
>
> Halted on the summit of a hill, and with a couple of guns made a demonstration which stopped the enemy's advance till the column got down the hill to the valley of Constantino; beyond that took up a position for the enemy, where the troops bivouacked.[3]

Alexander Gordon wrote in his journal that an unsuccessful attempt was made to blow up a bridge 'betwixt' Nogales and Constantino:

> Near this spot the guns of the mule brigade, as it was called, which had never been fired, were spiked and thrown down a precipice. These pieces, three-pounders, were remarkably light,

and constructed so as to be conveyed on the back of mules, through roads and into positions inaccessible to ordinary artillery. Three mules were attached to each gun: one carried the barrel, another the carriage, and the third was loaded with ammunition. Several casks of dollars and doubloons were also rolled down the steep side of the road into the valley beneath, just in time to prevent their capture.[4]

This is how the subject was handled by the British Army's historian Sir John Fortescue:

On the 5th the Reserve marched from Nogales; and the French cavalry, somewhat delayed by two unsuccessful attempts to blow up the bridge at Puente Ferreira, on the road a little north-west of Nogales, kept in touch with the British rear-guard all day. At about two o'clock in the afternoon the waggons, containing British treasure to the amount of 25,000, broke down; and the barrels holding the money were thrown over a precipice and abandoned. la Houssaye's dragoons filled their pockets, but did not on that account relax their pursuit, and late in the evening came up with the British rear-guard at the bridge of Santa Maria de Constantin.[5]

Moore's military secretary, who was with the rear-guard at this stage, also gives us this place. 'About 5 or 6 o'clock, we retired quickly down the hill in front of Sobrado or Constantin and we passed the rivulet or river before the enemy could discover that we were in full retreat.'[6] This is echoed by D.W. Davies, who wrote that at about 17.00 hours, 'the Reserve reached Santa Maria de Constantin, a parish of Neira de Jusá on the right bank of the Neira'.[7]

The Regimental Record of the 52nd Regiment states that: 'A few miles in the rear of Nogales, the road to Lugo leads over a steep mountain. Here the weary oxen were unable to drag along the heavy-laded carts, and as the enemy were pressing upon the rear-guard, it was found impossible to save the military chest.'

From the above accounts we can, with some certainty, place the spot where the money was discarded somewhere between Nogales and a place called Constantine, Constantino or Constantin.

A note in the diary of Ensign William Gavin of the 71st Highland Regiment, states that, 'the treasure casks [were] thrown over a precipice … on January 4th [sic] between Nogales and Cerezal. This is reinforced by the historian D.W. Davis, who wrote: 'About noon the rear guard reached Cerezal where two wagons laden with dollars were stopped on the road'.[8] Unfortunately, there is no such place shown on Michelin Guide to Galicia, nor on Google Earth.

A Spanish interpretation has been provided by Cyril Falls, former Professor of the History of War, Oxford University:

> The money, food, baggage, light arms, cannon and ammunition that the British were dropping over the precipices of the imposing strength of Piedrafita would have been saved, and on the other hand they would have taken the equivalent material from their enemies.[9]

So, we now have another name that should help us pinpoint the place where the military chest was disposed of – the precipitous slopes of Piedrafita. This actually draws its name from Piedrafita do Cebreiro, a small village in Lugo province, and the Pass of Piedrafita lies between Piedrafita do Cebreiro and Nogales. However, we know that the money was disposed of after Nogales, not before it, so this reference can be discounted.

We certainly know that Captain Nathaniel Steevens was with the rear-guard and watched the military chest being thrown over the precipice, and he tells us that, contrary to Blakeney's account, some of the money was indeed taken by the British soldiers and that this was known about by the military authorities: 'We had a great laugh, a year or two afterwards, at several of my officers of my regiment who were very zealous in some in carrying some dollars; they little thought Government would have called upon them to return what they received, for the money would have been lost if they had not carried it. However, one morning … very unexpectedly, an order was received for the refunding of the whole of the money with which these zealous officers had trudged along the road many a weary hour, and they were obliged to hand out what they had received, and might think themselves lucky they had not the interest to pay; of course it was a great inconvenience to many, and a great annoyance to all, to refund the money they had every reason to suppose was their own.'[10]

In describing the place where the money was discarded, Sergeant Robertson wrote: 'The next part of the wreck of the army were the carts containing the money which we had to make away with, rather than let them fall into the hands of the enemy. The horses were shot and the casks with the money rolled down the side of the hill, which is very steep and high, having at the bottom a deep and woody ravine.'[11]

This is the only reference to the ravine being 'woody', but if this is the case, then our chances of finding anything among thick vegetation after 200 years, compared to a barren mountainside, will be considerably diminished.

Just how much money was lost is difficult to determine. Even if we knew how much had been sent to Moore, we have no knowledge of how much had been spent during the campaign, or even how much actually reached the army. That Moore did not receive all the money allocated to him is revealed in General Charles Count Alten's account published in *The United Service Journal and Naval and Military Magazine*, in 1831:

> While we were wind-bound in Vigo, I was most opportunely joined by Brig.-Gen. Peacock, who was on his way from Lisbon to Sir John Moore with part of the military chest. This supply enabled me to issue a month's subsistence to the troops, and to furnish Major Martin with money for the conveyance and subsistence of the sick and stragglers, the want of funds for whom had caused Major Martin to suffer much ill-will and annoyance from the Spanish authorities and inhabitants.

Equally, Captain Gordon recorded the following:

> Our regiment was destined to form the rear-guard as usual, and halted under the walls of Lugo, near the Corunna Gate, at eleven o'clock, to allow time for the infantry, who had not yet come up, to join the line of march. During this interval the left squadron was ordered to the town-house to take charge of 35,000 dollars,

which must have been left as a prize for the enemy. Sealed bags, each containing 500 dollars, were distributed to the troopers, and in this manner about £8,000 was saved to the nation; but our poor horses were much oppressed by the addition of nearly two stone to the weight they already carried.[12]

We are then told that when the men of the 15th Hussars reached Guitiriz, mules were found by Adjutant Jones and the dollars were transferred to them under the charge of a Sergeant Roberts. Roberts was able to deposit 27,000 of those dollars with the paymaster general at Corunna.[13]

   This was confirmed by the adjutant of the 15th Hussars:

Several hundred thousand dollars having been left at Lugo, they were distributed among the Cavalry Regiments, 500 to each man in a sack and so brought on the road … proceeded on the route for Betanzos the 7th and 10th Regts. forming the rear guard. Procured mules by dint of force and sent 30,000 dollars from this place to Corunna, under escort of Sergt. Roberts, with orders to them safe at any rate and by any means.[14]

Captain Henry Evelegh of 'C' Troop Royal Horse Artillery recorded the retreat:

Wednesday, 4th January, 1809. Nothing for the horses to eat, and miserable accommodation for the men and officers. At 7 marched for Nogales. The Troop and three regiments went a mile further to the bridge. This was a dreadful march over an immense snow mountain, with ruts cut into the snow ice two feet deep and large, so that the horses could scarce move. The road strewed and blocked up with ordnance-carriages and others of every description; numbers of dead horses; men, women, and children frozen to death. Got into Arerias (Herreira) about 4 o'clock, with Chester and Barlow and four guns. Walcott, in the rear with two guns, did not arrive till 7. An immense quantity of dollars left on the road, and thrown over the hill on this day's march.[15]

However, on Friday 6 January, Evelegh wrote that: 'About 10,000 pounds' worth of dollars thrown over the hill this day.'[16]

The Journal of the 3rd Hussars of the King's German Legion adds a little more information:

> Among the resources of the army which it was found necessary to abandon, was part of the military chest. This sum, amounting to about £25,000 in dollars, was contained in casks and carried on bullock-carts; but the tired animals were no longer equal to their load, and the casks were ordered to be left behind. Lieutenant Hugo, who commanded the rear-guard of the German hussars, thought, however, that he might be able to save a part of the treasure, and halting, made each man of his detachment, which amounted to about five-and-twenty, to take an equal weight of dollars in his corn-sack; these sums were brought on and safely delivered to the commissariat at Corunna; the remainder was rolled down the side of the mountain, and fell into the hands of the enemy and Spanish peasants.[17]

Schaumann had a slightly different take on this, stating that:

> A hussar regiment had, indeed, been furnished with bags, in order that they might carry some of it on their saddles; but as the men could not endure the load, they put as much of it as they could in their pockets, and flung the rest away.[18]

Carrick Moore, in his justificatory monologue on his brother's campaign, wrote:

> There were even two carts with dollars to the amount of five and twenty thousand pounds, which fell behind. This money had been brought forward from Corunna with Sir David Baird's corps, and was under the charge of Mr. Courtney belonging to the Paymaster-general's department. The means provided for its conveyance were insufficient; for the carts were drawn by tardy bullocks who were quite exhausted by fatigue and could not be got on. After every effort had been made in vain, the casks were at length rolled down a precipice on the side of the road, and the advanced-guard of the French passed the place in five minutes afterwards. It was afterwards learnt by some prisoners, that this money was found by the Spanish peasants.[19]

In today's terms, £25,000 would be the equivalent of a little less than £1,500,000 – a very considerable sum to throw away.

Richard Bogue, the 2nd Captain of Downman's troop of the Royal Horse Artillery, recorded the following in his diary of 3 January 1809:

> One mountain that we had to pass was seven leagues over-covered with frost & a deep snow, on the top of which we found sticking [in the snow] a great many sick cars – with men & women dead & dying in all directions, two brigades of English & all the Spanish Artillery, as well as thirty thousand pounds in doubloons & dollars, 20 thousand pounds of which was destroyed afterwards as it was found impossible to bring them on. [20]

Colonel Digby Hamilton of the Royal Waggon Train, wrote of 5 January: 'Upon the day that $250,000 was thrown over the mountain for want of means to convey the Casks, I saw in the line of Baggage thrice as many carts as would have carried this specie loaded with women, children, and articles apparently of plunder.'[21]

A report in *The Times* of 30 January also gave a very high figure:

> The Dispatches packet is returned to Falmouth, from Corunna, with the mails which she sailed with from the former port on the 12th. She arrived off Corunna on the 21st, where she met with His Majesty's brig *Resolute*, Capt. Joyce, who informed him the French were in possession of Corunna, and that he was stationed there to prevent any British vessels entering that place. The Military Chest, on the retreat of our Army towards Astorga, contained dollars to the amount of six hundred thousand pounds, and about fifteen hundred pounds in gold coin. To prevent this money falling into the hands of the enemy, it was thrown into rivers, caves, &c.; and to this circumstance, we hear, a large portion of our loss of men on the march is imputable, many persons having dropped behind under various pretences, in the hope of recovering part of the specie so disposed, who were afterwards unable to regain their respective corps.

The total, according to this report, is £601,500, which today would amount to a staggering, and probably unrealistic, £35,000,000. *The Times* report also mentions gold to be amongst the coins in the military chest.

The notable French historian M.A. Thiers had this to say on the matter: 'We collected a lot of artillery and a considerable amount of money along the way, which the English had thrown over precipices. Our soldiers filled their pockets with no fear of descending into the deepest ravines. A sum of piastres worth about 1,800,000 francs could be saved'[22] Research indicates that 1 pound Sterling was equivalent to 21 francs in 1800, which would give a sum of more than £85,000, which is a remarkable amount to have recovered by the pursuing troops and is hard to accept.

William Napier gives the usually stated sum of £25,000 and at the same time provides a cogent explanation of why other figures were banded about at the time:

> Towards evening the French army, recovering their lost ground, passed Nogales, galling the rear-guard with a continual skirmish, and it was here that dollars to the amount of twenty-five thousand pounds were abandoned. This small sum was kept near headquarters to answer sudden emergencies, and the bullocks that drew it being tired, the general [Paget], who could not save the money without risking an ill-timed action, had it rolled down the hillside ... The returns laid before parliament in 1809 made the sum 60,000*l*., and the whole loss during the campaign nearly 77,000*l*., but it is easier to make an entry of one sum for a treasury return, than to state the details accurately; the money-agents were, like the military-agents, acting independently, and all losses went down under the head of abandoned treasure. Officers actually present, agree, that the only treasure *abandoned* by the army was that at Nogales, and that the sum was 25,000*l*.

What Napier, of the 43rd Regiment, points out is that when Paget ordered the chests to be thrown over the precipice, the paymaster responsible for the treasure remonstrated with the general, exclaiming 'It is *money!*' Paget wisely countered by saying, 'so are shot and shell'. Putting that into context, the disposal of the military chest was of little consequence in terms of the cost to Britain of the military operation as a whole and the loss of enormous quantities of stores and equipment during the retreat.[23] It is certainly true that greater efforts could have been made to save the money, as others have suggested, but this constituted the load of just two carts among the many hundreds that had been intentionally destroyed or abandoned.

The Regimental Record of the 52nd Regiment provides these details:

> Casks containing dollars to the amount of £25,000 were thrown over the precipice on the right-hand side of the road, and rolled from one declivity to another, till they at last settled in the bottom of a rugged, narrow ravine, quite out of reach of the column. The rear regiments of the Reserve only were present when the money was cast away, and certainly not a man of those left their ranks in the hope of obtaining a portion. This discipline, however, did not extend to the 'followers', who, as soon as they arrived at the spot where the dollars were rolling over the mountain-side, at once began a scramble, in which the wife of the regimental master-tailor, Malony (who was a merry one, and often beguiled a weary march to the men with her tales), was so successful that her fortune was apparently made. The poor woman went through all the subsequent perils and hardships of the retreat, but on stepping from the boat to the ship's side on embarking at Coruña, her foot slipped and down she went like a shot, and, owing to the weight of dollars secured about her person, she never rose again.[24]

Just how much money was taken by the men who hung back is another imponderable. Blakeney recorded the following on 10 January:

> A guard was thrown across the road at the entrance to our position, through which all the stragglers must pass. Each man as he came up had his pack and haversack taken off and closely searched; and all the money found upon them which it was fully ascertained could have been acquired by robbery only was collected in a heap and distributed among the men who never swerved from their colours, thus rewarding the meritorious and well disciplined to the mortification of those who disgraced their profession. The sum thus collected amounted to a great deal.[25]

D.W. Davis in his thorough 1974 study offers a somewhat different version of events, stating that; 'The oxen pulling them [the treasury wagons] were lying down, too exhausted to move. It has usually been assumed that the dollars were travelling with Moore's column and were part of the military chest. It seems more probable that the money was part of the million and a half dollars shipped from England to La Coruña for Moore on 24 November, and that the oxen were pointed east, on the way toward Moore when they gave out. Fearing that if the money were [*sic*] simply left on the road the men would make a rush for it, with consequent delay, confusion and even danger, Sir John Moore ordered the casks to be rolled over the cliff and instructed an officer of the 28th to shoot the first man who interfered with the task.'[26] There are obvious errors in this, if we assume Blakeney's entirely believable first-hand account is correct, and the statements of others who had passed the bullock cart or carts earlier in the day. The cart was, quite clearly, travelling with the army, not in the opposite direction. Yet there is some logic to Davis's comment. We know from Moore's despatch to Castlereagh eleven days' earlier that he was virtually penniless, and that Baird had spent all the money he had received. Where then did this money come from? It is quite likely, therefore, that this was in fact a second instalment of the money promised by the Exchequer, which had reached the army from Corunna at some point during the retreat. This also explains why there is so much uncertainty regarding the amount of money disposed of.

The official French view, as given in the *Bulletin de l'arméed'Espange*, was as follows:

> The enemy were obliged to destroy considerable numbers of carriages and the baggage and munitions carts. The precipices were filled with this debris. There was disorder amongst the divisions Lorge and Lahoussaye because of a trove among abandoned carts filled with gold and silver; it was a part of the treasure of the English army. We evaluate what is in the hands of the divisions to be two million [francs, presumably].

Despite all these imponderables, if we take the usually stated sum of £25,000, we can actually arrive at a precise number of coins.

With reference to the system mentioned in Chapter 2, we know that the British Government had to purchase the Mexican silver dollars through agents. These were purchased by the Treasury at a rate of £212,500 per million.[27] This means that one pound equalled just less than five dollars. Therefore, £25,000 equalled approximately 125,000 silver coins.

Regardless of the precise sum, a considerable quantity of coin was thrown down the precipice. But what are the chances of any of it still being there?

There seems no doubt that some of the money was recovered on the spot, as Lieutenant General Charles Steevens of the 20th Regiment, who was in Paget's Reserve and actually watched the money being discarded, relates: 'One day, in consequence of the oxen being overcome with fatigue while drawing a cart laden with dollars, we were obliged to throw the money away amounting to about £25,000; it happened that, at the time we were in a high situation, that part of the road being on a hill and perfectly visible to the enemy. It was an unpleasant sight for us to see the little casks of dollars thrown down the slope into the valley on the side of the road, some of them breaking, when out threw the dollars in all directions. Many of the soldiers' wives went into the valley and loaded themselves with dollars, and several were, in consequence, taken prisoners; the French, not allowing any women to be with their army, sent them back into our lines in double-quick, *but without the money*. [Steevens' italics][28]

If Archibald Alison is correct, the rest of the money was collected later by the local peasants:

> Disorders went on accumulating with frightful rapidity along the whole line, and such was the general wreck of presence of mind, that at Nogales the military chest of the army, containing £25,000 in dollars, having stuck fast in the mud, the treasure was rolled in the cask in which it was contained over a precipice and became the property of the peasantry, who picked it up at the bottom.[29]

Napier was of the same opinion as Alison regarding the fate of the money: 'part of it was gathered by the enemy, part by the Galician

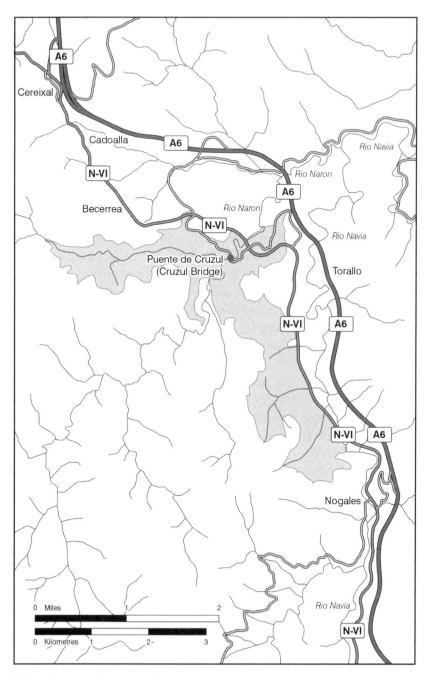

Nogales to Cereixal

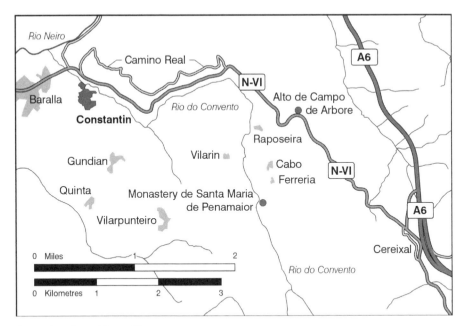

Cereixal to Baralla

peasants.'[30] Likewise, Charles Oman wrote: 'The silver shower lay scattered among the rocks at the bottom: part was gathered up by la Houssaye's dragoons, but the bulk fell next spring, when the snow melted, into the hands of the local peasants.'[31]

According to Moore's biographer, Roger Day: 'When the snows melted, hundreds of impoverished mountain herdsmen became rich beyond their wildest dreams.'[32]

But we can dream too of finding some treasure. So, we were:

Spain-Bound

There are a number of ways of reaching Galicia and the province of Lugo. It is, of course, possible to drive all the way down to northern Spain from the UK. But the distances involved are considerable. This was unanimously dismissed by the team.

The second route considered was the car ferry from Portsmouth to Santander. This, though, takes twenty-four hours each way which would be followed on the outward trip by a 200-mile drive to Benavente and on the return a discouraging 283-mile drive to Santander from Corunna. This was also dismissed.

This left just flying. There is, somewhat surprisingly, a direct route from Heathrow to Corunna, served by an airline called Vueling. This, an Iberia Airlines company, flies just once a day, every day. There are other airlines that fly into Corunna from the UK, but they all go via Madrid or Lisbon and can take anything up to twenty-two hours! There are other flights into nearby airports such as Léon and Salamanca, but these also go via Madrid and take an inordinate length of time.

The only problem with the Vueling service is that its one flight does not set off until 19.00 hours, arriving at Corunna at 22.00 hours. The return flight to Heathrow is also in the evening.

So, the route we chose was to fly into Madrid, pick up a hire car, conduct our investigations for a few days, then drop the car off at Corunna airport in time for the evening flight back to the UK.

There was not the remotest possibility of finding any coins merely lying on the surface of the ground after 200 years, so I had contacted the Spanish Embassy in London to seek permission to use a metal detector. They, in turn, passed me onto the Galician Tourist Board in La Coruña (or A Coruña to the Galicians) and then to Área Provincial de Turismo de Lugo, who in turn passed me onto the Ayuntamiento de As Nogais. Finally, Dr Jesús Manuel Núñez Diaz of the Concello da as Nogais gave us permission to metal detect in the area, but under the supervision of a Lugo municipal technician. I was asked for the evidence supporting my estimation of where the military chest was disposed of and of the documentary research I had undertaken. This was submitted and, with a top-of-the-range metal detector packed carefully in my baggage, we set off for Spain.

Arriving at Madrid airport at 12.40 hours, and armed with our Michelin guide, and lots of Google Earth screenshots, we set the GPS for our first major stop at Sahagun. The hotel I had chosen proved, quite by chance, to be almost adjacent to the fields over which the 15th Hussars and the 1st Provisional Chasseurs galloped as the French tried to escape the onslaught of the British troopers. The Puerta de Sahagún, a modern hotel built in response to the increasing number of pilgrims passing through on their way to

Santiago de Compostela, sits at the eastern edge of the town and the area of the battlefield, and the bridge over which the few chasseurs managed to escape to warn Soult, is easily found by following the path at the back of the hotel.

Day 2 was to Noceda, with a first stop at Astorga. It is easy to see why this town was an important point along the road to Corunna, sitting on top of a steep-sided hill and surrounded by its still-impressive walls. It is generally said that it was at Astorga that the brigades under Craufurd and Alten split from the main body. There are, though, reports from at least two sources that state that the army stayed as one until Foncebadon.

We followed the line of the retreat through Bembibre. Here, the British found the place full of wine vats and the town is still noted for its quality wines. Surprisingly little has changed in many of the places in this part of Spain, with many old, and in not a few cases, abandoned buildings that must have stood at the beginning of the nineteenth century.

We crossed the Cua at Cacabellos, where Rifleman Plunkett brought down General Colbert, and then onto Villafranca, its narrow, winding streets seemingly all facing the mountains, which form a towering skyline to the north. The troops must have shuddered at the prospect of the struggle ahead. From Villafranca our next stop was at Hotel El Urogallo, Noceda, Nogales, our Galician base for our search for Moore's lost treasure.

In consultation with highly-regarded specialist historians (whose identities I will not disclose) who have travelled the full length of the retreat to Corunna numerous times, I received widely varying opinions on where the military chests had been abandoned, ranging from, 'The exact spot is not really known,' to 'it would appear to be a fairly obvious place'.

What we do know is that the Reserve was on the road just as dawn was breaking. We also know from meteorological data that sunrise on 5 January in that region of Spain is around 09.05 hours. We also know that the military chest was disposed of around midday or possibly a little later. If the rear-guard reached the spot where the military chest was disposed of, we have a march of no more that three hours. What we don't know is how fast the men marched in the terrible conditions they encountered and how much time was spent stationary in repelling the attacks of the French. Blakeney wrote that: 'scarcely was darkness succeeded by light when the fight again commenced and continued until darkness again returned. 'We also know, according to Blakeney, that the Reserve 'remained at our post beyond the bridge for about an hour'. This reduces the length of the march to just two hours, the troops fighting much of the way.

With all the evidence we could gather, including advice from a number of the locals, we set off from Nogales along the old road out of the town at a brisk pace, a good marching speed. Frequent halts to take photographs and to make notes might well have mirrored the actions of the rear-guard standing at bay to fire a volley or two to ward off the pursuing cavalry.

After twenty-three minutes we reached the bridge over the Rio Navia which the engineers endeavoured to destroy. There is a section of the bridge on one side that is very obviously different to the rest and, presumably, is the rather clumsy repair to the damage caused by the explosion.

We reached the bridge so graphically described by Blakeney, the name of which he could not recall, after 105 minutes. This bridge is in fact that which spans the Rio Cruzul. Here the Reserve stood for approximately an hour before moving off again. If the men began their day's march at around 09.00 hours and reached the point where the money was discarded at midday, this would have left them only fifteen minutes or so to have travelled 'several' miles to where they came across the military chest. Our timings were clearly out. The men must have been up and on the road before daylight. The adjutant of the 15th Hussars recorded that on the 2 January, just three days earlier, the rear-guard set off from Bembibre at 07.00 hours, as did Captain Evelegh of the RHA on 4 January.

This was repeated on the 5th, as Evelegh wrote: 'Pickets drove in about seven in the morning.' This, then, allows us two more hours. We have seen in the previous chapter that, on average, the men achieved a pace of around 2 miles per hour. This is confirmed by Captain Gordon who states that the 15th entered Nogales about 09.00 hours on the 4th, halted for a couple of hours to feed the horses, and then pushed on to Constantin, where they arrived between 15.00 and 16.00 hours, having marched, generally at a walk, 64 miles in twenty-five hours, during twenty-two of which they were actually on horseback. This gives us a speed of 2.56 miles per hour, though a large part of the march had been on horseback. A speed of 2 miles per hour therefore seems fairly accurate.

With the possibility that the Reserve marched for two hours before encountering the distraught paymaster, this would mean that place would be approximately 4 miles from the bridge over the Cruzul. We covered this distance and found ourselves at Constantin which was also shown on the large-scale maps that had been kindly given to us by one of our local contacts.

We have also been told that the military chest was disposed of around Cerezal, which was short of Constantin. The only place that this could be is Cereixal, which is about two miles short of Constantin. Certainly, this is where Professor Oman believes the place to have been – between Nogales and Cerezal – and so we focused our search in this area along the old road to Lugo. The modern National N-VI high road now bypasses the hamlet of Cereixal. We walked along the old road through Cereixal and, at the southern end of the village, it meets the N-VI. At this spot, there is a steep precipice that drops away for a very considerable distance. It is also, unlike so many of the narrow roads in the area that are almost hidden from view by trees, a relatively open position that tallies with Steevens' account of it being 'on a hill and perfectly visible to the enemy'. This became our favoured location for the disposal of the military chest.

In order to eliminate other possible locations, we endeavoured to journey along every other road in the vicinity. We proceeded beyond the previously elusive Constantin to the bridge over the Rio Neira (Puenta de Senro) at Baralla. From Baralla we drove south-east, back towards the approach of the retreating army, which was approximately parallel to the old road we had used to reach Baralla. This narrow country lane wound through the hills and various tiny hamlets, such as Gundian, Vales, Lexocairo and Lexo, but realised that we were too far to the west of the road of the Serra da Pena do Pico and the road of the retreat. We therefore made our way to Becerrea and the old, royal highway.

We also tried the road on the right of the old road through Saa, but it led downhill to the bottom of a ravine and was clearly not the route of the British army. Another road from Cereixal led upwards. This, though, only led to the Escuela Capc. Agraria where it terminated. Finally, we tried to drive and walk up a steep and rough road north-west of Becerrea into the Serra da Pena do Pico. It proved to be a series of hairpin bends and it degenerated into a narrow, rocky track and was clearly not a major thoroughfare. We walked or drove every road between the Rio Cruzal and Constantin in a very long and tiring day, having stopped and spoken to countless Spaniards. One thing we did discover, or failed to discover, was the place Gallegos referred to by Blakeney. This is because there is no such place. Galegos is what the people of Galicia call themselves; Gallegos is what the rest of Spain call them. This shows how easy it is for a mistake to be made, and for the error to be repeated by others.

According to Professor Javier Gomez, who studied the roads through the region for his doctorate, in some parts the Camino Real followed the route of the old Roman road and in other parts they are separate. This is also the case with the Camino Real – the Royal Highway between Madrid and Corunna, also known as the Camino Carlos III – and the more recent N-VI. This may have confused other visitors who were not fortunate in having such in-depth local knowledge, which has led them to mistake the exact route of the retreating army.

At this stage, we had a meeting with a number of key local historians. There is no tradition or folklore relating to the discovery of large amounts of money, nor of anyone suddenly becoming extravagantly wealthy. There was, though, an intriguing event that happened around the time in question. The owner of a considerable estate, called Vicente Rivera, possessed a large number of farms worked on by peasant farmers. At the end of the Peninsular War, the Guerra de la Independencia Española to the Spanish, Señor Rivera was able to sell all his farms enabling him to move out of the area. He was able to do this because the peasants suddenly found the money to buy the farms for themselves. More on this story later.

Local folklore also has it that Moore's treasure is hidden in the galleries of the Torres de Doncos, an abandoned medieval ruin. At first consideration, this can be safely discounted.

As might be expected, over the years people from outside the region have been to this part of Galicia looking for the military chest. A lady in Noceda relates that years ago she remembers going to a field, the property of her husband's family, and sitting on a rock called the 'stone of the treasure'. She recalls that some 'drilling' had been done on the rock looking for the treasure. The place in question is in the tiny hamlet of Torallo (population twenty-one) between Nogales and Becerrea. The only problem with this is that Torallo is not on the known line of the retreat and we have confirmation of the route of the retreat along this section from Alberto Blas Ferreiro, who published his findings in 1992. From this, we know that the Roman road, the Camino Real on its route from Becerrea to Baralla did not pass through Torallo.[33]

A resident of Cereixal, Vincente Poy, aged 97 in 2018, recalled that when he was about 9 years old, a man conducted a search for buried treasure 'in a hollow between two rocks'. It was understood that this was not where the money had been discarded, but where it had been buried for safekeeping.

Interestingly, the opinion of some local individuals regarding the route of the retreat is the similar to the Spanish version of events provided by Cyril Falls. A number of those that stated they knew about the retreat declared that the British army took the road from Pedrafita do Cebreiro to Becerrea. There are two roads that run between these two places, the N-VI/Camino Real and the one to the east which runs through Villanova. This is the old Roman road that was still in use in the 1800s. As the opinion of the local authorities is that this is the road taken by the British army, it could not be ignored. Guided by the former major of the region, we travelled over this ancient track. This was a very steep climb and there were numerous places that would fit perfectly the eye-witness accounts. It branches near Nogales, with one branch dropping down to Nogales and one beyond this town.

There is another story of treasure, this time in almost exactly the place we had identified. This is at Cadoalla, immediately south of

Cereixal. The story, unearthed by Angel Rodil, goes as follows: There were stories of buried treasure in a place where several people had searched without finding anything. Fifty years ago, a man came with two miners to undertake a serious excavation. They brought with them what the man called 'pendulums' to help locate the exact spot where the treasure was buried. The individual who related this story actually assisted these men with the digging. He said they dug down more than 2 metres but found nothing. The place in question can be reached from the N-VI, signposted Cadoalla. Upon entering the hamlet there is a crossroads and a fountain. It is there when the men dug. The GPS co-ordinates for this spot are:

42°51'58.4"N 7°10'17.7"W
42.866211, -7.171582

The problem with this location is that, while there is a steep incline to the west, there is no corresponding ravine to the east as Cadoalla sits near the bottom of the hill. There is a slope to the east from the N-VI but this is an entirely new road along this section. The old road through Cadoalla, as confirmed by the inhabitants, is the Camino Real.

From low-lying Cadoalla, the Camino Real ran up the mountainside to Cereixal, This is confirmed by the work of Professor Benito Sáez Taboada, who states that the road passed between Cereixal and Cadoalla.[34]

There is still a small road that runs from Cadoalla to Cereixal, but there are no steep slopes along its route until it joins the N-VI and runs up to the precipitous spot we had found earlier.

Beyond Cereixal, the road continues along fairly steep mountainside, and it is not impossible that the treasure was disposed of after Cereixal. This road reaches its highest point at Alto de Campo de Arbore, which is 794 metres above sea level. This point has been remarked on as being the place where the military chest was discarded by others who have travelled the route of the retreat.[35] There is certainly a considerable slope on the eastern side of the road at this point but being at the top of the mountain means there is no corresponding incline on the western side. Also, time and distance must again be considered, as the Reserve marched on beyond the point where the treasure was dumped for a number of hours before reaching Constantin.

A anonymous senior French officer of Soult's II Corps recorded the following in his *Souvenirs*: 'At Cerezal, the dragoons of 18 and 19 regiments, of the Lahoussaye division, seized a convoy of money laden in cars abandoned by the drivers. The English army only took forty-eight hours to make the journey of twenty-five leagues from Villafranca to Lugo.'[36]

Further confirmation of what would appear to be the place where the military chest was abandoned comes from the *Catholic Diary* of 1897, written by Dr Antonia Correa of Pena de Neira de Rey, who wrote that the British army travelled the 'route that exists from Villafranca del Vierzo to Cerezal and Campo del Arbol. During this day, the artillery and ammunition that the Marquis de la Romana and, furthermore, near Nogales in Cruzul and when climbing from Becerrea to Cerezal threw the sum of 120,000 pesos by order of General Moore in silver, which came in barrels, boxes and other deposits.

'All this indicates the state of disorganization of that army and the little military expertise of its leaders who, dominated by an inexplicable terror, squandered the precious positions and advantages that the land offered them at every step.'[37]

Dr Correa goes on to write: 'On January 5, 1809 and at the point called Retorta, which includes the descent that is on the road to Castilla, from the village of Camp de Arbol to Constantin and Baralla, there was a clash of arms between the rear of the British Army of General Moore, the vanguard of the French Army, which pursued with courage first, commanded by Marshal Soult, the battle would have been formalized if the English did not undertake hastily and in the midst of the greatest disorder, attacking wounded, sick, armaments, canons, clothing and others impedimenta and portions of the great convoy they were carrying.

'The tradition still conserve this fact, and many, deluded by their greed, after consulting with fortune-tellers and readers of [tarot] cards, have been practicing for a long time numerous excavations in different points of the mentioned Retorta and that here the road suffered severe damage, believing to find barrels full of currency and other valuables; as if the retreating fugitives had given time to such operations.'

Of course, nothing was found by these treasure hunters because, as Dr Correa pointed out, the military chest was disposed of 'when climbing from Becerrea to Cerezal'.

Until this point, we had assumed that when diarists and earlier historians wrote of Cerezal, we presumed they were referring to the present-day Cereixal. However, there was, it seems, a Cerezal in the eighteenth century which was not quite the same as the Cereixal of today. To explain: Becerrea which is today a lively town, was an insignificant village 200 years ago. This is why it is not usually shown on maps of the retreat, nor mentioned much in contemporary accounts. What is now the district of Becerrea, of which Cereixal is a part, was formerly the district of Cerezal. So, whereas the naming of the location where the treasure was discarded as Cerezal might mean anywhere in that district. It extended from Becerrea to a point beyond Campo del Arbol. The exact place where this district ends is at GPS Co-ordinates 42°53'41.3"N 7°13'02.3"W, 42.894798, -7.217315.

In conclusion, then, the most likely place where the military chest was disposed of was somewhere in the approximate area of:

42°52'08.8"N 7°10'33.6"W
42..869119, -7.175987

This is because:

a) This is the approach to highest point on the road between Nogales and Constantin with severe slopes on either side.
b) Its aspect is 'stupendous' and, because of the fall of the road it is a point 'on a hill and perfectly visible to the enemy'.
c) It is the approximately correct distance from Nogales.
d) It conforms to local traditions.
e) People have been investigating in this area in the past.

Finally, it might be recalled that a number of peasants, indeed all the peasants who worked the land belonging to Vicente Rivera, were able to buy their farms in this impoverished region. Where then was this estate? Exactly at the place above. It seems that those who stated the peasants had recovered the money were correct – as we had always suspected. Much of Vincente Rivera's estate, possibly that which had been farmed directly by him, is an uncultivated, overgrown tangle. Señor Rivera, it seems, took the money and ran.

Unfortunately, after eliminating other possible locations, we only had time for half-a-day with our metal detector and a trowel at the place we had identified.

However, all this might not be as clear cut as it seems. A number of diarists give 4 January as the date the money was disposed of. This is usually ignored, it being assumed that such people got their dates muddled up. But could it be that there were two occasions when money was discarded and that these individuals were recording the events they had witnessed, unaware of the other instance of the army's chest being abandoned? Who is to say that the total money of the army was just £25,000, which we have seen was a very small sum to provide for such a considerable number of men? Could it be that there was more than two cart carrying the money of the paymaster general? Could this explain why some say the money was coming from Corunna and others that it was travelling with the army? It might account for the varying amounts offered by numerous commentators.

If this was the case, it might also enable us to reconcile what we know with some degree of certainty with the seemingly contradictory versions of events which state that money was disposed of as the army marched over the Piedrafita pass – on 4 January.

There is also another problem with the place that we have identified, which is that Blakeney, as well as the Regimental Record of the 52nd Regiment, stated that the steep hill was on the left as the Reserve turned to face the enemy, and at Cereixal the steep slope is on the right if facing rearwards. Along the road from Becerrea all the way to Campo del Arbol, the ascent, if facing towards where the French would have been approaching, is on the right. It is only after Campo del Arbol, as the road travels down to Constantin that this swaps round. As said before, such a place does not fit into the timings given by Blakeney. However, the Camino Real follows a different route between Campo del Arbol and Constantin. This road is no longer passable for vehicles and passes through Retorta, mentioned by Dr Correa as the place where the rear-guard clashed with its pursuers. The slope here also conforms with Blakeney's description of the descent being on the left, facing southwards. The only problem with this is that it is only a short distance from Constantin.

The hunt for Moore's missing military chest, therefore, is not over. In fact thanks to the ongoing investigations by my acquaintances, especially Angel Rodil, in trawling through the documents in the Archivo Historico de Lugo and the Archivo del Reino de Galicia amongst other sources, as well as interviewing the ancient families of the region, the search has only just begun.

Notes

Chapter 1: Cintra Shame

1. M. de Bourienne, *Memoirs of Napoleon Bonaparte,* Vol. II (London, 1836), p. 18, quoted in David Chandler, *The Campaigns of Napoleon* (Macmillan, New York, 1966), p. 586.
2. Robert Harvey, *The War of Wars, The Epic Struggle Between Britain and France 1793–1815* (Constable, London, 2006), p. 449.
3. Charles Oman, *A History of the Peninsular War* (Greenhill, London, 1995), Vol. I, pp. 30–1.
4. W.F.P. Napier, *History of the War in the Peninsula and in the South of France, From the Year 1807 to the Year 1814* (Constable, London, 1992), Vol. I, pp. 24–7.
5. J. Gurwood [ed.] *The Dispatches of Field Marshal the Duke of Wellington, during His Various Campaigns* etc. (John Murray, London, 1837), p. 121.
6. R.M. Johnston, *In the Words of Napoleon, the Emperor Day by Day* (Frontline, Barnsley, 2015), pp. 207–8.

Chapter 2: Blind Confidence

1. James Carrick Moore, *A Narrative of the Campaign of the British Army in Spain Commanded by His Excellency Lieutenant General Sir John Moore* (Joseph Johnson, London, 1809), Appendix A, pp. 241–5
2. Arthur Bryant, *Years of Victory, 1802–1812* (Collins, London 1951), p. 236.
3. Moore to Lieutenant General Robert Brownrigg, Military Secretary to the Duke of York, 17 January 1803, quoted in David Gates, *The British Light Infantry Arm c. 1790–1815* (Batsford, London, 1987), p. 92.
4. The Duke of Wellington [ed.], *Supplementary Despatches, Correspondence and Memoranda of Field Marshal Arthur Duke of Wellington* (John Murray, London, 1860), pp. 130–1.

5. John Gurwood [ed.], *The Dispatches of Field Marshall the Duke of Wellington: during his Various Campaigns etc.* (John Murray, London, 1837), Vol. IV, pp. 144–5.
6. Moore to J.W. Gordon, quoted in Charles Esdaile, *The Peninsular War, A New History* (Allen Lane, London, 2002), p. 142; Napier, pp. 330–1.
7. Moore to Castlereagh, 9 October, TNA WO 1/236.
8. Castlereagh to Dalrymple 2 September 1808, quoted in Oman, Vol. I, p. 486.
9. Oman, p. 488.
10. Quoted in Christopher Hibbert, *Corunna* (Batsford, London, 1961), p. 37.
11. James Moore, Appendix A.
12. Oman, pp. 31–2.
13. Quoted in Hibbert, p. 38.
14. Sir John Fortescue, *History of the British Army,* Vol.6, 1807–1809 (Macmillan, London, 1910), p. 293.
15. Quoted in Hibbert, p. 39.
16. James Moore, Appendix A.
17. Maurice, J.F., *The Diary of Sir John Moore*, Vol. II, (Edward Arnold, London, 1904) hereafter referred to as *Diary*, p. 261.
18. Dalrymple had actually sent Brigadier-General Robert Anstruther to take command of the fortress of Almeida and he had been asked to provide information on the roads through which he travelled.
19. Francis Culling Carr-Gomm, *Letters and Journals of Field Marshal Sir William Maynard Gomm From 1799 to Waterloo, 1815* (John Murray, London, 1891), p. 110.
20. Hibbert, 34–5.
21. *Diary*, p. 326.
22. Hope to Moore, 24 October 1808, Murray Papers, National Library of Scotland, Add. MSS 46 f, in Paul P. Reese, '*The Ablest Man in the British Army*': *The Life and Career of General Sir John Hope*, p. 154.
23. Carr-Gomm, pp. 111–12.
24. James Moore, p. 13.
25. David Chandler, *The Campaigns of Napoleon*, (Macmillan, New York, 1966), pp. 628–9.
26. Jan Read, *War in the Peninsula* (Faber & Faber, London, 1977), p. 93; James Moore, p. 13.
27. Fortescue, p. 266.
28. *Diary*, p. 273
29. James Moore, p. 14.
30. James Moore, p. 15.

Chapter 3: Portugal Adieu

1. Julian Sturgis (ed.), *A Boy in the Peninsular War, the Services, Adventures and Experiences of Robert Blakeney, Subaltern in the 28th Regiment* (John Murray, London 1899), hereafter referred to as Blakeney, p. 22; Bryant, 260.
2. Robert Kerr Porter, *Letters from Portugal and Spain, Written During the March of the British Troops under Sir John Moore* (Longman etc., London, 1809), p. 68.
3. James Moore, p. 13.
4. Written at Villafranca on 27 October, *Diary*, 273.
5. G.C. Moore-Smith, *Life and Letters of John Colborne* (John Murray, London, 1903), p. 384.
6. T.E. Hook, *The Life of General the Right Honourable Sir David Baird*, Volume II, (Richard Bentley, London 1832), p. 205.
7. John Dobbs, *Recollections of an Old 52nd Man* (Privately published, Waterford, 1863), p. 5.
8. R.D. Henegan, *Seven Years' Campaigning in the Peninsula and the Netherlands from 1808 to 1815* (Henry Colburn, London, 1846), p. 19.
9. Boothby, *Under England's Flag 1804–1809, The Memoirs, Diary and Correspondence of Charles Boothby, Captain of Royal Engineers* (Adam & Charles, London, 1900), p. 186.
10. Dobbs, pp. 7–8.
11. A.L.F. Schaumann, *On the Road with Wellington, Diary of a War Commissary in the Peninsular Campaign* (Frontline, Barnsley, 2015), pp. 60–1.
12. Henry Curling [ed.], *Recollections of Rifleman Harris* (H. Hurst, London, 1948) hereafter referred to as *Harris*, p104.
13. Porter, p. 98.
14. Oman, p. 495.
15. ibid.
16. Letter to Castlereagh, 24 November, in James Moore, Appendix L.
17. Blakeney, pp. 22–4.
18. Adam Neale, *Letters from Portugal and Spain* (Richard Phillips, London, 1809), p. 24; Blakeney, p. 195.
19. Fortescue, pp. 294–5.
20. Jean Sarrazin, *History of the War in Spain and Portugal from 1807 to 1814* (Edward Earle, Philadelphia, 1815), pp. 50–1.
21. Wellesley to Castlereagh, 19 October 1808, quoted in D.W. Davis, *Sir John Moore's Peninsular Campaign 1808–1809* (Springer, The Hague, 1974), p. 81.

22. Thomas Sadler (ed.), *Diary, Reminiscences and Correspondence of Henry Crabb Robinson*, Vol. I. (Fields Osgood, Boston, 1870), pp. 274–5.
23. Fortescue, p. 305.
24. *Diary*, 278.
25. Roger Parkinson, *Moore of Corunna* (Purnell, Milton, 1976), p. 184.
26. *Diary*, p. 279.
27. Blakeney, p. 28.
28. James Moore, pp. 264–29.
29. Marquess of Londonderry, *Story of the Peninsular War* (James Blackwood, London, 1857), p. 83.
30. James Moore, p. 20.
31. ibid, p. 38.
32. Andrew Leith Hay, *A Narrative of the Peninsular War* (Hearne, London, 1839), pp. 59–60.
33. *Harris*, pp.104.
34. Major Patterson 'Leaves from the Journal of a Veteran', in W.H. Maxwell, *Peninsular Sketches by Actors on the Scene* Vol. I, (Henry Colburn, London, 1845), p. 36.
35. Dobbs, p. 9.
36. Quoted in Hibbert, pp. 53–4.
37. Neale, p. 54.
38. Chandler, 639.
39. James Moore, 62.
40. Hibbert, p. 64.
41. James Moore, p. 261.
42. Chandler, p. 641.

Chapter 4: The Fate of Spain

1. Thomas Stephen Sorell, *Notes of the Campaign of 1808–1809 in the North of Spain*, (John Murray, London, 1848), p. 4.
2. Quoted in Hibbert, p. 60.
3. Oman, p. 499.
4. Napier, pp. 339–40.
5. Moore to Castlereagh, Salamanca, 24 November, quoted in James Moore, Appendix L; Hibbert, p. 60; Oman, p. 499. According to Davis, p. 100, the news that Baird, in the course of a few days had spent most of the 500,000 dollars caused Spencer Perceval, the Chancellor of the Exchequer, considerable embarrassment, as he had estimated that the expense of the entire force in the Peninsula would not exceed £50,000 per month. Baird commanded only about

a quarter of the army and, according to the Chancellor's predictions, should have spent less than £25,000 by 24 November. But in that time, Baird had spent the £40,000 he had got from Frere (Davis gives this as £50,000), £17,000 by bills of exchange on the Treasury, the £8,000 received from Moore plus the 500,000 dollars, making a total of around £180,000!

6. Claud Vivian, *Richard Hussey Vivian, First Baron Vivian, A Memoir* (Isbister, London, 1897), p. 67.
7. Quoted in John Mollo, *From Corunna to Waterloo with the Hussars, 1808 to 1815* (Pen & Sword, Barnsley, 1997), p. 52.
8. ibid, p. 47.
9. John Brumwell, *The Peninsular War, 1808–1812. Letters of a Weardale Soldier*, [William Egglestone, ed.], (Ann Arbor, University of Michigan, 2012), p. 14.
10. Sorell, p. 12.
11. Hook, p. 229.
12. Moore to Castlereagh, 24 November 1808, in James Moore, Appendix M.
13. Quoted in Anthony Brett James, *General Graham, Lord Lynedoch* (Macmillan, London, 1959), p. 150.
14. Quoted in Roger William Day, *The Life of Sir John Moore, Not a Drum was Heard* (Leo Cooper, Barnsley, 2001), pp. 148–9.
15. *Diary*, pp. 282–3.
16. Vivian, pp. 74–5.
17. ibid, p. 75.
18. James Moore, p. 64.
19. ibid, p. 83.
20. G.C. Moore-Smith, p. 95.
21. Quoted in Nick Lipscombe, *Wellington's Guns, The Untold Story of Wellington and his Artillery in the Peninsula and at Waterloo* (Osprey, Oxford, 2013), p. 55.
22. Charles Stuart's secretary had ridden 476 miles from Tudela to Madrid and then from Madrid to Salamanca in six days, and he then went on with despatches to Corunna, accomplishing the 790 miles in eleven days, including two day's stay at Madrid, see Fortescue, p. 311.
23. *Diary*, pp. 153–4.
24. Fortescue, p. 311.
25. James Moore, pp. 69–70.
26. Londonderry, p. 84
27. Joseph Sinclair, *A Soldier of the Seventy-First, From De La Plata to the Battle of Waterloo, 1806–1815* (Frontline, London, 2010), p. 46.

28. Archibald Alison, *History of Europe from the Commencement of the French Revolution in 1789 to the Restoration of the Bourbons in 1815*, Volume VI (Blackwood, London, 1847), p. 830.
29. Vivian, pp. 82–3.
30. Napier, pp. 440–1.
31. Hope to Moore, 20 November 1808, Letters from Hope to Moore, The British Library, Add. MSS 57541 f. 112, in Reese, p. 159.
32. Londonderry, p. 89.
33. Quoted in Vivian, pp. 87–8.
34. Londonderry, p. 89.
35. *Diary*, p. 284.
36. James Moore, Appendix Q.
37. In all fairness to Frere he had passed on Moore's complaints to the Spanish authorities. They, in the form of a letter from Martin de Garay, responded very positively, explaining to the British representative, to some degree, why Moore had been left in the dark, and by stating that they had a formidable body of 70,000 infantry and 6,000 cavalry assembled ready to cooperate with the British army. Frere made the perfectly understandable mistake of believing the Spaniards.
38. James Moore, p. 87.

Chapter 5: In Fortune's Way

1.   James Moore, pp. 97–8.
2.   ibid, p. 111.
3.   *Diary*, p. 284.
4.   Chandler, p. 645.
5.   Moore's reference here refers to the city of Saragossa which, under the direction of Palafox had famously resisted the French throughout the summer of 1808. It was to suffer another prolonged siege from 20 December 1808 to 20 February 1809, in which most of its civilian population and its military garrison died.
6.   James Moore, Appendix BB.
7.   Sorell, p. 34
8.   Sorell, p. 40.
9.   Brett-James, p. 160.
10. Leith Hay, *Narrative*, p. 64.
11. Londonderry, p. 92.Mollo, p. 58, says that the combat at Rueda took place on the night of the 13th.
12. Carr-Gomm, p. 114.

13. Sorell, p. 36.
14. Hibbert, p. 83. Captain Boothby also mentions a French despatch being captured on 6 December. As it would have taken a few days to reach Moore, one wonders if the two stories are describing the same event, even though the circumstances are quite different. This is what Boothby wrote in his diary for 7 December: 'Yesterday General Alton intercepted the imperial mail from Burgos to Madrid. It was carried by a Spanish courier, and guarded by two French officers and a French courier. The party was attacked by about twenty peasants a few leagues from Burgos. One French officer and the French courier were killed. The other Frenchman made his escape, and the Spanish courier set off at full speed for the English outposts. The mail had many letters for Napoleon and his dukes and nobles.
15. James Moore, Appendix GG. The letter is also reproduced in full in *Diary*, pp. 399–401.
16. Londonderry, p. 94.
17. Boothby, p. 195.
18. Sinclair, p. 46.
19. Stanley Monick [ed], *Douglas's Tale of the Peninsula and Waterloo 1808–1815* (Leo Cooper, London, 1997), p. 62.
20. Alexander Gordon, *A Cavalry Officer in the Corunna Campaign, The Journal of Captain Gordon of the 15th Hussars* (John Murray, London, 1913). p. 83.
21. William Gavin, *The Diary of William Gavin, Ensign and Quarter-Master 71st Highland Regiment, 1806–1815*, (privately published, 1921), p. xii.
22. Gareth Glover, *From Corunna to Waterloo, The Letters and Journals of Two Napoleonic Hussars, 1801–1816* (Frontline, Barnsley, 2015), p. 78.
23. Glover, p. 79.
24. Mollo, p. 60.
25. Gordon, pp. 103–7.
26. Oman, p. 536.
27. Augustus Paget, *The Paget Papers* Volume II (Heineman, London, 1896), p. 388.
28. Glover, *From Corunna to Waterloo*, pp. 81–2.

Chapter 6: Risking too Much

1. Brett-James, p. 162.
2. Quoted in N. Ludlow Beamish, *History of the King's German Legion* (Buckland & Brown, London, 1993) vol.1, p. 157.

3. *Harris*, p. 89.
4. ibid.
5. James Clavell Library, Woolwich, catalogue reference MD 2566, General G. Cookson, *The Journals of Lieutenant George Cookson, The Retreat to Corunna.*
6. James Moore, p. 166.
7. *Diary*, pp. 286–7.
8. Londonderry, p. 97.
9. Gareth Glover, *From Corunna to Waterloo*, p. 82.
10. Anthony Hamilton, *Hamilton's Campaign with Moore and Wellington During the Peninsular War,* (Privately published, 1847), p. 28.
11. William Surtees, *Twenty-five Years in the Rifle Brigade* (Blackwood, London, 1833), pp. 80–1.
12. Porter, pp. 234–5.
13. James Sterling, *Memoir of Campaign of 1808 in Spain under Lieutenant-General Sir John Moore, K.B.*, p. 74, quoted in *Diary*, pp. 375–6.
14. Vivian, p. 81.
15. Anonymous, *The Personal Narrative of a Private Soldier, Who Served in the Forty-Second Highlanders, for Twelve Years, During the Late War* (London, 1935, Ken Trotman, Cambridge, 1996)
16. ibid, p. 101.
17. James Moore, pp. 322–3.
18. Quoted in Oman, p. 542.
19. Quoted in Chandler, p. 650.
20. Arthur John Butler, *The Memoirs of Baron de Marbot* (Longmans, Green & Co., London, 1903), Vol.1, p. 278. Also, see Davis, pp. 183–4.
21. Chandler, p. 651.
22. Vivian, p. 100.
23. Eric Hunt, *Charging Against Napoleon, Diaries & Letters of Three Hussars* (Leo Cooper, Barnsley, 2001), p. 30.
24. Sinclair, pp. 47–8.
25. ibid, p. 48.
26. James Moore, pp. 176–7.
27. Sarrazin, p. 47.
28. Schaumann, pp. 94–5.
29. Gareth Glover, *The Corunna Journal of Captain, C.A. Pierrepoint AQMG* (Ken Trotman, Huntingdon, 2005), p. 14.
30. ibid, pp. 14–15.
31. Quoted, unsourced, in Andrew Rawson, *The Peninsular War, A Battlefield Guide* (Pen & Sword, Barnsley, 2009), pp. 54–5.
32. *Harris*, pp. 170–1.

33. *Diary*, p. 381.

34. Quoted in Hunt, p. 30 but the source is Oman, p,548.

35. Hunt, p. 31

36. Jean-Roch, Coignet, *The Notebooks of the Captain Coignet, Soldier of the Empire* (Frontline, Barnsley, 2016), p. 160.

37. Just how difficult it had been for the chasseurs to ford the river was explained by Vivian, who wrote the following in his diary: 'From passing the river I had an opportunity of judging of the difficulties the enemy must have encountered. I was mounted on an English horse, considerably stronger and larger than the best of theirs, and in going I found it an operation of difficulty, and several minutes on returning my horse swam and was nearly carried down with the current. Count Grazinsky afterwards came to my side of the water, and would have actually been lost but for one of the men of the 7th, who assisted him on shore.'

38. Beamish, vol.1, p. 164.

39. Napier, vol.1, pp. 476–7.

40. Butler, *Marbot*, p. 279.

41. Dobbs, p. 11.

42. Vivian, p. 103.

43. Quoted in Edward Ryan, *Napoleon's Shield and Guardian, the Unconquerable General Daumesnil* (Frontline, Barnsley, 2015), p. 181. Lefèbvre-Desnoëttes was sent as a prisoner to England and housed at Cheltenham where he lived for over two years. As was the custom, he gave his parole as a French officer that he would not try to escape. He was even allowed to be joined by his wife Stephanie. It seems that the couple: 'were in demand socially and attended social events around the district.' However, it seems that he was in possession of a fine signet ring of considerable value which had been given him years earlier by Napoleon. Lefèbvre-Desnoëttes used this ring as a bribe to gain his escape and he was able to return to France, where he re-joined the Chasseurs, Stephen Lewis, https://thewildpeak. wordpress.com/the-authors.

44. Leith Hay, pp. 69–70.

Chapter 7: Retreat

1. Schaumann, pp. 100–1.

2. Londonderry, p. 101.

3. Sinclair, p. 50.

4. Vivian, p. 104.

5.   Michael Glover and Jonathon Riley, *That Astonishing Infantry: Three Hundred Years of the History of the Royal Welch Fusiliers (23rd Regiment of Foot), 1689–1989* (Pen & Sword, Barnsley, 1989), p. 51.
6.   Surtees, p. 82.
7.   Gareth Glover, *Pierrepoint*, pp. 10–11.
8.   James Moore, pp. 184–5.
9.   Robert Southey, *History of the Peninsular War* Vol.1 (John Murray, London, 1823)p. 784.
10. ibid.
11. *Harris*, pp. 225–6.
12. Sinclair, p. 50.
13. *Harris*, p. 114.
14. Londonderry, pp. 101–2.
15. Gordon, pp. 145–6.
16. James Moore, p. 84.
17. Chandler, p. 652; R.M. Johnstone [ed.], *In the Words of Napoleon* (Frontline Books, Barnsley, 2015), p. 212; Glover, p. 116.
18. Butler, *Marbot*, p. 280.
19. ibid, p. 281.
20. Oman, pp. 560–1.
21. For more details of these two French forces, see Philip Haythornthwaite, *Corunna 1809, Sir John Moore's Fighting Retreat* (Osprey, Oxford, 2001), p. 16.
22. Oman, p. 564.
23. *United Services Journal*, 1831, Part III, quoted in Beamish, p. 362.
24. Schaumann, pp. 103 & 107.
25. Sinclair, pp. 51–2.
26. Glover, *Pierrepoint*, p. 18.
27. Quoted in Reese, p. 170.
28. Schaumann, pp. 109–10.
29. Quoted in Charles Esdaile, *Peninsular Eyewitnesses, The Experience of War in Spain and Portugal 1808–1813* (Pen & Sword, Barnsley, 2008), p. 66.
30. *Harris*, pp. 181–2.
31. *Anon., Memoirs of a Sergeant late in the Forty-Third Light Infantry Regiment previously to and during the Peninsular War* (London, 1835), p. 52.
32. Maxwell, *Peninsular Sketches*, p. 49.
33. Blakeney, pp. 49–50.
34. W.H. Maxwell, *Peninsular Sketches by Actors on the Scene* Vol. I, (Henry Colburn, London, 1845), p. 50.
35. *Memoirs of a Sergeant*, p. 53.
36. Blakeney, pp. 50–1.

37. Oman, p. 568.
38. John and Dorothea Teague, (eds.), *Where duty calls me: Napoleonic war experiences of Rifleman William Green* (Synjon Books, Borden, 2007), p. 15.
39. Dobbs, p. 10.
40. Gordon, pp. 163–4.
41. Blakeney, p. 59
42. Anthony Brett-James, (ed.), *The Peninsula and Waterloo Campaigns – Edward Costello* (Longmans, London, 1967), p. 11; Oman, p. 569, says that it was not Colbert's trumpet-major who was shot after the general, but his aide-de-camp, Latour-Maubourg.
43. Anthony Brett-James, *Costello*, p. 11.
44. R. Rutherford-Moore, 'Plunkett's Shot', *First Empire*, Issue 24; 1998.

Chapter 8: The Loss of the Military Chest

1. Hibbert, p. 120.
2. Blakeney, p. 68.
3. Benjamin Miller, *The Adventures of Serjeant Benjamin Miller* (Naval & Military Press, Heathfield, 1999), p. 34.
4. Anonymous, p. 63.
5. Gordon, pp. 165–6.
6. Vivian, pp. 106–7.
7. Schaumann, p. 115.
8. ibid, pp117–8.
9. Porter, pp. 263–4.
10. Hook, p. 310.
11. Sinclair, p. 53.
12. *Memoirs of a Sergeant*, pp. 61–4.
13. O. Robertson, *The Journal of Sergeant D. Robertson, late 92nd Foot* (Perth 1842), p. 55.
14. Dobbs, pp. 10–11.
15. Brett-James, *General Graham*, p. 164.
16. Dobbs, p. 12.
17. Londonderry, p. 102.
18. Mollo, p. 73.
19. MacBride, MacKenzie, *With Napoleon at Waterloo and Other Unpublished Documents of the Waterloo and Peninsular Campaigns* (Francis Griffiths, London, 1911), p. 74
20. Hook, p. 311.
21. William Mahon, *Messenger, The Life of Henry Percy, Peninsular Soldier and French Prisoner of War* (Pen & Sword, Barnsley, 2017), p. 34.

22. Albert J.M. de Rocca, *Memoires sur la guerre des Francais en Espagne* (Paris 1814) pp. 96–100.
23. M. de Naylies, *Mémoires sur la guerre d'Espagnependnant les années 1808, 1809, 1810 et 1811* (Paris: Magimel, Anselin et Pochard, 1817), p. 37.
24. ibid, p. 38.
25. Gordon, p. 168.
26. Vivian, p. 121
27. *Memoirs of a Sergeant*, p. 52.
28. Nathaniel Steevens, *Reminiscences of My Military Life From 1795 to 1818 by the Late Lieut.-Colonel Chas. Steevens, Formerly of the XX Regiment* (Warren & Son, Winchester, 1878), pp. 66–7.
29. Oman, p. 572.
30. Southey, p. 792.
31. Schaumann, p. 121.
32. Glover, *Pierrepoint*, p. 23.
33. Londonderry, p. 106.
34. Gareth Glover [ed.], *The Diary of a Veteran, The Diary of Sergeant Peter Facey, 28th (North Gloucester) Regiment of Foot 1803–1819* (Ken Trotman, Godmanchester, 2007), p. 10.
35. Stephen Morley, *Memoirs of a Sergeant of the 5th Regiment of Foot* (Ken Trotman, Cambridge, 1999), p. 61.
36. Francis Arthur Whinyates, *From Corunna to Sevastopol: The History of 'C' Battery … Royal Horse Artillery* (G. Francis Smith, 1990), pp. 44–5.
37. Vivian, p. 107.
38. Blakeney, p. 78.
39. Fortescue, p. 369.
40. Londonderry, p. 106.
41. Schaumann, pp. 121–2
42. Londonderry, p. 106.
43. Southey, p. 792.
44. Glover, *Pierrepoint*, p. 23.
45. Steevens, p. 70.
46. Davis, p. 216.
47. Londonderry, p. 108.

Chapter 9: At Bay: The Battle of Lugo

1. Archibald Alison, *History of Europe from the commencement of the French revolution to the restoration of the Bourbons* (Blackwood, Edinburg, 1860), Vol. VI, p. 840.
2. Maxwell, pp. 45–6.

3. Carrick Moore, p. 194.
4. Esdaile, *Peninsular Eyewitnesses*, p. 68.
5. Gavin, p. xiii. Together Graham and Gavin arrested the dragoon and marched him off to the provost and he was locked up. But in the confusion of the retreat that followed, the affair was forgotten.
6. *Regimental Journal of the 15th Light Dragoons*, p. 26, quoted in Davis, p. 217.
7. Oman, p. 574.
8. James Moore, p. 196.
9. *Memoirs of a Sergeant*, p. 43.
10. Fortescue, p. 370.
11. Sinclair, p. 57.
12. Cowan, p. 49.
13. Brett-James, *General Graham*, p. 165.
14. Napier, p. 494.
15. ibid, p. 200.
16. Sinclair, p. 58.
17. Morley, p. 62.
18. Cookson, quoted in Lipscombe, p. 70.
19. Capt. A. Wall, *Diary of the Operations in Spain under Sir John Moore by Captain Adam*, Royal Artillery Institute Proceedings, vol. XIII, p. 126, quoted in Lipscombe, p. 69.
20. Neale, pp. 313–4.
21. Schaumann, p. 128.
22. Glover, *Pierrepoint*, p. 25.
23. Cowan, p. 49.
24. Gordon, p. 184.
25. Schaumann, p. 130.
26. Maxwell, p. 45.
27. Hibbert, p. 142.
28. Teague, pp. 14–15.
29. Hussey-Vivian, pp. 111–2.
30. *Peninsular Sketches*, pp. 44–5.
31. Hussey Vivian Memoir, p. 111.
32. Morley, pp. 63–4.
33. Morley, pp. 58–9.
34. Gavin, xiv.
35. Gordon, pp. 190–1.
36. Hook, p. 320.
37. Cowan, p. 53.
38. Blakeney, pp. 90–1.

39. Beamish, pp. 362–3.
40. Brumwell, p. 17.
41. Gordon, p. 195.

Chapter 10: A Melancholy Aspect of Affairs

1. Sinclair, p. 59.
2. Quoted in Brett-James, p. 167.
3. Blakeney, pp. 94–5.
4. ibid, p. 97.
5. Mollo, p. 77.
6. Glover, *From Corunna to Waterloo*, p. 88.
7. Fortescue, p. 375.
8. Surtees, p. 94.
9. *Harris*, p. 236.
10. Carrick Moore, p. 206.
11. Blakeney pp. 101–2.
12. Londonderry, p. 111.
13. Blakeney, p. 102.
14. Teague, p. 18.
15. Porter, pp. 274–5.
16. Napier, Vol. I, pp. 499–500.
17. Quoted in Lipscombe, pp. 71–2.
18. Hamilton, p. 56.
19. Blakeney, p. 106.
20. Gordon, pp. 199–200.
21. Sinclair, p. 60.
22. Oman, p. 582.
23. Beamish, pp. 179–80.
24. Schaumann, p. 134.
25. Basil Hall, *Voyages and Travels of Captain Basil Hall RN* (Nelson & Sons, London, 1895), p. 230
26. Schaumann, p. 133.
27. Londonderry, p. 111.
28. Oman, p. 583.
29. Boothby, pp. 215–6.
30. James Moore, p. 207.
31. Leith Hay, *Memoirs*, p. 26.
32. Quoted in Esdaille, *Peninsular Eyewitnesses*, p. 70.
33. William H. Cope, *The History of the Rifle Brigade* (Chatto & Windus, London, 1877), p. 37–8.

Chapter 11: 'I Hope the People of England Will be Satisfied!'

1. Hibbert, p. 169.
2. Quoted in Mark Urban, *The Man Who Broke Napoleon's Codes, The Story of George Scovell* (Faber and Faber, London, 2001), p. 15.
3. Quoted, unsourced, in Sommerville, pp. 183–4.
4. Basil Hall, p. 230.
5. Quoted in Lipscombe, p. 75.
6. Urban, p. 16.
7. Sir William Francis Patrick Napier, *The Life and Opinions of General Sir Charles James Napier, G.C.B.*, pp. 94–5.
8. Blakeney, p. 114.
9. Delavoye, Alexander M., *Life of Thomas Graham, Lord Lynedoch. (London: Marchant Singer, 1880), p. 801.*
10. James Moore, pp. 359–60.
11. Anonymous, p. 83.9
12. Napier, *Life and Opinions*, p. 96
13. ibid, p. 98.
14. ibid, p. 99.
15. ibid, pp. 99–100.
16. *Delavoye, pp. 297–8.*
17. Hibbert, p. 182.
18. Delayoye, pp. 297–8.
19. Napier, *Life and Opinions*, pp. 95–6.
20. Blakeney, pp. 116–7.
21. Dobbs, p. 14.
22. Moore-Smith, p. 109.
23. Moore, p. 227.

Chapter 12: Consequences

1. Grehan and Mace, p. 51.
2. Blakeney, p. 118.
3. Dobbs, p. 15.
4. Adam Neale, *Letters from Portugal and Spain* (Richard Phillips, London, 1809, p. 326.
5. Vivian, p. 118.
6. Schaumann, pp. 144–5.
7. Quoted in Roger Knight, *Britain Against Napoleon, The Organization of Victory 1793–1815* (Allen Lane, London, 2013), p. 205.
8. TNA WO 55/1194, quoted in Lipscombe, pp. 74–5.
9. Oman, p. 596.

10. ibid, pp. 646–7.
11. Moore-Smith, p. 17.
12. C.G Gardyne, *The Life of a Regiment: The History of the Gordon Highlanders* (The Medici Society, London, 1929), Vol.1, p. 164. Quoted, unsourced, in Hibbert, p. 198.
13. Gordon, pp. 209–10.
14. Gareth Glover, *From Corunna to Waterloo*, p. 89.
15. Schaumann, pp. 135–6.
16. Moore-Smith, pp. 104–5.
17. Andrew Leith Hay, *Memoirs of the late Lieutenant-General Sir James Leith, G.C.B., with a precis of some of the most remarkable events of the Peninsular War. By a British Officer* (Privately published, Barbados, 1817), pp. 24–5.
18. Kerr Porter, p. 272.
19. Neal, p. 338.
20. Edmund Warre [ed.] *Letters from the Peninsula 1808–1812 by Lieut.-Gen. Sir William Warre* (John Murray, London, 1909), p. 48.
21. Fortescue, p. 408.
22. Letter from George Napier to his mother, dated 13 January 1809, quoted in Davies, p. 241.
23. Quoted in Brett-James, p. 166.
24. Esdaile, *Peninsular War*, p. 153.
25. Hansard, House of Commons Debates, Vol. 12, 1157–1119, 24 February 1809.
26. Moore-Smith, p. 108.
27. Hussey Vivian, p. 120.
28. Napier, p. 360. This caused a major rift between Castlereagh and Canning, which resulted in them fighting a duel with pistols on 21 September 1809 on Wimbledon Common. Canning missed and was hit in the thigh by Castlereagh. Strangely, up to this point, Canning had been fulsome in his praise of Moore's advance against Napoleon's line of communication, declaring in the House that: 'In this movement he acted as a statesman no less than as a soldier ; because even though he might fail he must have gained an advantage for the south of Spain, whose exertions had never been relaxed, by drawing off the French army from Madrid and the prosecution of operations against the capital and the southern provinces. Every operation of that campaign had proved glorious for the character of the British army. If we had been obliged to quit Spain, we had left that country with fresh laurels blooming upon our brows.' *Diary*, p. 392.

26. H.R. Milburne, *A Narrative of the Circumstances Attending the Retreat of the British Army Under Sir John Moore, With a Concise Account of the Memorable Battle of Corunna, and Subsequent Embarkation of his Majesty's Troops* (T. Egerton, London 1809), p. 38.
30. Oman, p. 598.
31. James Moore, pp. 204–5.
32. Oman, p. 556.
33. Diary, pp. 380–1.
34. 'Memorandum of Operations in 1810' in Gurwood, Vol.7, pp. 291–313.
35. Oman, p. 598.
36. Oman, p. 556.
37. Diary, pp. 380–1.
38. Weller, p. 68.
39. Hansard, House of Commons Debates, 25 January 1809 vol. 12 cc138–44.
40. 'Guerra de la Independencia Española 1808–181', reproduced courtesy of the Napoleon Series.
41. Hussey Vivian memoir, p. 129.
42. ibid.
43. TNA WO 55/1193
44. Sorrel, pp. 41–2.
45. Chandler, pp,657–8.
46. James Moore, Appendices, p. 32.
47. Sorrel, p. 2.
48. Dominique Eugène Paul Balagny, *Campaign de l'empereur Napoléon en Espagne (1808–1809)* (Berger-Levraut, Paris, 1902), cited in Fortescue, p. 394.
49. de Rocca, ibid.
50. Parkinson, p. 235.

Chapter 13: The Hunt

1. Blakeney, pp. 78–81.
2. Cadell, pp. 56–7.
3. *Life of Thomas Graham*, p. 294.
4. Gordon, pp. 176–7.
5. Fortescue, p. 369.
6. Moore-Smith, p. 389.
7. Davis, p. 215.
8. Davis, p. 214.

9. 'Guerra de la Independencia Española 1808–1814', reproduced courtesy of the Napoleon Series.

10. Steevens, p. 72.

11. MacBride, MacKenzie, p. 74.

12. Gordon, pp. 184–5.

13. Glover, *From Corunna to Waterloo*, p. 88: Mollo, p. 76.

14. Jones, Charles and Major Lord Carnock, 'Cavalry in the Corunna Campaign: As Told in the Diary of the Adjutant of the 15th Hussars' *Society for Army Historical Research*, No.4, 1936, p. 27.

15. Whinyates, p. 45.

16. ibid.

17. Beamish, vol.1, pp. 176–7.

18. Schaumann, p. 122.

19. James Moore, pp. 192–3.

20. John Henry Leslie, *The Services of the Royal Regiment of Artillery in the Peninsular War, 1808 to 1814* (Hugh Rees, London, 1908), p. 62.

21. TNA WO 1/237, f.383, quoted in Davies, p. 215.

22. M.A. Thiers, *Histoire du Consulat et de L'Empire* (Paris, 1849), Volume 9, p. 526.

23. Whinyates, p. 46.

24. Napier, *History*, p. 490.

25. Blakeney, p. 92.

26. Davis, p. 214.

27. Davis, p. 68.

28. Steevens, pp. 70–1.

29. Alison, p. 108.

30. Napier, *History*, p. 490.

31. Oman, p. 572.

32. Day, p. 184.

33. Alberto Blas Ferreiro, 'John Moore pasa por Lugo' *Taboa Redonda*, 3 de junio de 1992.

34. See http://www.asociacioncastanoynogal.com

35. Correspondence with Clare Harding, who accompanied Julia Page on her trips to the Peninsula.

36. Anonymous, *Souvenirs Militaires Du Temps de L'Empire Par Un Officer Supérieur du Deuxième Corps* (Paris, 1841), p. 64.

37. Antonia Correa, *El Lucense, DiarioCatolico*, 9 January 1897.

Appendix I

Reasons for the loss of equipment during the Corunna Campaign

The following is an extract from the introduction of the report of the of Board of Claims, Great George Street, London, on 26 May 1809. Parts of these introductory paragraphs are reproduced here to show how the losses in the Corunna campaign, including that of the military chest, were regarded by the British authorities:

> The very peculiar circumstances in which the British Army was placed during the late campaign, particularly on the retreat to Corunna and Vigo … the difficulties and privations it experienced and the losses it sustained, have long been a matter of too general notoriety to admit of a doubt. The Board nevertheless considering the great importance of the trust confided in them, both with respect to the nature and extent of the claims, on which they would have to decide, and the consequent magnitude of the indemnification to be granted at the public expense … felt it their duty not to deviate from any of the usual or established rules, without first calling for evidence to prove the facts … With this view, they have … examined several General and other Officers, upon the subject and the result of such examinations has formed the basis of various opinions and resolutions … of which the following is a summary:

Causes of the Losses

1. It appears that large quantities of Regimental accoutrements and appointments, of Officers' Baggage, and camp equipage, and of

N.C.O.'s and men's necessaries, were left behind, or destroyed, at various times, and places, for want of the means of conveyance, the horses and mules having been so worn out with fatigue, want of forage, shoes as to be unable to proceed, and it consequently became necessary to destroy them. That in the town of Lugo alone, not less than from 200 to 250 horses were shot under these circumstances. That in the case of one Regiment – the 15th Lt. Dragoons – there consisting of 700 men, not more than 300 men were mounted on the return of the Regt. to Corunna. That the horses were constantly falling down on the road, and their backs were so offensive, from being in a state of mortification, that the stench was frequently intolerable.

2. That in addition to the hardships which the Army had to encounter, from these and other circumstances, the inhabitants in almost every part of the country through which the troops passed were continually watching opportunities to plunder both Officers and Men, so that no vigilance on the part of either, could protect them from depredations of this kind which appear to have been committed to a very great extent.

3. That verbal orders were at various times given by General and other Officers to destroy or throw away, accoutrements, Baggage, Camp equipage and necessaries, and to destroy horses.

4. That Baggage was sometimes left behind from the necessity of employing the horses and mules on services of greater importance. No recorded attempt was made to use either horses or oxen from other Army transport to even save the Army's treasure.

5. That from the hurry and confusion which prevailed on the re-embarkation of the Army at Corunna, as well as from the want of Boats to convey accoutrements, baggage, etc., on board the transports, very considerable losses were sustained.

6. That many articles of various descriptions were lost in consequence of Regiments not embarking in the same transport with their baggage, which upon their arrival in England, was found to be in a very deficient state.

7. It appears also from the testimony of, and from Documents produced by the Military Superintendent of Hospitals, that considerable quantities of clothing and necessaries belonging to sick men of different Regiments, were destroyed in the several Hospitals upon

their landing in England, to prevent infection, and that a very considerable loss of accoutrements was likewise sustained from the same and other causes.

The rest of this report deals with the sums of money the board was willing to pay for the various losses suffered by officers, men and regiments. This can be found in the National Archives, WO 26/41, compiled here by Keith Raynor and reproduced courtesy of Access Heritage Inc. Claims were still being investigated by the War Department more than two and-a-half years later.

Appendix II

British Losses in The Corunna Campaign

By Steve Brown

J ust how many men did Sir John Moore's force lose in Spain? The question has long vexed historians. Appendix XIII of Oman Volume 1 provides figures based upon a comparison of returns between October 1808, 19 December 1808 and January 1809, at which time men missing from their regiments may not have re-joined. I have recently discovered a return in WO 1/904 which computed the total men lost in Portugal and Spain as of 6 May 1809, in other words, nearly four months after Corunna. This reveals considerable differences in the losses in some regiments as stated by Oman.

There are two possible problems with Oman's numbers. Firstly, he based them upon 'Effective Strength' – i.e. men fit to take the field – rather than Total Strength, i.e. the sum of fit men plus sick men or 'On Command'. A second problem is that his disembarkation strengths in England in January 1809 may not include various men who were detached or lost and sailed with other regiments to other ports in the confusion. It is reasonable to assume that by May 1809 these men were well and truly accounted for with their parent battalions.

The 'Total Other Ranks left in Portugal' number in the WO return – 1,353 other ranks – accords reasonably well with the men used to form the two battalions of Detachments (see http://www.napoleon-series.org/military/organization/c_detach.html) which show a slightly higher number (by only fifty or so), but with the knowledge that these units contained some men who were described as 'escaped from the French' or 'from the frontiers,' (in other words formerly listed amongst those 'missing in Spain' in the War Office return), which would account for the difference.

It also seems reasonable to assume that the vast majority of men still missing in Spain as of May 1809 were either dead, deserted or POWs, and would not be seen again until (at best) the termination of the war in 1814 – if ever.

The one deficiency within the May 1809 War Office return is that it provides no data for;

- 1st and 3rd Foot Guards
- KGL units
- Cavalry
- Royal Artillery
- Staff Corps

Therefore, these units have not been included in the following summaries but have been discussed at the end. The 3rd Foot and the 5/60th Rifles, who left Moore before Corunna and returned to Portugal, are excluded.

Sources Used:

1. WO 1/904, National Archives
2. Andrew Bamford, *British Army Unit Strengths 1808–1815*; returns for 1 November 1808 (although where regiments joined later, the 1 December numbers are used)
3. Oman, *History of the Peninsula War*, Volume 1 Appendix XIII.

Losses In Portugal and Spain According to WO 1/904 and Oman

The following table is compilation of data from all three sources used:

Unit	Brigade	Total Other Ranks 1 November 1808 [2]	Effective Strength 19 December 1808 [3]	Disembarked England January 1809 [3]	Total Other Ranks left in Portugal as of 6 May 1809 [1]	Total Other Ranks missing in Spain as of 6 May 1809 [1]	Oman's Reported 'Deficiency' [3]	% Original Other Ranks lost in Spain based on [1]
1/6th Foot	Beresford	940	783	491	33	410	391	43.6%
1/9th Foot	Beresford	939	607	572	0	344	373	36.8%
2/43rd Light	Beresford	702	411	368	111	211	230	30.5%
1/28th Foot	Disney	1032	750	624	111	285	302	27.7%
2/23rd Fusiliers	Beresford	575	496	418	0	152	172	26.4%
2nd Foot	Hill	755	616	461	93	194	205	25.8%
1/50th Foot	Bentinck	943	794	599	71	234	264	25.0%
2/81st Foot	Manningham	719	615	478	0	164	241	22.8%
51st Foot	Leith	630	516	506	0	139	107	22.1%
3/1st Foot	Manningham	871	597	507	0	190	216	21.8%
1/26th Foot	Manningham	866	745	662	0	187	208	21.6%
1/91st Highlanders	Disney	895	698	534	154	190	212	21.3%
1/5th Foot	Hill	969	833	654	83	188	239	19.6%
1/82nd Foot	Fane	879	812	602	92	166	228	19.3%
1/32nd Foot	Hill	875	756	619	70	158	187	18.1%
2/14th Foot	Hill	621	550	492	0	108	138	17.4%
2/59th Foot	Leith	636	557	497	0	107	143	16.8%
1/52nd Light	Anstruther	877	828	719	0	139	143	15.9%

Unit	Brigade	Total Other Ranks 1 November 1808 [2]	Effective Strength 19 December 1808 [3]	Disembarked England January 1809 [3]	Total Other Ranks left in Portugal as of 6 May 1809 [1]	Total Other Ranks missing in Spain as of 6 May 1809 [1]	Oman's Reported 'Deficiency' [3]	% Original Other Ranks lost in Spain based on [1]
20th Foot	Anstruther	580	499	428	43	90	113	15.5%
1/71st Highlanders	C Crawfurd	850	724	626	100	129	138	15.2%
1/42nd Highlanders	Bentinck	937	880	757	21	139	161	14.9%
1/4th Foot	Bentinck	960	754	740	73	138	149	14.4%
76th Foot	Leith	779	654	614	0	112	170	14.4%
1/38th Foot	Fane	955	823	757	55	136	143	14.2%
1/36th Foot	C. Crawfurd	862	736	561	67	113	243	13.2%
1/79th Highlanders	Fane	989	838	777	59	130	155	13.2%
1/92nd Highlanders	C. Crawfurd	975	900	783	66	126	129	12.9%
2/95th Rifles	R. Craufurd	780	702	628	0	78	96	10.0%
2/52nd Light	R. Craufurd	625	381	462	112	60	161	9.6%
2/60th Foot	Corunna garrison	272	0	0	0	22	0	8.1%
1/95th Rifles	Anstruther	857	820	706	31	68	157	7.9%
1/43rd Light	R. Craufurd	898	817	810	0	66	85	7.3%
TOTALS		26043	21492	18452	1445	4973	5899	
% 1 Dec 1808 Strength		100%	82.5%	70.9%	5.5%	19.1%	22.6%	

In summary: Applying Oman's disembarkation numbers to the total strengths on 1 November gives a 29 per cent loss for the campaign, or 7,591 men. WO 1/904 arrives at a total of 6,418 men. The Oman-derived figure is probably too high since it excludes men detached from their regiments on disembarkation in England who subsequently re-joined, suggesting that the 6,418 figure is probably close to the true number.

Losses by Brigade

The same data, represented by brigade, shows some interesting comparisons:

Given that Beresford's and Disney's brigades were only lightly engaged at Corunna on 16 January 1809, the above figures do not flatter those commanders. Bentinck, Manningham, and to a lesser degree Hill had borne the brunt of the French attacks on that day.

Robert Craufurd's 2nd Light Brigade had retreated via Vigo and thus was spared the battle at Corunna, nonetheless his brigade's low wastage rate supports all we know about 'Black Bob's' reputed iron discipline during the retreat.

Interestingly, because Oman's 'Deficiency' figures are based upon differences between October returns and disembarkation returns, it does not take into account losses amongst drafts of reinforcements who joined the expedition in December, whereas the WO 1/904 do so. Hence the 6,418 figure will probably be a more reliable indicator than Oman's 5,899 men lost.

Brigade	Total Other Ranks as per return of 1 November 1808 [2]	Effective Strength 19 December 1808 [3]	Total Other Ranks left in Portugal as of 6 May 1809 [1]	Total Other Ranks missing in Spain as of 6 May 1809 [1]	% Original Men Lost in Spain based on [1]	Total Losses in the Peninsular since 1 November 1808 from [1]	Oman's Reported 'Deficiency' [3]
Beresford	3156	2297	144	1117	35.4%	1261	1166
Disney	1927	1448	265	475	24.6%	740	514
Manningham	2456	1957	0	541	22.0%	541	665
Hill	3220	2755	246	648	20.1%	894	769
Bentinck	2840	2428	165	511	18.0%	676	574
Leith	2045	1727	0	358	17.5%	358	420
Fane	2823	2473	206	432	15.3%	638	526
Caitlin Crawfurd	2687	2360	233	368	13.7%	601	510
Anstruther	2314	2147	74	297	12.8%	371	413
Robert Craufurd	2303	1900	112	204	8.9%	316	342
Corunna Garrison*	272	250	0	22	8.1%	22	0
TOTAL	**26043**	**21742**	**1445**	**4973**		**6418**	**5899**

*Oman's numbers do not include the 2/60th Foot which was garrisoning Corunna town.

The Missing Data

The WO 1/904 returns excludes some units. These have been re-constructed using the returns from Oman and applying the same factors.

Unit	Brigade	Total Other Ranks 1 November 1808 [2]	Effective Strength 19 December 1808 [3]	Disembarked England January 1809 [3]	Total Other Ranks left in Portugal as of 6 May 1809 [1]	Total Other Ranks missing in Spain as of 6 May 1809 [1]	Oman's Reported 'Deficiency' [3]
1/1st Foot Guards	Warde	1359	1300	1266	no data	no data	74
2/1st Foot Guards	Warde	1110	1027	1036	no data	no data	66
7th Hussars*	Paget	676	497	575	no data	no data	97
10th Hussars	Paget	677	514	651	no data	no data	24
15th Hussars	Paget	675	527	650	no data	no data	24
18th Light Dragoons	Paget	671	565	547	no data	no data	77
3rd Light Dragoons KGL	Paget	563	347	377	no data	no data	56
1st Light Battalion KGL**	Alten	939	803	706	no data	no data	163
2nd Light Battalion KGL***	Alten	937	855	618	no data	no data	262
Royal Artillery****		1378	1297	1200	no data	no data	255
Staff Corps		134	133	99	no data	no data	38
TOTALS		9119	7865	7725			1136

These regiments are known to have had about 430 men 'sick absent' on 1 December. If we assume for the sake of the argument that Oman's Deficiency figure is slightly low as was the case for the previous study, this would give a total loss amongst these units of 1,000 men after deducting the sick absent. As can be seen below, nearly 300 of these occurred after the campaign had ended.

* The 7th Hussars lost fifty-six men drowned on the return voyage to England.

** The 1st Light Battalion lost twenty-two men drowned on the return voyage to England.

*** The 2nd Light Battalion lost 187 men drowned on the return voyage to England.

**** The Royal Artillery lost thirty-one men drowned on the return voyage to England and in Corunna Harbour.

ANALYSIS

All of this suggests that 1,445 men were left behind in Portugal and 4,973 were lost in Spain, based upon the WO 1/904 return of May 1809, or 6,418 in total. As this return does not include the Guards, cavalry, KGL light battalions or artillery, these estimated losses need to be added. Losses amongst those units appear to be about 1,000 men, of whom it is assumed few or any ended in Portugal other than the 'sick absent'. This gives a total estimated campaign loss of 7,400 men.

The total number of men lost in Spain according to our figures appears to be 4,973, plus the lion's share of the 1,000 losses amongst the Guards, cavalry etc. So, this number might be 6,000 men. This is almost identical to the 5,998 men 'actually lost in Spain' according to Oman in the conclusion to his Appendix. Of these, documentary evidence tells us that 2,189 ended up as prisoners in France. By a different route, and using different data, Oman's overall figures appear to be validated, although there are obvious discrepancies if studied on a unit-by-unit or per brigade basis.

Most brigades lost between 12 per cent and 20 per cent of their men on the campaign.

As an addition to Steve Brown's analysis, it might be of interest to give Napier's assessment of the losses during the campaign. On page 625 of Volume I of his *History*, he quotes from a General Return received at the Horse Guards which, he says, 'contains the whole number of non-commissioned officers and men, lost during Sir John Moore's campaign':

> Lost at or previous to the arrival of the army at the position of Lugo: Cavalry 95; Infantry 1,302. Total = 1,397.
>
> Of this number 200 were left in the wine-vaults of Bembibre, and nearly 500 were stragglers from the troops that marched to Vigo.
>
> Lost between the departure of the army from Lugo and the embarkation at Coruña: Cavalry 9; Infantry 2,627. Total = 2,636

Napier states that 'of the whole number, 800 contrived to escape to Portugal'. This, then, would give a total of: 4,033 – 800 = 3,233. As we can see, this is far different from the figure arrived at in Steve Brown's careful investigation.

Source Information

Unpublished Documents

The National Archives, Kew

WO 1/236, Europe and the Mediterranean. viii. British Army in Spain, Portugal and France (1808–1820). Moore and Baird.

WO 26/41, War Office: entry books of warrants, regulations and precedents.

WO 55/1193, Ordnance Office, Artillery Letters and Letter Books, Foreign.

James Clavell Library, Royal Arsenal, Woolwich

Catalogue reference MD 2566, General G. Cookson, *The Journals of Lieutenant George Cookson, The Retreat to Corunna*.

Florida State University

Reese, Paul P., *'The Ablest Man in the British Army': The Life and Career of General Sir John Hope*, Doctoral Dissertation, 2007.

Published Works

Alison, Archibald, *History of Europe from the Commencement of the French Revolution in 1789 to the Restoration of the Bourbons in 1815*, Volume VI (Blackwood, London, 1847)

Anonymous, *Memoirs of a Sergeant late in the Forty-Third Light Infantry Regiment previously to and during the Peninsular War* (London, 1835, Ken Trotman, Cambridge, 1996)),

Anonymous, *Personal Narrative of a Private Soldier in the 42nd Highlanders* (Ken Trotman, Cambridge,1996).

Anonymous, *Souvenirs Militaires Du Temps de L'Empire Par Un Officer Supérieur du Deuxième Corps* (Paris, 1841).

Beamish, N. *Ludlow, History of the King's German Legion* (Buckland & Brown, London, 1993)

Boothby, Charles, *Under England's Flag 1804–1809, The Memoirs, Diary and Correspondence of Charles Boothby, Captain of Royal Engineers, Compiled by the Last Survivors of his Family* (Adam & Charles, London, 1900)

Brett James, Anthony, *General Graham, Lord Lynedoch* (Macmillan, London, 1959).

Brett-James, Anthony (ed.), *The Peninsula and Waterloo Campaigns – Edward Costello* (Longmans, London, 1967)

Brownrigg, Beatrice Smith, *The Life and Letters of Sir John Moore* (Blackwell, Oxford, 1923)

Brumwell, John, *The Peninsular War, 1808–1812. Letters of a Weardale soldier*, [William Egglestone, ed.],(Ann Arbo,: University of Michigan, 2012)

Bryant, Arthur, *Years of Victory, 1802–1812* (Collins, London 1951)

Butler, Arthur John, *The Memoirs of Baron de Marbot, Late Lieutenant General in the French Army* (Longmans, Green & Co., London, 1903)

Cadell, Charles, *Narrative of the Campaigns of the Twenty-eighth Regiment, Since Their Return from Egypt in 1802* (Whittaker, London, 1835)

Carr-Gomm, Francis Culling, *Letters and Journals of Field Marshal Sir William Maynard Gomm, From 1799 to Waterloo, 1815* (John Murray, London, 1891)

Chandler, David, *The Campaigns of Napoleon*(Macmillan, New York, 1966)

Coignet, Captain Jean-Roch, *The Notebooks of the Captain Coignet, Soldier of the Empire* (Frontline, Barnsley, 2016)

Cope, William H., *The History of the Rifle Brigade* (The Prince Consort's Own) Formerly the 95th (Chatto&Windus, London, 1877)

Correa, Antonia, *El Lucense, Diario Catolico*, 9 January 1897.

Curling, Henry (ed.), *Recollections of Rifleman Harris* (H. Hurst, London, 1848)

Davis, D.W., *Sir John Moore's Peninsular Campaign 1808–1809* (Springer, The Hague, 1974)

Day, Roger William, *The Life of Sir John Moore, Not a Drum was Heard* (Leo Cooper, Barnsley, 2001)

Delavoye, Alexander M., Life of Thomas Graham, Lord Lynedoch. (London: Marchant Singer, 1880)

Dobbs, John, *Recollections of an Old 52nd Man* (Privately published, Waterford, 1863)

Esdaile, Charles, *The Peninsular War, A New History* (Allen Lane, London, 2002)

Esdaile, Charles, *Peninsular Eyewitnesses, The Experience of War in Spain and Portugal 1808–1813* (Pen & Sword, Barnsley, 2008)

Ferreiro, Alberto Blas, 'John Moore pasa por Lugo' *Taboa Redonda*, 3 de junio de 1992

Fortescue, Sir John, *History of the British Army*, Vol.6, 1807–1809 (Macmillan, London, 1910)

Gardyne, Charles Greenhill, *The Life of a Regiment: The History of the Gordon Highlanders From Its Formation in 1794 to 1816*, Volume 1 (The Medici Society, London, 1929)

Gates, David, *The British Light Infantry Arm c. 1790–1815* (Batsford, London, 1987)

Gavin, William, *The Diary of William Gavin, Ensign and Quarter-Master 71st Highland Regiment, 1806–1815*, (privately published, 1921)

Glover, Gareth, *The Corunna Journal of Captain, C.A. Pierrepoint AQMG* (Ken Trotman, Huntingdon, 2005)

Glover, Gareth, *From Corunna to Waterloo, The Letters and Journals of Two Napoleonic Hussars, 1801–1816* (Frontline, Barnsley, 2015)

Glover, Michael, and Riley, Jonathon, *That Astonishing Infantry: Three Hundred Years of the History of the Royal Welch Fusiliers (23rd Regiment of Foot), 1689–1989* (Pen & Sword, Barnsley, 1989)

Gordon, Alexander, *A Cavalry Officer in the Corunna Campaign, The Journal of Captain Gordon of the 15th Hussars* (John Murray, London, 1913)

Gurwood, John [ed.], *The Dispatches of Field Marshal the Duke of Wellington, during His Various Campaigns* etc. (John Murray, London, 1837)

Hall, Basil, *Voyages and Travels of Captain Basil Hall RN* (Nelson & Sons, London, 1895)

Hamilton, Anthony, *Hamilton's Campaign with Moore and Wellington During the Peninsular War* (Privately published, 1847)

Harvey, Robert, *The War of Wars, The Epic Struggle Between Britain and France 1793–1815* (Constable, London, 2006)

Haythornthwaite, Philip, *Corunna 1809, Sir John Moore's Fighting Retreat* (Osprey, Oxford, 2001)

Henegan, R.D., *Seven Years' Campaigning in the Peninsula and the Netherlands from 1808 to 1815* (Henry Colburn, London, 1846)

Hibbert, Christopher, *Corunna* (Batsford, London, 1961)

Hook, T.E. *The Life of General the Right Honourable Sir David Baird*, Volume II (Richard Bentley, London 1832)

Hunt, Eric, *Charging Against Napoleon, Diaries & Letters of Three Hussars* (Leo Cooper, Barnsley, 2001)

Jones, Charles and Major Lord Carnock, 'Cavalry in the Corunna Campaign: As Told in the Diary of the Adjutant of the 15th Hussars'*Society for Army Historical Research*, No.4, 1936)

Johnston, R.M., *In the Words of Napoleon, the Emperor Day by Day* (Frontline, Barnsley, 2015)

Kenward, Denis & Nesbitt-Durfort [eds.], *A Sussex Highlander, The Memoirs of Sergeant William Kenward 1767–1829* (Whydown, Sedlescombe, 2005).

Knight, Roger, *Britain Against Napoleon, The Organization of Victory 1793–1815* (Allen Lane, London, 2013)

Leith Hay, Andrew, *Memoirs of the late Lieutenant-General Sir James Leith, G.C.B., with a precis of some of the most remarkable events of the Peninsular War. By a British Officer* (Privately published, Barbados, 1817)

Leith Hay, *A Narrative of the Peninsular War* (Hearne, London, 1839)

Leslie, John Henry, *The Services of the Royal Regiment of Artillery in the Peninsular War, 1808 to 1814* (Hugh Rees, London, 1908)

Lipscombe, Nick, *Wellington's Guns, The Untold Story of Wellington and his Artillery in the Peninsula and at Waterloo* (Osprey, Oxford, 2013)

Londonderry, Marquess of, *Story of the Peninsular War* (James Blackwood, London, 1857)

MacBride, MacKenzie, *With Napoleon at Waterloo and Other Unpublished Documents of the Waterloo and Peninsular Campaigns* (Francis Griffiths, London, 1911)

Mahon, William *Messenger, The Life of Henry Percy, Peninsular Soldier and French Prisoner of War* (Pen & Sword, Barnsley, 2017)

Maurice, J.F., *The Diary of Sir John Moore*, Vol. II, (Edward Arnold, London, 1904)

Maxwell, W.H., *Peninsular Sketches by Actors on the Scene* Vol. I, (Henry Colburn, London, 1845)

Milburne, H.R., *A Narrative of the Circumstances Attending the Retreat of the British Army Under Sir John Moore, With a Concise Account of the Memorable Battle of Corunna, and Subsequent Embarkation of his Majesty's Troops* (T. Egerton, London 1809)

Miller, Benjamin, *The Adventures of Serjeant Benjamin Miller Whilst Serving in the 4th Battalion of the Royal Regiment of Artillery 1796 to 1815* (The Naval & Military Press, Heathfield, 1999)

Mollo, John, *From Corunna to Waterloo with the Hussars, 1808 to 1815* (Pen & Sword, Barnsley, 1997)

Monick, Stanley [ed], *Douglas'sTale of the Peninsula and Waterloo 1808–1815* (Leo Cooper, London, 1997).

Moore, James Carrick, *A Narrative of the Campaign of the British Army in Spain Commanded by His Excellency Lieutenant General Sir John Moore* (Joseph Johnson, London, 1809)

Moore-Smith, G.C., *Life and Letters of John Colborne, Field Marshal Lord Seaton* (John Murray, London, 1903)

Napier, William Francis Patrick, *The Life and Opinions of General Sir Charles James Napier, G.C.B.* (John Murray, London, 1857)

Napier, William Francis Patrick, *History of the War in the Peninsula and in the South of France, From the Year 1807 to the Year 1814* (Constable, London, 1992)

Naylies, M. de, *Mémoires sur la guerre d'Espagnependnant les années 1808, 1809, 1810 et 1811* (Paris: Magimel, Anselin et Pochard, 1817)

Neale, Adam, *Letters from Portugal and Spain, Comprising an Account of the Operations of the Armies under their Excellencies Sir Arthur Wellesley and Sir John Moore from the Landing of the Troops at Mondego Bay to the Battle at Corunna* (Richard Phillips, London, 1809)

Oman, Charles, *A History of the Peninsular War* (Greenhill, London, 1995)

Paget, Augustus, *The Paget Papers, Diplomatic and other Correspondence of the Right Honourable Sir Arthur Paget 1794–1807*, Volume II with Two Appendices 1808 & 1821–1829 (Heineman, London, 1896)

Paget, Eden, *Letters and memorials of General the Hon. Sir Edward Paget K.C.B. Collected and arranged by his daughter Harriet M. Paget* (Privately published, London, 1898)

Parkinson, Roger, *Moore of Corunna* (Purnell, Milton, 1976)

Porter, Robert Kerr, *Letters from Portugal and Spain, Written During the March of the British Troops under Sir John Moore* (Longman etc., London, 1809)

Rawson, Andrew, *The Peninsular War, A Battlefield Guide* (Pen & Sword, Barnsley, 2009)

Read, Jan, *War in the Peninsula* (Faber & Faber, London, 1977)

Robertson, Ian C., *Wellington at War in the Peninsula 1808–1814, An Overview and Guide* (Leo Cooper, Barnsley, 2000)

Robertson, O., *The Journal of Sergeant D. Robertson, late 92nd Foot* (Perth 1842)

Rocca, Albert J.M. de, *Memoires sur la guerre des Francais en Espagne* (Paris 1814)

Ryan, Edward, *Napoleon's Shield and Guardian, the Unconquerable General Daumesnil* (Frontline, Barnsley, 2015)

Sadler, Thomas (ed.), *Diary, Reminiscences and Correspondence of Henry Crabb Robinson*, Vol. I. (Fields Osgood, Boston, 1870)

Sarrazin, General Jean, *History of the War in Spain and Portugal from 1807 to 1814* (Edward Earle, Philadelphia, 1815)

Schaumann, A.L.F., *On the Road with Wellington, Diary of a War Commissary in the Peninsular Campaign* (Frontline, Barnsley, 2015)

Sinclair, Joseph, *A Soldier of the Seventy-First, From De La Plata to the Battle of Waterloo, 1806–1815* (Frontline, London, 2010)

Sorell, Thomas Stephen, *Notes of the Campaign of 1808–1809 in the North of Spain* (John Murray, London, 1848)

Southey, Robert, *History of the Peninsular War* Vol.1 (John Murray, London, 1823)

Steevens, Nathaniel, *Reminiscences of My Military Life From 1795 to 1818 by the Late Lieut.-Colonel Chas. Steevens, Formerly of the XX Regiment* (Warren & Son, Winchester, 1878)

Strurgis, Julian (ed.), *A Boy in the Peninsular War, the Services, Adventures and Experiences of Robert Blakeney, Subaltern in the 28th Regiment* (John Murray, London 1899)

Surtees, William, *Twenty-five Years in the Rifle Brigade* (Blackwood, London, 1833)

Teague, John and Dorothea (eds.), *Where duty calls me: Napoleonic War Experiences of Rifleman William Green* (Synjon Books, Borden, 2007)

Thiers, M.A., *Histoire du Consulat et de L'Empire* (Paris, 1849)

Urban, Mark, *The Man Who Broke Napoleon's Codes, The Story of George Scovell* (Faber and Faber, London, 2001)

Vivian, Claud, *Richard Hussey Vivian, First Baron Vivian, A Memoir* (Isbister, London, 1897)

Warre, Edmund [ed.], *Letters from the Peninsula 1808–1812 by Lieut.-Gen. Sir William Warre* (John Murray, London, 1909)

Wellington, Duke of [ed.], *Supplementary Despatches, Correspondence and Memoranda of Field Marshal Arthur Duke of Wellington* (John Murray, London, 1860)

Whinyates, Francis Arthur, *From Corunna to Sevastopol: The History of 'C' Battery … Royal Horse Artillery* (G. Francis Smith, 1990)

Internet Sources

Hansard, House of Commons Debates, http://hansard.millbanksystems.com/commons

The Napoleon Series, http://www.napoleon-series.org

www.asociacioncastanoynogal.com

www.militaryheritage.com/

Index

Abrantes, 22, 24, 32, 33–4
Alacantara, 24
Alison, Archibald, 64, 156, 247
Alexander I, Czar of Russia, 1, 2,
    3, 13
Almeida, 11, 17, 21–2, 24, 31–2,
    35–9, 230
Alten, Brigadier-General Karl, 25,
    85, 99, 123–4, 160, 170, 176,
    240, 251, 289
Alto de Campo de Arbore, 256, 258
Andalusia, 12, 45, 229, 231–2
Anstruther, Brigadier General
    Robert, 38, 286
Astorga, 53–5, 59–60, 62, 71, 73,
    77–8, 94–5, 99–100, 115–23,
    125–7, 130, 142–3, 147, 158,
    215, 222–6, 228, 243, 251
Asturias, 6, 17–19, 26, 78, 116, 215,
    228
Austria, 5, 13, 123

Badajoz, 21, 25, 32, 42, 72, 82–3, 93,
    225, 230
Bailén, Battle of, 12
Baird, Lieutenant General Sir
    David, 15, 20, 21, 25, 32–3,
    37–8, 40–2, 49–51, 54–5, 57–8,
    60–4, 69, 71, 73–5, 77–9, 83, 85,
    92, 97–8, 112, 115–6, 129, 138,

    153–4, 158, 168, 175, 186–7,
    193–4, 199, 205–6, 210, 222,
    224, 228, 230–1, 242, 246
Balagny, Commandant breveté
    Dominique, 232–3
Banks, Major Charles, 197
Baralla, 253, 255, 257
Barcelona, 7
Bathurst, Colonel, 88–9, 96
Bayonne, 6, 11, 13
Baxter, Rifleman Thomas, 165
Becerrea, 253–5, 257–8, 259
Beira, 22, 36
Belvedere, Count of, 26–7, 40
Bembibre, 128–30, 143, 150, 251,
    252, 291
Bennet, Lieutenant Joseph, 150, 237
Benevente, 54, 57–8, 75, 107–8,
    216, 218
Bentinck, Major General Lord
    William, 18, 24, 26–9, 36, 38,
    40–1, 195–7, 199, 203–4, 285,
    287, 288
Beresford, Major General William,
    9, 24, 33, 128, 212, 285, 287,
    288
Berlin, 2
Betanzos, 57, 164, 168–71, 173,
    186, 214
Bilbao, 26, 28

Blake, General Joachim, 26, 28, 37, 40, 44, 49, 55, 56, 57, 60, 77

Blakeney, Lieutenant Robert, 32, 36–7, 39, 129–30, 133, 135, 149–50, 165, 168, 170, 174–6, 178–9, 184, 195, 205, 209–10, 235–7, 239, 245–6, 252, 254, 259–60

Bonaparte, Joseph, King of Spain, 229, 232

Bonnet, General Jean-Pierre-François, 123

Boothby, Captain Charles, 34, 83, 187

Bowen, Captain James, 211–12

Braganza, House of, 3–4, 216

British Army,
Royal Artillery, 60, 94, 215, 163, 227–8, 289, 290
Royal Engineers, 106, 118, 137, 142–4, 178, 236, 252
Royal Horse Artillery, 52, 73–4, 86, 88, 94, 146–7, 241, 243
King's German Legion, 25, 92, 99, 109, 123, 146, 153, 183, 242
2nd (Royal North British) Dragoons, 57
2nd Foot, 25, 285
4th Foot, 24, 285
5th Foot, 285
6th Foot, 285
9th Foot, 24, 285
10th Light Dragoons (Hussars), 102, 109–10, 289
15th Light Dragoons (Hussars), 84, 86, 88, 92, 125, 130, 132, 142, 146, 157, 171, 176, 241, 250, 252, 289
18th Light Dragoons (Hussars), 92, 103, 108, 109
20th Foot, 124, 143, 152, 247, 286

23rd Foot, 117, 285
28th Foot, 24, 31, 37, 124, 130, 132, 145–6, 148–50, 174–5, 178–9, 184, 205–6, 236–7, 246, 285
32nd Foot, 34–5, 105, 285
38th Foot, 24, 286
42nd Foot, 97–8, 119, 125–6, 171, 194, 195–205, 286
43rd Light Infantry, 51, 96, 106–7, 110, 128, 130, 143, 159, 161, 170, 244, 285
50th Foot, 42–3, 128, 194–5, 197–203, 285
52nd Light Infantry, 16, 24, 33, 34, 106–7, 124, 131, 133–4, 139, 206–7, 238, 245, 259, 285
60th Foot, 24, 65, 284, 286, 288
71st (Highland) Light Infantry, 64, 84, 103, 116, 125, 138, 157, 162, 164, 169, 173, 183, 239, 286
79th Foot, 24, 286
91st Foot, 24, 124, 206, 285
92nd Foot, 25, 139, 212, 286
95th Rifles, 24, 35, 96, 106, 117, 124–5, 130, 132–4, 146–7, 165, 178–9, 189, 206, 286

British Government, 3, 15–16, 18–20, 27, 40, 50, 51, 54, 55, 58–9, 69–70, 78–9, 121, 219, 224, 226, 229, 231, 239, 247

Brodrick, General, 107

Bogue, Captain Richard, 88

Burgos, 25, 32, 40, 54, 61, 65, 75, 89

Burrard, Lieutenant General Sir Harry, 10, 16–18, 22, 24, 31, 33

Cacabelos, 129–32, 145

Cadell, Captain, later Lieutenant Colonel Charles, 236–7

Cadiz, 42, 59, 62, 227, 229, 231–2

Cadoalla, 256

Camino Carlos III (Camino Real), 254–6, 259

Canning, George, 50–1, 79, 219

Carlos IV, King of Spain, 6, 254

Carrion, 86–9, 89, 92–6, 107, 220

Castaños, General Francisco Javier, 24, 26, 27–9, 38, 40, 44, 55, 58, 60–1, 65, 69

Castellanne-Novejan, Lieutenant, 101

Castello Branco, 34, 36

Castlereagh, Robert Stewart, 2nd Marquess of Londonderry, 15, 17–23, 27, 30, 36–7, 41, 45, 52, 55, 62, 69, 77–8, 83, 99, 123, 184, 216–7, 226, 230, 231, 246

Castrogonzalo, 99, 108

Cathcart, William, 1st Viscount, 3–4

Celorico, 24

Cereixal, 253, 255–9

Cerezal, 239, 253, 257–8

Chandler, David, 229

Cintra, Convention of, 1–10, 17, 31

Ciudad Rodrigo, 17, 22, 24, 36, 39, 41, 62, 230

Coignet Captain Jean-Roche, 108

Coimbra, 22, 24

Colbert-Chabanais, General Auguste-François-Marie de, 132–4, 251

Clunes, Captain, 197

Colborne, Major John, 32, 59, 132, 191, 207, 215, 222

Constantin (Constantine, Constantino), 237–8, 252–4, 257, 258–60

Constantinople, 3, 5

Cookson, Lieutenant Colonel George, 94, 162, 180–1

Corunna, 15, 20, *et seq.*

Cork, 9, 25

Costello, Sergeant Edward, 133

Craddock, Lieutenant General Sir John, 31, 74, 79, 230

Craufurd, Brigadier-General James Catlin, 168

Craufurd, Brigadier-General Sir Robert, 85, 106, 123–4, 160, 170, 176, 222, 251, 287

Croatia, 3

Cruzulriver, 252–3, 257

Cua river, 130, 132, 251

Dalrymple, Lieutenant General Sir Hew, 8, 10–11, 17–18, 21–2, 29, 31

De Belle, Général de Brigade, 82

Delaborde, General Henri François, 9–10, 89, 188, 205

Delaney, Captain, 22

Denmark, 2, 3, 4

Diaz, Dr Jesús Manuel Núñez, 250

Dobbs, Captain John, 33–4, 43, 111, 131, 139–40, 206, 210

Doncos, Torres de, 255

Douroriver, 12, 100

Downman, Captain Thomas, 162, 243

Duhesme, General Guillaume, 7

Dupont, General Pierre, 12

Ebro river, 12, 14, 24, 26, 28, 40, 58, 231

Eguia, General Nazario, 45

El Burgo, 175, 177–9, 183–6

Esla river, 98, 99, 102, 106, 108, 111–2, 115

Elvas, 11, 21–2, 24–5, 230

Elviña, 186, 194–5, 197, 200–3, 206

Erfurt, 13

Erskine, Commissary General
    James, 19, 28
Escorial, 76
Espinar, 32
Evelegh, Captain Henry, 241–2

Falls, Professor Cyril, 239, 255
Falmouth, 15, 243
Ferdinand, Prince of Asturias, 6, 7
Ferrol, 58, 100, 153, 215, 227
Figueros, 7
Finland, 3
Fletcher, Lieutenant Colonel
    Sir Richard, 153
Foncebadon, 123, 216, 251
Fontainbleau, Treaty of, 6
Fortescue, Sir John, 37, 159, 176,
    233, 238
Franceschi, General Jean Baptiste,
    80, 82, 100, 123, 158, 174,
    179
Fraser, Lieutenant General
    Alexander Mackenzie, 85, 92,
    98, 118, 153, 158, 197
Frere, John Hookham, 41, 50, 51,
    53–4, 56, 58–9, 69–72, 73–4, 79,
    83–4, 89, 92
French Army
    Grande Armée, 5–6, 26, 123
    Imperial Guard, 13, 46, 101,
        109 10, 123, 230
    II Corps, 40, 61, 82, 89, 93, 100,
        213, 257
    VI Corps, 123
    Chasseurs à Cheval de la Garde
        Impériale, 102, 109–10
    1er Régiment des chevaux-légers
        (polonaise), 46
    3rd Hussars, 132
    15th Chasseurs à Cheval, 102, 132
Friedland, Battle of, 2, 3

Freire, Lieutenant General
    Bernardim, 9

Galicia, 21, 26, 37, 40, 44, 49–51, 54,
    78–9, 81–2, 85, 91, 95, 99, 108,
    119, 140, 144, 170, 206, 204,
    214–6, 220, 227–8, 231, 233,
    235–60
Gavido, 35
Gavin, Ensign William, 84–5, 157,
    168–9, 239
Germany, 7, 13, 123
Gibraltar, 5, 8–10, 59, 219, 227
Godoy, Manuel, Spanish Prime
    Minister, 6–7
Gomez, Professor Javier, 254
Gomm, Captain William
    Maynard, 22
Gordon, Captain Alexander, 84,
    87, 120, 132, 137, 142, 156, 164,
    168, 182, 213–4, 237–8, 240–1,
    252
Graham, Lieutenant John, 157
Graham, Colonel Thomas, 1st
    Baron Lynedoch, 55, 66, 74,
    75–6, 80, 139, 161, 196, 204,
    218, 237
Green, Rifleman William, 131, 136,
    147, 165, 179
Griffith, Major Edwin, 88, 96,
    176, 214
Guadarrama, Sierra de, 45, 66,
    101–2
Guarda, 24, 36–7
Guitiriz, 165
Gundian, 253
Gustav IV, King of Sweden, 3, 8

Hall, Captain Basil, 185, 192
Hamilton, Colonel Digby, 221, 243
Hardinge, Captain Henry, 205

Harris, Rifleman Benjamin
    Randell, 35, 42, 92, 106,
    119–20, 127, 177, 200
Henegan, Sir Richard, 33–4
Heudelet, Étienne General, 123, 188
Hill, Major General Rowland, 24,
    205, 285, 287, 288
Hood, Admiral Sir Samuel, 107,
    124, 212
Hodge, Major Edward, 54, 140
Holland, Elizabeth Vassall Fox,
    Baroness, 53

Ionian Islands, 3
Ireland, 9

Jackson, Francis, 3
Jeffs, Sergeant Major, 109
John VI, Prince of Portugal, 4–5
Joséphine de Beauharnais, 111,
    121
Junot, General Jean-Andoche,
    1st Duke of Abrantès, 4–10,
    12, 17, 19, 22, 36, 89
Junta, Central or Supreme, 27, 36,
    41, 45, 49, 51, 66–7, 69, 70, 72

Kennedy, Commissary-General
    Sir Robert Hugh, 115

la Houssaye, General, Armand
    Lebrun de, 123, 129, 134, 153,
    158, 194, 199, 203, 206, 238,
    246, 249, 257
Lapisse, General Pierre Belon, 101
Lannes, Jean, 1st Duc de
    Montebello, 61
Lefebve, Marshal François, 28
Lefebvre-Desnoëttes, General
    Charles, 111–2
Le Noble, Pierre, 189

Leon, 17, 37, 54, 56, 58, 75, 78, 82,
    85, 93, 250
Leith, Major General James, 17,
    160, 205, 285, 288
Leith Hay, Andrew, 17, 42, 80, 112,
    156, 188, 215
Lexocairo, 253
Lisbon, 4, 8, 9, 10, 11, 15, 18, 21–3,
    31–3, 35–6, 42, 52, 59, 61–2,
    74–5, 78, 80, 82, 93, 100, 225,
    227, 229–31, 233, 240, 250
Loison, General Louis Henri, 36
Lugo, 57, 130, 147, 153–4, 155–71,
    196, 216, 228, 238–41, 249–50,
    253, 257, 260

Maçeira Bay, 10
Mandeo river, 171, 174, 178
Madrid, 6–7, 11, *et seq.*
Majorga, 85, 98, 102
Malta, 5
Mascoso, Don Bernardo, 186
Manningham, Major General
    Coote, 85, 205, 285, 287, 288
Mansilla, 100
Marbot, General Jean-Baptiste
    Antoine Marcellin Baron de,
    101, 110, 120, 122
Mediterranean Sea, 5
Merle, General Pierre Hugues
    Victoire, 82, 123, 134, 158, 160,
    185, 194, 205
Mermet, General Julien Augustin
    Joseph, 123, 185, 194, 197, 202,
    203, 207
Mero river, 175, 178, 182, 183
Milburne Henry R., 222
Miller, Serjeant Benjamin, 136, 193,
    211
Minhoriver, 124, 158, 170
Moncey, General Jeannot de, 7, 28

Mondego Bay, 219
Monte Mero, 185, 187, 192, 194, 195, 197–9, 202–6
Monte Toleno, 125
Montgomery, Paymaster John, 198–9
Montbrun, General Louis Pierre, 46
Moore, Lieutenant General Sir John, 8–9, 10, *et seq.*
Moore, James Carrick, 44, 177, 242
Morley, Sergeant Stephen, 139
Mouton, General Georges, 7, 82
Murray, Quartermaster General, Colonel George, 17, 124

Napier, Major Charles, 194–203
Napier, Colonel George, 32, 153, 217
Napier, General Sir William Francis Patrick, 51, 65, 110, 151, 161, 180, 193–4, 244, 247, 291
Napoleon I, Emperor of the French, 1–7, 11, *et seq.*
Naviariver, 252
Naylies, sous-lieutenant Joseph de, 127, 142
Neale, Adam, 36, 139, 163
Neira, river, 238, 253
Ney, Marshal Michel, 40, 123
Niemen, river, 1, 2
Noceda, 251, 255
Nogales (As Nogais), 140–1, 143, 145, 235–9, 241, 244, 247, 251–3, 255, 257–8

Obidos, Combat of, 9
Odoards, Edouard de Fantin des, 153
Odoards, Captain Louis Florimond Fantin des, 192, 194
Oporto, 100

Orense, 67–8, 100, 116, 123–4, 143, 160, 170, 228
Otway, Colonel Loftus William, 108–10
Ottoman Empire, 3

Paget, Lieutenant General Henry William, 1st Marquess of Anglesey, 62, 67, 68, 77, 80, 83, 85–88, 91, 98, 99, 102, 106, 108–10, 124–5, 127, 137, 145, 173, 220, 289
Paget, Major General Sir Edward, 85, 98, 127, 129, 130–4, 148–50, 159–60, 164, 170, 175–6, 183–7, 193, 195, 197, 203–7, 220, 235, 244, 247, 289
Palafox, General José, 26, 29, 40, 44, 55
Pajares, 116
Pamplona, 7, 26
Paris, 123, 229–30, 238
Patterson Major John, 42, 128–9, 200
Pena do Pico, Serra da, 253, 254
Peñasquedo, Heights of, 186, 188–9, 192, 202, 207
Percy, Lieutenant Henry, 141
Piedrafita do Cebreiro, 239
Piedrafita Pass, 226, 239, 259
Piedralonga, 176
Pierrepoint, Captain Charles A., 117, 126, 145, 152
Plunkett, Rifleman Thomas, 133, 251
Ponferrada, 118–9
Ponsonby, MP George, 219
Porter, Robert Kerr, 31, 35, 79, 138, 179, 216
Portugal, 2–11, 15, *et seq.*
Portuguese navy, 19

Poy, Vincente, 255
Proby, Colonel Lord John, 218
Prussia, 1–2, 6, 13
Puente Ferreira, 238
Pyrenees, 4, 13, 26, 230, 231

Queluz camp, 23, 31
Quitterez (Guitiriz), 165

Rautenberg, Major K.H., 92
Retorta, 257, 259
Rey, Dr Antonia Correa of Pena de
    Neira de, 257
Reynosa, 40
Rivera, Vicente, 254, 258–9
Robertson, Sergeant David, 139,
    141, 240
Robinson, Henry Crabb, 38, 50
Rocca, Lieutenant Albert Jean
    Michel de, 142, 223, 233
Roliça, Battle of, 9
Romana, Don Pedro Caro y
    Sureda, 3rd Marquis de la, 9,
    26, 37, 56, 69, 75, 77, 78, 81, 85,
    93–5, 99–100, 116, 118, 120–1,
    123, 144, 145, 156, 185, 215,
    218, 224–5, 231, 233, 257
Royal Navy, 2, 3, 4–5, 8, 9, 192, 210
Rueda, 80, 91
Ruffin, General François Amable, 46
Russia, 1–5, 8, 13

Sahagun, 86–9, 98–99, 107, 184, 196,
    225, 250
Santiago de Compostela, 251
Saldana, 82, 88, 89, 220
Salamanca, 32, 36, *et seq.*
San Juan, General Benito, 45–7, 66,
    68
San Sebastian, 7
Sarrazin, General Jean, 37, 104–5

Savary, General Anne Jean Marie
    René, 46
Schaumann, Assistant Commissary
    A.L.F., 34–5, 116–17, 126–7,
    138, 144–5, 150–1, 163–5,
    171, 186, 209, 211, 214–15,
    217, 242
Sinclair, Joseph, 116, 119, 125, 138,
    159, 162, 173
Segovia, 81
Serra da Pena do Pico, 253, 254
Seville, 8, 42, 225, 229, 231–2
Shorncliffe Camp, 16
Sicily, 5, 9
Sorrel, Lieutenant Colonel T.S.,
    222, 228, 231
Spain, 3, 5, *et seq.*
Spanish Army,
    Army of Andalusia, 45
    Army of Estremadura, 26, 40, 45,
        54, 60, 93
    Army of Galicia, 40
    Army of the Centre, 40
Spencer, Major General Sir Brent, 9
Somerset, Field Marshal FitzRoy
    James Henry, 234
South Africa, 5
South America, 8
Stanhope, Lady Hester Lucy, 197,
    199, 201–2
Steevens, Captain Nathaniel,
    143–4, 152–5, 239, 247, 253
Sterling, Captain James, 97
Sterling, Lieutenant Colonel James,
    197
Stewart, Brigadier General
    Charles (later Marquis of
    Londonderry), 63, 67–8, 73,
    83, 95, 110, 116, 120, 136, 140,
    145, 151, 153–4, 184–5, 186–7
Stuart, Charles, 36, 65

Surtees, Quartermaster Sergeant
William, 96, 117, 177
Sweden, 2–3, 8, 10

Taboada, Professor Benito Sáez, 256
Tagus river, 17, 34, 61, 100, 233
Talavera, 25, 66, 70, 82, 100
Thorpe, Lieutenant Samuel, 117
Tigre, HMS, 52
Tilsit, Treaty of, 2–3, 13
Torallo, 255
Tordesillas, 80, 84, 102
Toro, 54, 77, 80, 83, 84
Treveake, Captain, 137
Tudela, Battle of, 44–5

Val des Orres, 160
Valencia, 8, 98, 112, 116
Valderos, 85, 98
Vales, 253
Valladolid, 24, 25–6, 32, 55, 60, 65,
79, 80, 82, 107
Vigo, 74, 78, 81, 83, 100, 123–4, 153,
160, 170, 176, 177, 185, 186,
212, 215, 222, 240, 280, 287,
291
Villacastin, 93
Villada, 92
Villapanda, 110

Villa Velha, 34–6
Vimeiro, Battle of, 10, 23, 103
Viney, Major James, 193
Vivian, Lieutenant Colonel Richard
Hussey, 52, 57–8, 64–5, 98,
102–3, 109, 111, 116, 137, 143,
147, 155–6, 165–7, 166–7, 210,
220, 227

Wall, Captain Adam, 60, 163
Warde, Major General Henry, 204,
289
Warre, Lieutenant William, 217
Weller, Jac, 225
Wellesley, Lieutenant General Sir
Arthur, 9–10, 11, 17, 37, 229,
230, 233, 234
West Indies, 5
Whittingham, Captain Samuel
Ford, 29
Wilmot, Captain Edward, 25, 36,
193, 212
Wynch, Lieutenant Colonel James,
199

York, Prince Frederick, Duke of, 16

Zamora, 54, 62, 74–5, 82, 93, 216